Bible and Justice

BibleWorld
Series Editor: Philip R. Davies and James G. Crossley, University of Sheffield

BibleWorld shares the fruits of modern (and postmodern) biblical scholarship not only among practitioners and students, but also with anyone interested in what academic study of the Bible means in the twenty-first century. It explores our ever-increasing knowledge and understanding of the social world that produced the biblical texts, but also analyses aspects of the bible's role in the history of our civilization and the many perspectives – not just religious and theological, but also cultural, political and aesthetic – which drive modern biblical scholarship.

Published:

Sodomy: A History of a Christian Biblical Myth
Michael Carden

Yours Faithfully: Virtual Letters from the Bible
Edited by Philip R. Davies

Israel's History and the History of Israel
Mario Liverani

Uruk: The First City
Mario Liverani

The Apostle Paul and His Letters
Edwin D. Freed

The Origins of the 'Second' Temple: Persian Imperial Policy and the Rebuilding of Jerusalem
Diana Edelman

An Introduction to the Bible (Revised edition)
John Rogerson

The Morality of Paul's Converts
Edwin D. Freed

The Mythic Mind: Essays on Cosmology and Religion in Ugaritic and Old Testament Literature
Nick Wyatt

History, Literature and Theology in the Book of Chronicles
Ehud Ben Zvi

Women Healing/Healing Women: The Genderization of Healing in Early Christianity
Elaine M. Wainwright

Jonah's World: Social Science and the Reading of Prophetic Story
Lowell K. Handy

Symposia: Dialogues Concerning the History of Biblical Interpretation
Roland Boer

Sectarianism in Early Judaism
Edited by David J. Chalcraft

The Ontology of Space in Biblical Hebrew Narrative
Luke Gärtner-Brereton

Mark and its Subalterns: A Hermeneutical Paradigm for a Postcolonial Context
David Joy

Linguistic Dating of Biblical Texts: An Introduction to Approaches and Problems
Ian Young and Robert Rezetko

O Mother, Where Art Thou?: An Irigarayan Reading of the Book of Chronicles
Julie Kelso

Sex Working and the Bible
Avaren Ipsen

Redrawing the Boundaries: The Date of Early Christian Literature
J.V.M. Sturdy, edited by Jonathan Knight

The Archaeology of Myth: Papers on Old Testament Tradition
N. Wyatt

Jesus in an Age of Terror: Scholarly Projects for a New American Century
James G. Crossley

On the Origins of Judaism
Philip R. Davies

The Bible Says So!: From Simple Answers to Insightful Understanding
Edwin D. Freed and Jane F. Roberts

From Babylon to Eternity: The Exile Remembered and Constructed in Text and Tradition
Bob Becking, Alex Cannegieter, Wilfred van der Poll and Anne-Mareike Wetter

Judaism, Jewish Identities and the Gospel Tradition: Essays in Honour of Maurice Casey
Edited by James G. Crossley

A Compendium of Musical Instruments and Instrumental Terminology in the Bible
Yelena Kolyada

Jesus Beyond Nationalism: Constructing the Historical Jesus in a Period of Cultural Complexity
Edited by Halvor Moxnes, Ward Blanton, James G. Crossley

The Production of Prophecy: Constructing Prophecy and Prophets in Yehud
Edited by Diana V. Edelman and Ehud Ben Zvi

The Social History of Achaemenid Phoenicia: Being a Phoenician, Negotiating Empires
Vadim S. Jigoulov

Biblical Resistance Hermeneutics within a Caribbean Context
Oral A. W. Thomas

Three Versions of Judas
Richard G. Walsh

Edward Said, Contrapuntal Hermeneutics and the Book of Job: Power, Subjectivity and Responsibility in Biblical Interpretation
Alissa Jones Nelson

Forthcoming:

Vive Memor Mortis: Qoheleth and the Wisdom of his Day
Thomas Bolin

The Joy of Kierkegaard : Essays on Kierkegaard as a Biblical Reader
Hugh Pyper

Charismatic Killers: Reading the Hebrew Bible's Violent Rhetoric in Film
Eric Christianson

Reading Acts in the Second Century
Edited by Rubén Dupertuis and Todd Penner

Queer Theory and the Marriage Metaphor
Stuart Macwilliam

Simulating Jesus: Reality Effects in the Gospels
George Aichele

Surpassing the Love of Two Women: The Love of David and Jonathan in Text and Interpretation
James Harding

The Grotesque Body in Early Christian Literature Hell, Scatology and Metamorphosis
István Czachesz

Delivering the Word: Preaching and Exegesis in the Western Christian Tradition
Edited by William John Lyons and Isabella Sandwell

BIBLE AND JUSTICE
ANCIENT TEXTS, MODERN CHALLENGES

Matthew J.M. Coomber

LONDON   OAKVILLE

Published by Equinox Publishing Ltd.
UK: 1 Chelsea Manor Studios, Flood Street, London SW3 5SR
USA: DBBC, 28 Main Street, Oakville, CT 06779

www.equinoxpub.com

First published 2011

British Library Cataloguing-in-Publication Data

A catalogue record for this book is available from the British Library.

ISBN-13 978 1 84553 526 1 (hardback)
          978 1 84553 527 8 (paperback)

Library of Congress Cataloging-in-Publication Data

Bible and justice : ancient texts, modern challenges / edited by Matthew J.M. Coomber.
        p. cm.—(BibleWorld)
    Includes bibliographical references and indexes.
    ISBN 978-1-84553-526-1 (hb)—ISBN 978-1-84553-527-8 (pb)
    1. Justice—Biblical teaching—Congresses. I. Coomber, Matthew J. M.
BS680.J8B54 2011
220.8'303372—dc22
                                2010012569

Typeset by S.J.I. Services, New Delhi
Printed and bound in Great Britain by Lightning Source UK Ltd, Milton Keynes

For my parents, Jim and Eleanor

CONTENTS

ACKNOWLEDGEMENTS

As with any project of this size, there are many people to thank. To all of those who made the 2008 Conference on Bible and Justice and this volume possible, from the speakers and the delegates to the staff at the Richard Roberts Auditorium, the Mappin Building, and Sheffield Cathedral, I express my immeasurable gratitude. I would like to use this space to also thank a few people and organizations, individually.

First of all I would like to thank Hugh Pyper and James Crossley, who were dedicated and patient mentors as I made my first attempt at organizing an academic conference. They always made themselves available to answer questions, help with various tasks, and offer their expert advice both leading up to and during the conference. Their help was truly invaluable. I am also especially grateful to Philip Davies, who was not only encouraging and supportive throughout the course of organizing the conference, but has also been a most gracious mentor throughout the process of editing this volume.

I am greatly indebted to the Department of Biblical Studies and the University of Sheffield, as a whole, for helping to make the conference possible. In particular, I am grateful for the help, support, and advice of Diana Edelman, Berry Matlock, Will Lamb, Keith Whitelam and Alison Bygrave. I would like to extend my special thanks to Gillian Fogg, who kindly and patiently endured all of the additional work that the conference added to her workload in the Department of Biblical Studies office. I would also like to thank the undergraduate and research students from the Department of Biblical Studies who offered their most welcome assistance during the course of the conference: Michelle Krejci, Cynthia Shafer-Elliott, James Anderson, Dohyung Kim, Aimie Hope and James Gould. Without their assistance in directing delegates through the labyrinth that is the Mappin Building and assisting with last minute details and all of the little surprises that came up, the chaos behind the scenes would have been far more noticeable. I would also like to thank my dear friends Jamie Hilton and Eleanor MacDonald, who ran countless errands and helped out in more ways than I could possibly count.

I am exceedingly grateful for the services and support that was provided by a number of organizations, making the conference both possible and enjoyable. Financial contributions from the Stephenson Trust and the Subject Centre for Philosophical and Religious Studies covered the travel and housing expenses for Stanley Hauerwas and Tim Gorringe and kept delegate fees low. I would especially like to single out Clare Saunders and Darlene Bird, whose Subject Centre research-training sessions inspired me to organize the conference. Sesame Catering's delicious vegetarian/vegan food, Sheffield Cathedral, and the Ethio Cubano Restaurant kept the speakers and delegates well fed and happy, for which I am very thankful. I would also like to extend my thanks to Paula Clifford and Christian Aid for helping to publicize the event.

Neither the conference, nor this volume, would have been possible without my family. I would first like to thank my parents, Jim and Eleanor Coomber, who flew all the way to England from Minnesota for the conference. While my mom helped my wife to take care of our son, who was only four-weeks old at the time, my dad used his vast conference-organizing experience to help me to make sure that everything ran smoothly on-site. Their help and support was limitless and invaluable, as it has always been. Finally, I would like to thank my wife, Sarah. Throughout the process of organizing the conference and putting together this volume, she has been a constant source of encouragement and support.

INTRODUCTION

Matthew J.M. Coomber[a]

From 29 May to 1 June 2008, around a hundred scholars and students from five different continents gathered together at the University of Sheffield to explore the various ways in which the ancient texts of the Bible could address a variety of forms of injustice in the modern world. As is the case with many interesting and worthwhile projects, there was a marked difference between what the 2008 Conference on Bible and Justice had initially set out to be and what it eventually became.

Origins and Development of the Conference

The idea for the 2008 Conference on Bible and Justice developed out of a research-training seminar that I attended during the first year of my PhD programme in the Department of Biblical Studies at University of Sheffield, where I was researching complaints against injustice in the Hebrew Bible. The seminar, which was run by the Subject Centre for Philosophy and Religious studies, included a session on how to organize an academic conference. The session leader did not take long to convince me that few

---

[a] Matthew Coomber received his Ph.D in biblical studies from the University of Sheffield in 2010, where he developed a cultural-evolutionary approach to understanding the hidden contexts behind prophetic complaints against injustice. His primary interests include the effects of political and economic structures on textual interpretation in ancient and modern societies and the reciprocal ways in which biblical texts affect and are affected by the cultures and societies into which they are absorbed. Coomber has published *Re-Reading the Prophets Through Corporate Globalization* (Gorgias, 2010) and edited *Political Theology* 11 (3), which contains papers from the 2008 Conference on Bible and Justice.

things could be more beneficial for a doctoral student than to invite a group of scholars to discuss his or her own area of interest.

With the enthusiastic support of the Department of Biblical Studies, I contacted a few academics to see if I could generate any interest in a conference that would focus on how justice teachings found in the Hebrew Bible/Old Testament could be applied to the various struggles for economic justice in the modern world. The response was both immediate and overwhelming. In addition to receiving encouraging words from those who kindly accepted invitations to present papers at the conference, people offered the names of other scholars that would be interested in the project and other justice topics that should be considered. As the list of speakers grew, so did the subject matter: quickly spreading into the New Testament and covering issues from ecojustice to a wide range of human-rights concerns. What I had originally intended to be a gathering of perhaps a dozen scholars quickly developed into something much larger.

By the time that Philip Davies, John Rogerson, Hugh Pyper, James Crossley, Timothy Gorringe, Louise Lawrence, David Horrell and Stanley Hauerwas were scheduled to present papers, I began to receive unsolicited emails from people who had heard about the conference and were interested in being involved. With the encouragement of Hugh Pyper, James Crossley and Keith Whitelam, the conference was allowed to grow and a call for abstracts was issued. In the end, what had started as a symposium on economic-justice in the Hebrew Bible became an international conference in which over 30 papers were presented on topics ranging from potential Pauline contributions to environmental justice and the use of the Bible by international human rights organizations to the development of a deaf hermeneutic. However, the size and scope of justice issues covered were not the only unexpected developments; the issues that arise when scholars and/or activists apply biblical texts to modern justice concerns became a central part of the conversation.

Ancient Texts, Modern Challenges

The first full day of the conference was opened by Yvonne Sherwood, who suggested that the title of the conference, "The 2008 Conference on Bible and Justice", might have been more aptly named with a question mark at the end. Her observation was very helpful, as it allowed the proceedings to begin by addressing the elephant in the room: the vast and complex challenges that accompany any attempt to wrest the texts of the Hebrew Bible and New Testament out of their contexts and apply them to modern justice concerns. Indeed, this was a theme that recurred throughout the conference, both in the presentations and in the question and answer sessions that followed. The conference papers that were chosen for this volume address these issues in detail and, therefore, a lengthy discourse is not included in this introduction. However, a brief overview of some of the broader issues that are posed by the theme of *Bible and Justice* may be useful to the reader.

Attaching Ancient Texts to Modern Justice Issues, and Vice Versa
From my initial conversations with potential presenters, it became apparent that the larger questions surrounding the use of texts from a radically different time and culture to address modern concerns would need to be a part of the conversation. Notions of "how" the Hebrew Bible and New Testament can speak to injustices in the twenty-first century was quickly accompanied by questions pertaining to whether they could, or even should, be applied. It is easy to find passages that state "you will not do x to y" or "you must protect the ..." and latch on to them for the immediate purposes of a social cause. What is far more difficult, and is addressed by several of the authors in this book, is taking the important steps of giving due consideration to the actual intent of the text and contemplating its relevance, if any, to the injustice to which it is being applied before bringing it into the conversation.

As campaigns for various forms of human rights and environmental justice concerns engage with biblical texts, some difficult questions need to be asked if they are to do so in an open and honest manner. Could the authors of Deut. 20:19 have conceived of the human-made threat of global warming that motivates people to struggle against the clear cutting of rainforests? Were prophetic authors who lived in a society that did not have a functioning monetary system equipped to address the complexities of the World Bank's structural adjustment programmes, which have been blamed for fatal levels of poverty in the developing world? The simple answer is "no", and when people fail to exercise caution in their use of biblical texts, the works of Hellenistic theocrats or Roman-era apocalyptic communities quickly come to be treated as if their writings were recorded to either specifically support or denounce western democracy, communism, fascism, capitalism, socialism or some other system of governance or finance that would have been entirely alien to their realm of understanding. In cases such as this, the scholar and/or activist begins to go astray by trading what the biblical authors actually wrote for what he or she wishes that they had written. To impose modern worldviews and concepts such as these on to the biblical authors is to engage in a kind of cultural or paradigmatic imperialism that is dishonest to both the text and the practitioner, as it forfeits one's integrity and the potential for a more effective application of the passage. Rather than using a text as a quick sound bite for a particular cause, a better understanding of the text may reveal levels of relevance not previously known. Conversely, a closer examination may also reveal that a text is of little use in addressing a particular justice issue.

To make things even more complicated, there is a flipside to the complexities that are involved in using the ancient texts of the Bible to address issues that their authors could not have conceived: whether we actually *want* to be bringing ancient Near Eastern notions of justice into the modern world. As is addressed in Philip Davies' contribution to this text, "Rough Justice?", people should be careful when they make calls for biblical justice; they might not fully understand what they are asking for. Can notions of collective justice leave behind notions of collective punishment, which were an integral part of Iron Age worldviews? Can we draw out biblical calls to care for the widow and the orphan but leave the stoning and destruction behind? The question of "how can we use the Bible to address modern injustice" is naturally followed by questions regarding the parameters and implications for doing so. Is it acceptable to cherry pick those biblical ideas that we are comfortable with or support our immediate needs and leave behind those that disturb us, even though they are sometimes coexist in the same passage? The answers to this question are sure to be varied and may even change, for some, depending on the situation. The complex nature and varied answers that come from questions such as this and the others posed above highlight the attention that they deserve from those who seek to bring the justice(s) found in the Bible into struggles for justice today.

Whose Justice is It Anyway?
Another important issue that was addressed during the Conference on Bible and Justice, and is given specific attention in the first section of this book, is the nature of the concept of "justice", itself. While navigating the significant discrepancies between ancient and modern concepts of justice presents the modern reader with one set of challenges, navigating the varied notions of justice that exist within the modern world presents yet another.

The word "justice" is often assumed to represent a single and eternal ideal that can be applied to any situation, even though the concept is often defined on a cultural, or even an individual, basis.[1] While, from an early twentieth-first-century white-male-American-English-speaking-academic-Episcopalian-democratic[2] point of view, I hope that caring for the poor, the environment, and treating one's neighbours with respect could be agreed upon as a basis for justice. However, even others who share this very narrow and artificially-constructed demographic entertain different notions of "justice", let alone an elderly woman from Bogotá or a middle-aged businessman in Taiwan. It is the fluid nature of concepts of "justice", which change their shape in order to fit into different personal and cultural contexts, that makes a rigid approach to the issue of justice both awkward and unhelpful. To simply impose one's own notions of justice or remedies for injustice on to another culture, without considering its specific needs or definitions of justice, can be as harmful as imposing an economic or governmental system. While an effective use of Bible and justice demands a greater understanding of the biblical context, if "justice" is used to intervene on behalf of others, it also requires a greater understanding of the context to which it is to be applied.[3] The difficulty in pinning down a single definition of justice is vividly reflected in the varied approaches and attitudes that the authors of this volume offer in relation to the topic of Bible and justice.

The Potential Applicability of Bible and Justice

For some, the challenges presented above are the end of the conversation; the cultures and the times in which biblical teachings on justice were written are too outdated to bear any relevance to the modern human condition, or would only inflict further harm on the target of injustice, whether applied internally or by an outsider with good intentions. In certain cases, both concerns are likely to be valid. However, to allow these concerns to develop into a nihilistic outlook that is quick to abandon all biblical texts on justice, and in all circumstances, is unnecessary.

While the challenges that face those who apply biblical texts to modern injustice are both numerous and complex, they should not be prohibitive. Arguments against using biblical texts to address modern justice issues that are either based on the irrelevance of certain texts to a particular issues or are based upon a general mistrust of the Bible due to misogynist and other intolerant views found within, can be the basis for valuable discourse. But to entirely dismiss the possibility of using the Bible to address modern injustice would be to shut the door on both social and academic possibilities. While neither CO_2-induced global warming nor harmful structural adjustment programmes existed within the biblical authors' worldviews, those who wrote against injustice in the ancient world were keenly aware of such issues as economic exploitation, political corruption, and the need to take care of the environment, as is particularly evidenced in the final section of this book. It is because of the ongoing presence of these kinds of challenges in human societies, although they may manifest themselves differently across time and culture, that the idea of Bible and justice should be examined. Whether used in a secular sense to provide examples of the enduring pursuit of justice in its many different forms and to compare and contrast with modern notions, or to be used in a religious context to provide encouragement and support for those who oppose overwhelming forces of injustice, value can be found in these ancient texts. The papers that have been included in *Bible and Justice: Ancient Texts, Modern Challenges* address these issues and offer examples of how the Bible may be effectively used to address the economic, environmental and human rights concerns that we face in the world today. Whether you are an academic, social justice practitioner, a person who found the title interesting, or a mixture of all three, I hope that you will enjoy the varied perspectives on the topic of Bible and justice that this book has to offer.

Layout of the Volume

The book has been divided into sections that represent three different aspects of Bible and Justice that were predominant throughout the conference: challenges and understandings of Bible and justice, previous uses and approaches to Bible and justice, and prospects for the application of Bible and justice. A brief synopsis of the papers that have been included is given below.

1. Challenges and Understandings of Bible and Justice

Yvonne Sherwood – "On the Genesis of the Alliance Between the Bible and Rights" explores the role that the Bible is currently playing in debates on liberalism and justice. Through examining a variety of arguments on the viability of applying biblical texts to politics and justice concerns, ranging from those who see the Bible as indispensable to the conversation to others who believe that justice cannot truly exist without an abandonment of biblical texts, Sherwood addresses the effects of differing biblical interpretations on a variety of governing issues and offers a valuable perspective on the role of the biblical scholar.

Philip Davies – "Rough Justice?". Through addressing the rift that has developed between philosophical and religious approaches to ethics since the Enlightenment, Davies explores the Bible's potential as a source for philosophical discourse on matters of social justice. Rather than approaching the Bible and religion as the antithesis of philosophy, "Rough Justice?" illuminates the continuous philosophical debates on justice that take place throughout the Bible in order to reveal the benefits and limitations of using biblical texts to address the ongoing search for justice, and its meaning.

John Sandys-Wunsch – "Is the Belief in Human Rights Either Biblical or Useful?". This article argues three points about inalienable human rights. First one should bear in mind that this notion was the product of debates in England about legitimate government in the seventeenth century. Second, the Bible properly understood provides motivation and examples but not exact guidance in social matters. Third, Jeremy Bentham's attack on inalienable human rights is supported by more recent discussions of the matter.

Stanley Hauerwas – "Jesus: The Justice of God" considers the notion of "doing justice" in relation to Christian practice. Hauerwas engages the work of Daniel Bell to confront the problematic ways in which Christians often treat injustice as an external event that Christians "go out" to address. Through confronting how this relationship between Christianity and injustice often removes Christians from direct engagement with injustice, rendering them as the underwriters of secular/political justice movements, Hauerwas offers an alternative view of how the figure of Jesus provides an avenue for a more direct involvement.

2. Uses and Approaches to Bible and Justice

Walter Houston – "Justice and Violence in the Priestly Utopia" addresses the charge that the grant of "dominion" to human beings in Genesis 1 has authorized the exploitation of the earth. The world created in Genesis 1 is a utopia without predation or violence. Humanity is charged with preserving this just order, and fails. After the flood, "violence" – the brutal violation of another's rights or life – is accepted as a fact of life, but restrained by law. Houston argues that the ethical stance of the priestly writer against violence needs to be embraced by us today to restrain our destruction of the natural world.

Louise J. Lawrence – *"A Signs Source: Approaching Deaf Biblical Interpretation".* This essay documents contextual bible studies among the Deaf. The Deaf are here understood not primarily by their sensory impairment, but rather their minority language group status (using British Sign Language). Deaf interpretation of biblical stories is revealed as midrashic in nature, frequently biblical traditions are elaborated on in reference to Deaf experience and culture.

Gerald West – *"From a Reconstruction and Development Programme (RDP) of the Economy to the RDP of the Soul: Public Realm Biblical Appropriation in Postcolonial South Africa".* This chapter explores how the mechanism that had been adopted by the African National Congress' tripartite alliance with trade unions and the South African Communist Party to transform South Africa into a more equitable society quickly became a vehicle for neo-liberal reforms and the development of a non-interventionist movement. Accomplished, in part, through the biblical rhetoric of former President Thabo Mbeki, a programme that had been intended to transform the South African economy was reshaped to transform South African morality. West analyses this shift in detail and reflects on the return of the Bible to the public realm in post-apartheid, postcolonial South Africa.

3. Prospects for the Application of Bible and Justice

J. W. Rogerson – *"The Old Testament and the Environment".* Any attempt to address the current ecological crisis involves a form of recreating the natural world in a human image, for example, by intervening to save threatened species from extinction. The fundamental question is that of the values that are brought to this process of re-creating, and what they imply for what it means to be human. The Old Testament has much to contribute to this debate not by way of prescription, but by examples that can be the starting point and inspiration for reflection and action in regard to today's problems.

David Horrell – "Ecojustice and the Bible? Pauline Contributions to an Ecological Theology". Horrell wrestles with different viewpoints on whether or not Bible provides an eco-friendly message. Through a critical analysis of a wide range of views within this debate, the need for an ecological hermeneutic is revealed, as well as the potential value of Paul's writings on salvation and reconciliation. Using God's act of cosmic reconciliation through Christ as a doctrinal lens, Horrell proposes that God's act of cosmic reconciliation in Christ might serve as a "doctrinal lens" at the centre of what he calls "an ecologically reconfigured Pauline theology".

Simon Woodman – "Can the Book of Revelation Be a Gospel for the Environment?". The "good news" of the book of Revelation is often understood as "bad news" for the environment. However, Woodman argues that Revelation's scenes of environmental destruction should be understood as "images of warning", designed to provoke repentance on the part of the nations through representations of the inevitable impact of imperial violence on the earth. Hope for creation-under-empire is seen to lie in John's prophetic call to the church to enact a faithful witness to a non-exploitative vision of humanity and the earth, challenging alternative formulations of environmental ethics – if you do not serve the Emperor, just whom do you serve?

Diana Lipton – "The Kindness of Strangers: Biblical Hospitality and the Politics of Intervention". This chapter reads Amos and Genesis 18–19 to determine when third-party intervention is morally obligatory and when it is ethically unsound. A common bond justifies intervention on behalf of fellow community members, but what justifies intervention on behalf of strangers? Through considering Michael Walzer's characterization of Amos' oracles against the nations as Geneva conventions and themes of righteousness and hospitality in Genesis 18–19, Lipton explores the moral issues that surround military intervention.

Matthew J.M. Coomber – "Prophets to Profits: Bringing Ancient Voices into the Struggle Against the Abuses of Corporate Globalization". The social injustices that are perpetrated through the neoliberal policies of corporate globalization have sparked a debate on the ethical significance of our daily economic decisions. While prophetic complaints against landownership abuse in eighth-century Judah might seem like an unlikely resource for justice advocates, these texts appear to contain a previously unknown level of relevance. Coomber argues that the recurring societal patterns of exploitation that are evidenced in both Judah's absorption into the Assyrian trade-nexus and in agrarian societies that are being absorbed into corporate globalization could offer valuable insights that has been missing from the debate.

Notes

1. James Crossley's book *Jesus in an Age of Terror*, London: Equinox, 2008 provides a very helpful account of how a universal view justice has been adopted by many neo-conservatives in the so-called War on Terror.
2. The latter trait refers to being raised in a (western) democratic system of governance, not in relation to the American political party.
3. Which may very rightly result in a rejection of the use of *Bible and Justice*, altogether.

Part I

CHALLENGES AND UNDERSTANDINGS OF BIBLE AND JUSTICE

ON THE GENESIS OF THE ALLIANCE BETWEEN THE BIBLE AND RIGHTS

Yvonne Sherwood[a]

And God said, "Let there be rights; and there were rights" (Gen. 1:3a, adapted)

1. The Bible and the Public Square

While we biblical scholars have been busy in our introverted corners, discussing etymologies of the personal names in the Mari tablets and *hapax legomena* in the Pastoral Epistles, the Bible has been equally busy playing a lead role in heated contemporary debates about liberalism and justice. In his widely discussed *Justice: Rights and Wrongs*, philosophical theologian Nicholas Wolterstorff dedicates no less than 65 pages to showing how the Bible provides a theistic ground for rights (Wolterstorff 2008).[1] Countering origin stories that appeal to beginnings in pagan/Christian antiquity, the nominalism of the fourteenth century, or the individualism of the seventeenth, Wolterstorff seeks to establish the Bible as an alternative – more trustworthy and explicitly Christian – origin for rights. At the other end of the spectrum, Mark D. Lilla, Professor of Humanities at Columbia, has recently argued that the preservation of liberalism relies on the

[a] Professor Yvonne Sherwood is senior lecturer in Old Testament/Tanakh at the University of Glasgow, Scotland. She has authored or edited seven books including *The Prostitute and the Prophet* (T. and T. Clark, 1996; repr. 2004), *A Biblical Text and Its Afterlives: The Survival of Jonah in Western Culture* (Cambridge, 2000), *Derrida and Religion: Other Testaments* (Routledge, 2004, co-edited with Kevin Hart) and *Derrida's Bible* (ed; Palgrave, 2004). In recent articles she explores the "liberalization" of the Bible and the relationship between secularization and the Bible. She is currently writing a monograph exploring these issues in relation to the sacrifice of Isaac/Ishmael.

"Great Separation" between Christianity and the secular state. According to Lilla's *The Stillborn God: Religion, Politics, and the Modern West* (Lilla 2007), liberal justice can only be sustained by bravely holding the line established by founding heroes such as Hobbes, Locke and Hume. Its maintenance depends on constant vigilance against the ghost of "political theology" – a term that Lilla regards as synonymous with mysticism and theocracy.

Many such resurrections are taking place, even as Lilla is busy trying to push political theology firmly down into its grave. In these, the Bible stands for the very inverse of autocracy, just as clearly (that is to say starkly and crudely) as it represents autocracy for Lilla. According to John Milbank and Stanley Hauerwas – representatives of very different Christianities who nevertheless unite in the belief in Christianity's uniquely redemptive political potential – the Bible is not just liberal, but post-liberal, counter-liberal. It is a massive soteriological-critical force to be pitched against the current order; a symbol of exhorbitant justice that chastises a mealy-mouthed and individualistic (selfish/secular) discourse of rights. In the myriad giddy theological-political visions currently rolling off the press, "Christianity emerges with an uncompromising theopolitical praxis that outflanks the current liberal deadlock"; or the One and Only God opposes idolatrous human political Oneness (be that hypersovereignty or totalitarianism); or redemptive power is made manifest in Paul's "overtly counter-imperial" theo-politics or "the hypostatic descent of the Spirit" that heralds "counter-sovereignty", radical communitarianism and even "eucharistic anarchism".[2]

These arguments – from Lilla and his allies and from those who seek to usher in the redemptive-corrective force of the Christian anti-kingdom – seem at once highly sophisticated and crude in their rough-handling of the perceived struggle between the Christian and the secular, cast as rival forces in a Manichean struggle between darkness and light. The argument seems to be yet another example of what Régis Debray calls an "operatic duet" of "alternating voices", a "dialogue of the deaf between neopagans and neobiblicists" governed by an either-or logic, in which religion must feature either as "liberation" or "plague" (Debray 2004: 4). At the level of their simplified antagonistic framing conflicts, these high academic arguments come uncommonly close to more "vulgar" battles being fought out on a very public stage. In the central battlefield of the USA, the latest phase of the Religion-Secular Civil Wars has involved a major skirmish between the Constitution and the Bible – the latter being led, appropriately enough, under the Commandership of the Ten Commandments. The bugle-call sounded in 2003 when Roy Moore, the former chief Justice of the Supreme Court of Alabama, erected a two and a half ton granite monument of the Ten Commandments in the grounds of the Alabama courthouse. The counter-attack was launched in the law-courts and the mediasphere by blogs such as "The Swift Report". In 2005 (the year that several European nations voted out the European constitution) the Swift Report announced that Americans were on the verge of voting out the Constitution, which had "lost market share to more muscular governing documents, including the Ten Commandments and the Patriot Act" (Swift 2005). Since the Constitution is "abstract" and "cluttered with amendments", it cannot fight against the simplicity and glamour of the Ten Commandments, endorsed by the authority of Moses/Charlton Heston, the blog laments. The high academic battles are fought on the more abstract grounds of history, ethics, and theology – with less crude announcements about the implications for the polity – and they are aimed at a different (though perhaps overlapping) demographic. A two and a half ton monument is a very different kind of thing to an academic monograph, but they can still share the aim of publicly placing the Bible/ Christianity at the origin of modern liberal/legal justice.

It is interesting that Wolterstorff and Moore feel called – albeit in very different ways – to restore the deep connection between the Bible/ Christianity and rights. For this alliance seems to be built in deep into the self-understanding of the democratic West. The front cover of Brian Tierney's *The Idea of Natural Rights* displays a gavel resting on a Holy Bible and an ancient Hebrew manuscript (Tierney 1997).[3] The equation seems, well, natural, at least at the level of cover-design. Though swearing on a Bible in a court of law is now optional in the UK, swearing on *Das Kapital* has never been an option. The Bible and the so-called Judeo-Christian tradition seem to have a self-evident relation to justice and rights. Alongside the idea that religion is a particular problem for democracies (the view expressed by Lilla) we encounter the widespread assumptions that: (a) the particular scriptures and religious tradition of the "West" are a natural ally, and even foundation, for modern notions of justice; and (b) the Christian God (and his Bible) does not seek direct theocratic governance over the state. So broad is this consensus that it is affirmed not just by those representing a specifically Christian position but also by theorists of the origins of secularism and human rights.

For example, the 2007 *Human Rights Reader*, subtitled "Major Political Essays, Speeches and Documents from Ancient Times to the Present" was called, in its first edition in 1997 "Major Speeches, Essays and Documents from the Bible to the Present" (Ishay 2007). The second edition expands the origins of rights to a more global-inclusive base in "secular, Asian and Monotheistic Traditions". In order to counter criticisms that a particularized, Western history jeopardizes a "universal" declaration, it seeks to extend the domain of rights as far as possible in time and space. Select pages from the ancient texts are used to show that the ancient and the modern are essentially on the same page when it comes to crucial core topics such as "Liberty, Tolerance and Codes of Justice", "Social and Economic Justice" and "Justice War and Peace". The citations are framed by introductory comments such as: "One can only marvel at how the same precepts as one encounters in Buddhism are also found in monotheism. The Ten Commandments of the Hebrew Bible represented a code of morality, justice and mutual respect shared by the three monotheistic religions" (Ishay 2007: 31), or "Like the secular and Asian traditions, these three religions preached universalism" (Ishay 2007: 31) or "The pacifist conviction ... found expression in the Hebrew Bible, when Micah demanded that a "nation shall not lift a sword against nation (Mic. 4:3)". Yet if a war was unavoidable, despite all efforts to avert it, "the Hebrews ... would have to treat their prisoners humanely" (Ishay 2007: 63). The logic of the Reader is that the ancient biblical (and expanded "religious" sources) are generally on the right evolutionary lines, even as the need for progress is indicated by a poor record on slaves, women and homosexuals.

The idea that Christianity and its Bible lay the foundation for an inevitable trajectory of progress is also a curiously constant theme in theories of secularization/democratization. Robert Bellah argues that the Protestant–Puritan concept of the priesthood of all believers quite logically "eventuated" in the secular democratic theory of John Locke (Bellah 1976: 68). Francis Fukuyama locates the origins of "democracy" and "political equality" in the Christian doctrine of the "universal dignity of man" (Fukuyama 2006).[4] John Berger argues that the transcendent and supernatural God of the Hebrew Bible granted the world a kind of independence from the beginning, thus anticipating the separation of God and state (paradoxically by divine design) (Berger 1967: 127). In a similar vein Marcel Gauchet sees Christianity as the "seed" that flowered into secular humanism, making possible the terrestrial autonomy at the heart of Western democratic society. For Gauchet, the potential for democracy is in the open Bible in a way that it is not in the closed Qur'an (Gauchet 1997: esp. 80).[5]

These origin myths of democracy/secularization disagree about the precise elements in the Bible or the Christian that led so inexorably to the modern "West". It may have been the Hebrew/Christian God's hands-off transcendentalism. (This is an interesting twist – and one we shall return to – where transcendentalism is read as an expression of the divine desire to devolve earthly-secular political power.) It may have been the notion of universal priesthood. Or it might have been the divine declaration in Gen. 1:26–27 that human beings were all created in God's image (hence equal, hence destined for rights). Whatever the particular point of contact between the ancient text and the modern constitution, the biblical seems to fuse seamlessly and unproblematically with cherished modern principles such as religious toleration, rights and government by contract or consent.

Exactly the same fusion is assumed by Roy Moore in his autobiography *So Help Me God*:

> The god [sic] of Islam commands that no other faiths are to be tolerated by the government. In contrast, the God [sic] of the Christian faith prohibits government from interfering in that relationship which lies solely between God and his creation. Our forefathers recognized that essential truth and adopted the First Amendment to protect freedom of conscience from government interference. (Moore 2005: 109)

If Moore is a cruder Wolterstorff, he is also a populist Gauchet. For Moore, it is self-evident that the First Amendment lies, in utero, in the verse "Render therefore unto Caesar the things which are Caesar's; and unto God the things that are God's" (Mt. 22:21). Moreover, the "God of the Holy [Christian] Scriptures" is a God who guarantees "freedom of conscience and thought" and "equal treatment under the law" – unlike the God of the Qur'an (Moore 2005: 73).

This self-evident truth seems to be affirmed across the Christian spectrum just as easily as it is affirmed in histories of secularization and human rights. The evangelical political activist and founder of *Sojourners* magazine, Jim Wallis, would disagree with Roy Moore on numerous issues. But in *God's Politic*s he affirms, exactly like Moore, that fundamentalism and theocracy, as practised by Al Qaeda or Jerry Falwell, can only be "a betrayal of biblical faith". For biblical faith in no way supports the desire to enforce a "religious agenda" through the "power of the state" (Wallis 2005: 67). Once again, the Christian God typically devolves power and supports democratic human government. And, once again, this fundamental disposition of the Christian God and his Bible is tied to the key text of Gen. 1:27 – interpreted as a declaration of "equality" and "human rights" (Wallis 2005: xxx).

2. *In the Beginning*

The purpose of this essay is not to adjudicate between the Lillas and the Hauerwases and to enter the fray on one side or the other. (I shall go on to explain in my conclusion why any such definitive statements on the theo-political essence of the biblical would be futile and absurd.) Rather, far more modestly, I want to explore the genesis of the move that located the origin of rights in God's first words in the book of Genesis – at the very beginning of the world.

The book of Genesis is, of course, the famous battleground for another key struggle perceived to lie at heart of our modern Western identity: the battle between the Darwinians and the creationists (and their various offshoots including proponents of intelligent design). This battle is given a great deal of public airtime because it is presumed to sort out, once and for all, the true nature of the identity of the modern West and the Truth of the World. According to the logic of the either-or, it is assumed that this will either be acknowledged to be founded by the Christian God and his Bible – or it will be defined by the expulsion of the Bible and all its myths and fables, convicted of obfuscating the true Truth of the World.

Because we have become distracted by dinosaurs in Eden, we have forgotten an earlier modern battle that was also fought out – and conclusively decided – on the stage of the book of Genesis. This was a battle for nothing less than the theological–political identity of the Western world.

It is of course no accident that, in the quest for its identity, the West keeps going back to Genesis and the moment of creation. The origin is a crucial place; the most crucial place. It holds out the promise of a pristine "virginity of a story of beginnings" (Derrida 1974: 29); the idea of beginning as the source of the "most precious, most essential" (Derrida 1974: 21).[6] Hence the "superstitious reverence that surrounds the very notion of a Source" (something that we biblical scholars, with our relentless quest for sources, will understand) (Derrida 1974: 21). As Foucault puts it, the quest for the origin, the Ursprung, is an "attempt to capture the exact essence of things, their purest possibilities, and their carefully protected identities". It is a search that "assumes the existence of immobile forms that precede the external world of accident and succession"; a search for primordial truth as "that which was already there" (Foucault 1984: 78–79). The lure of the origin is that it is the presumed meeting point for the historical and transcendent, the contingent and the non-contingent. It marks the very first point in time and the transcendental guiding principle of the world.

In the English seventeenth century,[7] the desire or need to appeal to the
ultimate beginning was, if anything, even more acute. Any theo-political
vision worth its salt had to be related back to the "experience and Wisdom
of [our] Ancestors"[8] and notions of the "ancient constitution". The origin
was prized above originality. Claims of novelty would have rendered a
political–theological project invalid. This is in marked contrast to the era
self-designated as "modern" with its huge investment in the novel, the
neologism and the now. In this seventeenth century context, the book of
Genesis and the moment of creation became the battleground for two
radically different political–theological visions. These slogged it out for
supremacy just like those rival brothers – all those Abels and Cains, Isaacs
and Ishmaels, Esaus and Jacobs – who fight in the book of Genesis for the
prized place of the origin, the one.[9]

For the sake of simplicity, I shall pin these two political–theological
visions to the names of Sir Robert Filmer and John Locke respectively and
to the key works *Patriarcha* and Locke's *First Treatise of Government*. This
is not because I believe in the idea of the pure origin, Great Name or sole
inventor. Rather, these are the names traditionally pitched against one
another by constitutional historians and by Locke himself when he subtitled
the first treatise "in which the false principles and foundations of Sir Robert
Filmer and his followers are detected and overthrown". The specific
battleground for "Locke v. Filmer" is God's word in Gen. 1:26–28: "Then
God said, 'Let us make men in our image, after our likeness, and let them
have dominion." The intense exegetical battle (which has implications that
extend far beyond narrowed and self-enclosed "histories of biblical
interpretation") is over whether the addressee here is one man or all men,
and whether the emphasis is on the former or the latter half of the verse.

3. A Tale of Two (or Four) Bibles

This is a tale or two Bibles – or rather, four. One of the antagonists is Locke's
Bible. For the sake of argument I shall also refer to this as the Liberal Bible,
because of its connection with the nascent Whig or Liberal party.[10] The
other is Filmer's Bible. I shall also refer to this as the Patriarchal/Monarchical
Bible, because of its connection to the defence of the high Stuart monarchy
(particularly Charles II and James II), and its relation to the Tories, the
party of the Court. In order to understand the evolution of these two late
seventeenth-century Bibles, we need to look at two earlier Bibles, popular
at mid-century: the Active Republican/Revolutionary Bible and the
Deferential/Passive Bible. (Clearly, the different Bibles I am talking about

here are not different translations or editions, but different political-theological visions, understood to define the Bible's true essence. These different visions were understood to originate in the Bible, in both the historical and transcendental sense.)

The seventeenth century is infamous for drastic constitutional upheavals: the Civil Wars (1642–1651) and the brief Cromwellian experiment with a Parliament of Saints and a Republic; the execution of Charles I and the "Restoration" of the monarchy in 1660 with Charles II; and the forced abdication of Charles' brother, James II/VII, (r. 1685–1688) in favour of James' Protestant son-in-law William of Orange in the so-called "Glorious Revolution" of 1688. For those who lived through it, the seventeenth century must have felt like a turbulent place to be. But for present-day biblical scholars, visiting with a day pass, it's a strangely comforting place to be. This is a place where we – curiously biblically literate social misfits in the twenty-first century – can feel a strange sense of belonging. People speak Bible fluently and garrulously. They appeal to scripture as the "cultural matrix for explorations of virtually every topic" (Shuger 1990: 5–6, 9), including the domain that we now firmly separate out as "politics". The 1640s witnessed numerous Parliamentary Fast Sermons in which Old Testament texts were used as "England's looking glass", or "right parallels" in a directive and literal sense. Myriad "Hoseads" and "Jeremiads" invoked the Prophets as far more than a repository of a rather vague sense of "prophetic justice" – as they tend to be invoked across the political–theological spectrum today (Calamy 1970: 11–80; McGiffert 1983: 1151–76; Collinson 1991: 20–23).[11] Prophetic texts were understood as detailed inventories of the particular sins of England. They were invoked to keep up with a polity that seemed to be constantly and dramatically moving. Tropes of drastic reversal and sudden shifts in the divine mind seemed to lend themselves to upheavals in the state. When Parliament impeached Charles I's much-hated adviser, the Earl of Strafford, in 1640, MPs invoked the story of Rehoboam in 1 Kings 12 by accusing Strafford of asserting "that the king's little finger should be thicker than the loins of the law" (Wootton 2003: 27). Today this would be an obscure narrative, known only to specialists. But Parliament could reasonably expect that Charles would not only know the text, but also automatically decipher the biblical code and hear the accusation that he had overplayed his kingly hand. They could also assume that he would hear the not-very-veiled threat in the (delicately unspoken) biblical sequel: the rallying cry "To your tents, O Israel" and the start of Israelite-Judean Civil Wars (Hill 1993: 33).

4. Round One: The Active Revolutionary/Republican Bible Versus the Deferential/Passive Bible

For the sake of convenience, we can herd the sprawling applications of the Bible during the Civil War period into two different versions: the Active Revolutionary/Republican Bible and the Deferential/Passive Bible. The former was, in Christopher Hill's estimation, the Civil War's equivalent of Marx or Rousseau (1993: 49). This Bible drew on Protestant and Catholic resistance theory: the justification of opposition to the monarch-turned-tyrant who persecutes a Catholic or Protestant minority. This Bible is an unacknowledged predecessor for the radicalized Bibles that are currently reappearing in John Milbank and Stanley Hauerwas's visions of the Christian anti-kingdom. In the mid-seventeenth century, such Bibles tended to be sponsored by non-conformists and adherents of the Protestant "low" church, while the Anglicans and Catholics tended to support the quietist Bible of the Court. The seventeenth century could not have witnessed such easy alliances and transitions between the equivalent of the United Methodists, the Episcopalians and the Anglo-Catholics that Hauerwas and Milbank can take for granted.[12] Moreover, since democracy, let alone anarchy, was regarded as a political swearword, theological–poetic tropes of "eucharistic anarchism" would have seriously misfired.[13]

The Active Revolutionary/Republican Bible was a turbulent, volcanic document. It had a highly volatile and molten "core" made up of texts of social inversion, such as Ezek. 21:26 ("Thus says the Lord: Remove the turban, and take off the crown; things shall not remain as they are; exalt that which is low and abase that which is high"), Dan. 4:17 ("The most high rules the kingdom of men, and gives it to whom he will, and sets over it the lowliest of men"), and Ps. 113:7–8 ("He raises the poor from the dust, and lifts the needy from the ash heap, to make them sit with princes"). Key to this Bible was David's double appointment by God and by the people at Hebron, in 2 Sam. 5:1–5. This was regularly invoked to prove the accountability of the king to the people and their deputies – and even, in extremis, to make the case for armed opposition to the king. This Bible also had a strong predilection for apocalyptic – though not the individualist apocalyptic of contemporary *Left Behind* novels.[14] Rather it envisioned a very earthy millenarianism involving radical socio-political restructuring. It got its transcendental hands dirty by supporting campaigns for common land ownership and rallying opposition to exploitative Lord Esau's or Landlord Cains. This audacious scripture issued demands for the abolition of the law of primogeniture, according to which the eldest son inherited everything, as in the book of Genesis. It even went so far as to argue for universal male suffrage for the "poorest he" as for the "greatest he" (Hill 1993: 208–10).[15]

The Active Revolutionary/Republican Bible lent fervent support to radical groups such as the so-called Ranters, the Levellers and the Fifth Monarchists and fostered apocalyptic hopes of an imminent new millennium, presided over by King Jesus (hopes that receded in the wake of the "second coming", so to speak, of Charles, when the beheaded king, Charles I, was replaced by Charles II). It sponsored an accidental republic, led by a "Lord Protector" who modelled himself not on the Über-monarch of 1 Samuel 8, but on the humble, anti-monarchical thorn-bush of Judges 9 – though Cromwell became a king in all but name, nevertheless.[16] It supported a brief experiment with a "Parliament of Saints" and cried out for the literal enforcement of Old Testament law in capital punishment for blasphemy and adultery.[17] (Do those who recently pilloried Rowan Williams for his statements about the constitutional accommodation of Sharia Law know that, not so very long ago, there were moves to directly apply aspects of Old Testament law in the so-called Parliament of Saints?)

This dangerously renegade Bible could even advocate polygamy and come out as a supporter of highwaymen (Hill 1993: 443–46).[18] A popular ballad celebrated the notorious highwayman Dick Turpin as fulfilling Jesus's commands by clothing the naked and feeding the poor. The analogy was reversed by the Ranter preacher Abiezer Coppe who presented God as highwayman, warning the rich man "Thou has many bags of money, and behold, now I come as a thief in the night, with my sword drawn in my hand, and like a thief as I am – I say 'deliver your purse, deliver sirrah! Deliver or I'll cut thy throat!'". Arguably, this is no more shocking than biblical prophetic tropes in which God features as tramp, or wound, or aggressive militant against his own people.[19] But the apparition of a Bible orientated (or rather disorientated) around biblical tropes of decentring and inversion confirmed every fear about the dangers of a vernacular Bible, available to all. It also foregrounded the impossibility of controlling a book that structures (or rather de-structures) itself around principles of inversion: exalting the low, abasing the high, levelling the mountains. And it demonstrated the difficulty of closing and limiting scriptures that issue an ongoing interpretative command to take the literal and the Old and remake it spiritual and New.

The other Bible popular at mid-century attempted to put the brakes on this potential Bible chaos. This Bible, that we could call the Deferential/Passive Bible performed a crucial work of negation. It was an attempt to prevent the populace from taking the texts into their own hands and trying to bring any divine speech acts to pass. Its core was as stable as the Revolutionary/Republican Bible was unstable: Rom. 13:1, 1 Pet. 2:13–17, Jn. 19:11, Prov. 8:15, Dan. 4:17 and Lk. 20:25 – passages that exhorted quietism and non-resistance. The dominant divine speech act became, effectively, "Leave things to God and Caesar". This faithful courtier Bible gave Charles the slogan "Give Caesar his due" that he put on his standard when he took to the battlefield. In the aftermath of Charles I's execution, it supplied the language of the Prophets to describe the groans and convulsions of the God- and King-abandoned state (Kishlansky 1996: 151). It depicted Cromwell and his cohorts as the illegitimate usurpers and sinners of the Old and New Testaments.

The Active Republican/Revolutionary Bible was a complex and multi-faceted document. It was a shifting corpus founded on a wide-ranging vocabulary and grammar that you could parse and conjugate with your present situation in innumerable ways. The Deferential/Passive Bible was more of an inert icon. Its role is clearly demonstrated in the etching "The Royale Oake of Britayne" from Clement Walker's *Anarchia Anglicana* of 1649 (Fig. 1). Here the Deferential/Passive Bible as symbolic *Biblia Sacra*

Figure 1. "The Royall Oake of Brittayne" from Clement Walker, *Anarchia Anglicana* (1649). By permission of the Victoria and Albert Museum.

hangs on "The Royale Oake of Britayne", alongside those other stable-foundational documents: the Law and Magna Carta. Cromwell is depicted as Ahab, snarling "Let us kill and take possession". The Roundheads and revolting peasants are presented as the bad tenants of Matthew 21 taking the axe to the tree.[20] The none-too-subtle message of the engraving is clear. The Bible is an elevated icon or symbol, not to be manhandled at the level of the letter by the amorphous public. To take the letter of the text into one's own hands is tantamount to hubris, sin.

5. Round Two: The Liberal Bible versus the Monarchical/Patriarchal Bible, or Locke versus Filmer

5. 1 The Monarchical/Patriarchal Bible

The execution of Charles I, the cultural panic that followed, and the Restoration of the monarchy in 1660 placed the Cromwellian experiment and the wilder Bibles that had seemed to support it, beyond the pale. However, it is not true to say, as Christopher Hill claims, that this recoil resulted in the expulsion of the Bible. Seeking like Lilla to urge us forward to a purely secular state, Hill argues that the citizens of the seventeenth century wisely found the Bible guilty of incoherence and, moreover, convicted it of crimes of regicide, as if the Bible, like Cromwell, had killed a king. Instead, as the etching "The Royale Oake of Britayne" demonstrates, the default tendency was (and is) to blame not scripture, but evil perversions and mis-readings of scripture. (We keep compulsively returning to the origin of the Bible precisely to get behind all the corruptions, perversions and failed readings.) The Bible, like Charles, was a victim.

Hill wants to tell us that, in response to the excesses of Civil War, the good old commonsensical English passed "the gift of holy humbug" across the water, effectively sticking it in a boat with the Pilgrim Fathers, leaving the scurrilous "old authority" ever after to skulk in "dark corners" such as "Northern Ireland or the Bible belt of the USA" (Hill 1993: 428, 433). In fact in the 1680s a new and equally vigorous battle raged between two new mutations of the Bible. This took place long after the Bible, in Hill's scenario, fled to America, hanging its face in shame and trying to get the blood from its hands like Lady Macbeth. The conflict was between what could be called the Monarchical/Patriarchal Bible and the Liberal Bible or Filmer's Bible and Locke's Bible. To pre-empt my argument it's the Absolute Monarchical Bible that disappears into obscurity, like Ishmael or Esau trotting off into the desert. And it's the Lockeian Liberal/Whig Bible that emerges triumphant, like Isaac or Jacob. As Isaac and Jacob get to play a key role in the origins of Israel while their brothers are forgotten, so the Liberal Bible became the one and only theological–political vision deemed possible within the benign boundaries of the Christian and the biblical. It became the true Bible at our (Western) world's origin; the presumed foundation of modern democratic states.

Resurrecting the ghost of the Patriarchal/Monarchical Bible provides a salutary and shocking reminder of what was, relatively recently in "Western" history, not just a possible but the dominant reading of biblical politics. This Bible was consolidated by growing threats to the stability of the late Stuart monarchies of Charles II and James II/VII in the late 1670s and 1680s, and widespread anxieties about another major convulsion of the state. In the context of rebellions and attempted assassinations, sympathizers with the nascent "Tory" or court party wrote of fires in the palace of kingship, and cast themselves as the metaphorical firemen and those charged to defend the palace against rampant hooligans and pyromaniacs (Johnston 1686: a.2). A key foundation stone in the project of rebuilding and strengthening the palace of monarchy was the strategic republication of Sir Robert Filmer's *Partriarcha*, first written in the 1630s, together with the publication of various defences of monarchy that out-Filmered Filmer in their interpretation of high biblical-political power.

The Monarchical/Patriarchal Bible was not a minority document, but the institutional Bible. It was rehearsed by the University of Cambridge to Charles II in 1681 (Figgis 1896: 6). In contrast, Locke's riposte to Filmer in his *Two Treatises of Government* was a clandestine text that only saw the light of day in the wake of the so-called "Glorious Revolution" of 1688. It was hidden with friends and referred to under the code name the Morbo Gallico, the French disease or syphilis – a term that punningly invoked the political despotism associated with the Turks and especially, the French.[21] Locke was spied on by his colleagues at Christchurch College, who tried to lure him into traitorous pronouncements against the Crown. In 1683 he fled to the continent, just after the last major English bookburning in the Bodleian Quadrangle in Oxford. These late modern days – when we tend to regard Locke as a periwigged old colonialist and to deem Lockeian liberalism as way too little – it is important to remember that in the 1680s liberalism appeared as dangerous excess. Locke's contemporary, Algenon Sidney, wrote a lengthy riposte to Filmer in the manuscript posthumously published as *Discourses Concerning Government*. This was an essential part of the case of against him in 1683 – as a result of which he was sentenced to death (Laslett 1984: 32).

Bible and Justice

The patriarchal premises of the Monarchical/Patriarchal Bible are so blatant that it outflanks any latter day feminist critiques of the Bible and Christian theology, making them seem mild by comparison. Mary Daly's claim that "If God is male then the male is God" (1973: 19) can appear (or at least some say it can) as a stridently reductive over-reading when applied to politer, mildly androcentric theologies. But when it comes to Filmerian patriarchalism it seems but a gentle and moderate précis. *Patriarcha* is extremely useful for countering any suspicion that gender is a marginal topic: an optional special interest topic, or scholarship for girls. *Patriarcha* overtly displays the always-present bridge between the microcosm of the family and the macrocosm of the polity. It demonstrates that gender is not a private or a marginal issue in a very overbearing way. Through its exploration of the *jus paternum*, or "right of father", it shows how the gender of authority is key to the very conception of authority. Monarchy, theocracy and paternity are united in the holy trinity of God, father and king. At the heart of this Bible is the exegetical principle that when the Bible refers to one term in this trinity the two others can always be inferred. The theological and the familial therefore receive a direct and blatant political application. For whenever the Bible is talking about fathers or Gods, it is also, self-evidently, talking about kings.

The genealogical/reproductive model in the book of Genesis is monogenesis: from the body of the father to the body of the son. Purely male genealogies run like umbilical cord from father to son to grandson. Girls are hardly ever born and the matriarchs are commonly barren. Birth has to be substituted by sacrifice as "birth done better" or reproductive powers have to be given to the mother through the intercession of the father to a God gendered as male.[22] Filmer literalizes the familial politics of Genesis to produce a dystopia far more disturbing than the Genesis-based model imagined in Margaret Atwood's *The Handmaid's Tale*. In *The Handmaid's Tale*, a world that has been virtually destroyed by nuclear holocaust is ordered around what Foucault calls "biopolitics", the consolidation of political power in the micro-unit of the family (Atwood 1987).[23] A conservative Christian community re-instates the Genesis model of handmaids and concubines in order to secure the future of the human race. For Filmer, the familial politics of Genesis extend into the very heart of the body politic. The genealogies of Genesis relate to the reproduction of government itself.

Filmer invokes the first moment of creation as a first principle, *ab initio* (from the beginning). The moment of creation functions as: (a) the source of eternal principles that transcend the ebb and tide of history; and (b) the ultimate historical precedent; the first second on the world clock. Crucially for the high monarchists' strategy this is the one moment that cannot be preceded – or, in practical terms, usurped. Filmer's whole Bible is summarized in God's defining speech act in Gen. 1:26 and Gen. 1:28: "Let them have dominion". This is interpreted as a statement with performative power, like J. L. Austin's example "With this ring I thee wed" or God's original creative "Let there be light".[24] Thus God crowns King Adam and makes Adam the "universal Monarch" or first "World King" (Wilson 1684: 19). King Adam is succeeded by a whole chain of hereditary monarchs, including King Abraham and King Judah. Through the presumed homology of king-God-father, Abraham and Judah are kings *avant la lettre* (before the letter). The case for their kingship is then consolidated by proof of their absolute paternal power, demonstrated by their right to exceed the prohibition not to kill. Abraham's almost-sacrifice (Genesis 22), Judah's right to kill his daughter-in-law Tamar (Genesis 39) and the story of Jephthah's daughter (Judges 11) work as a textual trinity supporting the trinity God-king-father. These three texts are understood to prove the limitless reach of sovereign power as the "dominion of life and death" (Filmer 1884: 16).

In this vision of political power's generation-genesis, sovereign power is transferred down the male genealogical line and consolidated by exceptional powers over death. God, king and father have a double relationship to law. They are the source of law, and they are above the law. This is proven by the fact that Genesis, an account of the origins of kingship, comes before Exodus. According to Filmer, the fact that "there were kings long before there were any laws", provides "a proof unanswerable for the superiority of princes above laws" (1884: 20–21, 44). The Exodus is interpreted in a way that would make Gusavo Gutiérrez and the liberation theologians reel in horror. The dominant theological-political point is that "The Israelites had a sharp bondage under the Egyptians, and wanted not numbers to have made their party good: The Land was filled with them, and Pharaoh confesseth them the more mighty: yet they thought it better to quit the country than rebel" (Wilson 1684: 198–99).[25] This reading of the Exodus – which seems so deeply counter-intuitive to a late modern reader – is coupled with a similarly counter-intuitive reading of the prophet Samuel's warning against kingship in 1 Samuel 8. The original text seems to pose considerable problems for high monarchists like Filmer. Samuel and God seem to be tackling a problematic desire for a human king which originates with the people. Moreover, God seems to see this design as a rejection of his divine kingship (1 Sam. 8:7) implying a split, worked open

to the point of antagonism, between divine and human king. This split
between God and king (as divine fact and human notion) is mirrored in a
similar split between the king and the prophet/narrator. For the narrator/
the prophet gives a long and seemingly ironic inventory of the kind of
oppression that results from unlimited human-sovereign power. In the
biblical text, the king is seemingly mocked by satire from below and isolated
from God above. Filmer and the high monarchists deal with this potentially
dissident passage by divesting it of subversive irony and transforming it
into a "majestical discourse of the true law of free monarchy" (Filmer 1884:
198–99). Rifts are healed between king and prophet. Samuel's speech is
transformed into a straight-faced verbatim definition of the limitless scope
of "King [noun]" as set out in the very Dictionary of God.

To a late modern, Filmer's Bible seems alien to the true spirit of the
Bible. These late modern days, much is invested in the idea that the Christian
Bible is not retro-feudal, patriarchal-theocratic, or disposed to crude and
direct intervention in affairs of state. Our conviction on this score shows
that we are unassuming inheritors of the Liberal Bible. Contra the Liberal
Bible's own mythology, this Bible was not given at the moment of the
world's creation. Rather, it was relatively recently wrested from the text.

5.2 *The Liberal Bible*

We can see the Liberal Bible clearly emerging in Locke's *First Treatise of
Government*. But this is a treatise that, because of the success of the Liberal
Bible, remains unread. Biblical scholars, who have only recently awakened
from a devotion to ur-texts to begin to engage with cultural histories of the
Bible, still tend to prefer excurses into literature, film, art and "Culture"
than to trespass on the territory of Law and Politics. (Is this because we see
Bible more firmly separated from Law and Politics than it is from Culture,
or because the logic of secularization implies a separation of Bible from
Law and Politics while allowing it to still exert an influence in "Culture"?)
Meanwhile, political theorists and constitutional historians tend to
complain that the *First Treatise* is "unreadable" (Laslett 1984: 61) precisely
because it engages, in meticulous exegetical detail, with *Patriarcha*, the
Bible and even, Hebrew. And what could seem more obscure and specialist
than Hebrew? These late modern days, when the Bible tends to be seen
more as an iconic symbol, nothing could seem more curious than gets
involved, as Locke does with the precise meanings of חיה (to live) and רמש
(to creep, move lightly). The *First Treatise* smacks of times when a
smattering of Hebrew was a necessary accoutrement for the educated
gentleman. (Samuel Pepys proudly informs his Diary that he has just

purchased a Hebrew Dictionary.) But Hebrew and Bible seems so badly out of place in Locke – the figure who is meant to represent the birth of secular constitutionalism and to stand for the emergence of "rationalist arguments which simply could not be contained in Filmer's world of Biblical politics" (Locke 1984a: 158–59). Locke is meant to stand on the "Reason" side of the putative "Reason" versus "Revelation" conflict. In an influential modern myth still faithfully represented by Lilla, "Locke versus Filmer" demonstrates the crucial modern discovery that Divine Right/Theocracy can go so very wrong.[26]

In a sense Locke does seek to make in-depth political-biblical exegeses, like *Patriarcha* and the *First Treatise*, superfluous and unnecessary. But this is not to say that he wants to expel the Bible or "secularize" in any simple sense. Rather, he seeks to transform and redefine the nature of biblical and divine authority. He wants to change the nature of the force of the Bible, rather than negate or nullify it. To this end, the Liberal Bible puts forth a new version of the Bible that claims to represent a Christianity that dates back at least as far as the creation. In this Bible, the true nature of biblical and religious authority becomes apparent when God announces, in so many words in his very first words: "Let there be rights".

Locke battles Filmer for possession of the first moment of creation – or, more specifically, God's manifesto for true government and the very constitution of the world as announced in Gen. 1:26–28. Whereas Filmer hears a divine speech act establishing limitless dominion, for Locke, God's first words possess an overbearing force of negation. God's "Let there be rights" appears by way of strident negation of Filmer's position. If it is true, as Peter Laslett argues, that Locke's political position manifests itself more starkly because it is formulated against Filmer, the same seems to apply to Locke's Liberal Bible. It is because he seeks to negate Filmer's absolute Bible so absolutely, that Locke creates such a strident vision of the biblical vision of rights.

The Liberal Bible stands as a ban on absolute monarchy and modes of Filmerian exegesis. The emphasis in Locke's exegetical strategy is on the absences, the nots. Thus he deduces:

1. God gave no immediate Power to Adam over Men, over his Children, over those of his own Species, and so he was not made Ruler, or Monarch, by this Charter.
2. That by this Grant God gave him not Private Dominion over the Inferior Creatures, but right in common with all Mankind; so neither was he Monarch, upon the account of the Property here given him. (1984a: 157)

Not unlike those contemporary preachers of the redemptive force of post-liberal Christianity (who would of course be scandalized by being placed next to such an old modern liberal) Locke resists idolatrous human political Oneness in the name of the "Only One". As an alternative to the kind of divine father who spawns or clones human kings in his own image, Locke describes a divine father who distributes dominion equally among all his sons. The idea of shared human dominion over all the earth as property is not, of course, without its own immense problems (though these were rather less clear three centuries prior to postcolonial criticism, environmental theology and the work of Lynn T. White).[27]

Locke sees in kernel in Genesis not just a general statement of ethical righteousness but "right" in the modern sense of "subjective rights". Modern genealogies of rights, such as those in Ishay's *Human Rights Reader*, often lazily/usefully conflate ideas of righteousness with modern formulations of subjective rights. But there are important differences, as Charles Taylor points out. The ban on killing people (at least certain people under certain circumstances), may be reasonably widespread, but "That I have a right to life says more than that you shouldn't kill me. It gives me some control over this immunity. A right is something that in principle I can waive" (Taylor 2008: 143). In our desire to repeat that Filmerian/Lockeian move and trace our most precious concepts back to the very first moment of creation, we fudge terms and miss transitions. "Right" once referred to a particular concession to take tithes at this particular tollbooth or to act as magistrate on this particular bench. Similarly, "liberty" as a singular noun once referred to a particular concession – as in the phrase "taking a liberty". It is a considerable step to the idea of right and liberty as an intrinsic moral asset and universal possession "endowed by [the] Creator" (Taylor 1989: 11). Crucially, the clause "endowed by the Creator" is not detachable from the early modern formulation of rights. This is not just theological packaging for an argument that could be "secular" – in the sense of divested of any metaphysical underpinning. In Locke's logic, as Peter Laslett explains, "we are free of each other" and "equal to each other", because "we are not free of God's superiority and not equal to him" (1984a: 93). The two notions are inseparable. The transition to rights as an intrinsic moral asset requires the concept of the gift and will of the one divine universal king to bring it off. The transition, therefore, is not a simple one from the divine to the purely human, the theocratic to the self-determining, as in cruder versions of the secularization story. Rather, the enabling trope of proto-democracy was the idea that God gave us autonomy and that we possess self-determining freedom (under God).

In the Lockeian vision of creation as laid out by God on the first page of Genesis all men possessed executive power equally. The whole world was full of potential mini-kings with kingdoms over their own I's and their own property. All had the natural, God-given inalienable right to punish an infringement of their property and their person. But realizing that this would lead to chaos (Locke agrees with Hobbes on this point) human beings invested their natural right in the mode of government that they deemed most workable and wise. Charles Taylor describes the transition thus:

> The older notion that human society stands under a Law of Nature, whose origin was the Creator, and which was thus beyond human will, was now transposed. The fundamental law was reconceived as consisting of natural rights, attributed to individuals prior to society. At the origin of society stands a contract, which takes people out of a state of nature and puts them under political authority as a result of an act of consent on their part. (Taylor 2008: 143)

By describing a transition from Creator to contract, Taylor implies a move from theology to society that would fit with neater versions of the secularization story. But his wording obscures the fact that in both formulations the 'origin' is the 'Creator'. However 'origin' and 'Creator' are understood in different senses. In the first, the Creator establishes government through the expression of a will that transcends human will. In the second, the Creator's will expresses itself through the devolution of governmental power through contract. Government is still related to divine desire – but this is now redefined as the desire to respect rights. In the older view, there is only one form of legitimate government: that expressed by God's will, or natural law. Theoretically, the latter, contractual view, sponsors a range of different forms of government. But in practice there is a limit to the forms of legitimate government that this model will support. The true theological-political state cannot be theocratic, for example. Only when we see proof of the devolution of divine power in a constitution that is democratic or proto-democratic can we know that the state is underwritten by the true, new (Christian) God.

Locke claims that it has always been the nature of Christianity's God and his scripture to devolve power to human government and consensus. The roots of proto-democracy lie in a theo-political kenosis reminiscent of the self-emptying of Christ. Just as Christ, though "in the form of God" did not "count equality a thing to be grasped, but emptied himself, taking the form of a servant" (Phil. 2.6–7), so the Christian scriptures and the Christian God graciously devolve power. This is a key example of what Timothy

Fitzgerald astutely describes as the invention of religion and politics as "part of the same rhetorical movement" (2007: 14–15). As Fitzgerald argues, it is not that religion/theology and politics (or "Church" and "State") have always been self-evidently separate domains but that once upon a time they were confused. Rather, the notion of two distinct domains and the idea of their necessary parting were constructed fairly late in the day. These ideas, I argue, were first formulated within biblical/theological vocabularies. It makes a difference to our understandings of this constituting difference – between religion on one side and politics on the other – to realize that this difference was articulated, accommodated and sponsored from within the Bible/Christianity, as an act of the Bible/Christianity's expansive grace.

For Locke, God's inaugural command "Let there be rights", means that we can work within other vocabularies, like that of Law, while still operating within the founding spirit of the Bible and the graciously self-emptying deity that the Bible represents. If we follow the logic of Filmerian exegesis, he complains, the "Civil Lawyers" can only be seen as "meddling in a matter that belongs not to them". For "if all political power be derived only from Adam … by the Ordinance of God and Divine Institution, this is a Right Antecedent and Paramount to all Government; and therefore the positive Laws of Men, cannot determine that which is it self the Foundation of all Law and Government" (Locke 1984a: 233). In fact, Locke's vision also appeals to God and the Bible as a ground or foundation for law, but in a more subtle way. Locke's understanding of the relationship between the scriptural and the legal is spelled out by Locke's contemporary, the Whig lawyer Sir Richard Atkyns, thus:

> The laws of England (as all just and righteous laws) are grounded originally upon the divine law, as their foundation or fountain. The supreme and sovereign God among the heathen is supposed to have the name of Jupiter, quasi "Juris Pater" – But more immediately human laws have their force and authority from the consent and agreement of men. (Atkyns 1816: col. 1200–47)

The Liberal Bible and the Liberal God serve as the ultimate fountain, or foundation, beneath the everyday work of the political and the legal. This kind of God and this kind of Bible can clearly operate as the foundation of the modern state. At the same time, theocracy is associated with the God of the heathen. Over-literalism or over-dependence on the letter is the absolute antithesis of the spirit of the Liberal English Bible. In the early twenty-first century, it seems to be associated with the Qur'an. In the seventeenth century it was associated with the Turks and the French.

6. Locke's Jokes with Genesis

In his exegetical riposte to Filmer, Locke devotes a disproportionate amount of time to Genesis. This is because he is battling for the origin, but also because one doesn't need to go much further than Genesis to establish the kind of Bible he has in mind. For the Liberal Bible all that is needed is the inaugural moment where the Bible devolves power through the opening pronouncement "Let there be Rights". Revealingly, Locke's exegesis is split between an acknowledgement of the parochialism of the Bible and an appeal to the Bible as the source of universal, transcendent principle. Genesis is not a document that carries much weight with the Chinese, he jokes (1984a: 243). Other cultures have their own national heroes and their own origin stories, their own Abrahams, Adams and Hams. Temporally, the world of Genesis belongs to the world of the beginning, when, as Locke (in)famously puts it "all the World was America" (1984b: 301). Abraham and Adam are closer to the American "Indians" of the New World than they are to the developed governments of Europe. The Bible's temporal and geographical specificity prohibits any attempt to apply the Bible as a work of direct divine dictation to developed seventeenth-century European governments. But at the same time the Bible remains, for Locke, a source of universal principle. And this principle is expressed most neatly and powerfully at the origin, or genesis.

Filmer appeals to the origin in its historical and transcendent senses. For him, Genesis establishes transcendent governing principles and marks the historical beginning that sets the direct agenda for all time. Locke relativizes biblical beginnings in their contingent historical sense. But he still invokes the origin as transcendent guiding principle. And he still appeals to the two key repositories of self-evident truth: the origin and the letter or the plain sense of the Bible. In his counter-exegesis, he repeats the familiar gesture of freeing the "direct and plain meaning of the words" of scripture from the distorting force of "prejudice" and "ill grounded opinions" (1984). Just like the etching "The Royale Oake of Britayne" he makes the rhetorical move of recovering the true original/origin and releasing the poor distorted Bible from defamation and abuse. *Patriarcha* is not a true "Gospel" grounded on ancient authority. It is a "new nothing"; a pseudepigraphical-apocryphal-(Catholic) lie, authored not by the Holy Ghost but by "an English Courtier" (1984: 194, 138). The edifice of Bible that Filmer constructs is a phantom or man-made machine (1984: 145, 190). As an airy abstraction it floats high above the "nature of things", the self evident "constitution and order which God had settled in the World", and the joint testimony of "common sense and experience" and the "plain sense" of the biblical – the assumption being that common sense and the plain sense of the Bible agree (1984: 241). *Patriarcha* lacks the necessary grounding: in the ancient, in the divine-biblical, and in plain and common sense. The spurious "Fabric" "falls" and the "vast Engine of Absolute Power and Tyranny drops down of it self", once this lack of ground is spectacularly revealed (1984: 190).

Locke delights in hyper-literalism designed to strip the textual ground or plain sense from under Filmer's feet. The *First Treatise* is full of close-reading jokes that would have made biblically literate readers of the late seventeenth century chortle (although one has to confess that the comedy has rather aged as in Shakespeare's comic interludes). If Filmer is going to make so much of 'dominion over every living thing' as laid out in Gen. 1:28 and 9:2, then he must also concede that God has also licensed cannibalism, since dominion is also specified as the right to "eat every Living thing that moveth" (1984: 160). The creation narrative seems to put a "spade" into Adam's hand, rather than a "sceptre". Moreover, isn't it rather confusing that God banished the "world king" and consigned him to work as a day-labourer? (1984: 172) If "King" Isaac was really heir to "King" Abraham, then why didn't Abraham's servant – who goes to such trouble to list all his master's maid-servants, camels and asses – even mention it as one of his master's key assets when he seeks to woo Rebecca on his master's behalf (Genesis 24) (1984: 180)? If Judah's pronouncement of a death sentence over Tamar in Genesis 38 proves his sovereign right over her and all his subjects – and if it is acceptable biblical-rational reasoning to deduce a "right of doing" from "doing" – then surely we should add that "He lay with her also: By the same way of Proof, he had a Right to do that too" (1984: 235). If generation/procreation is the source of paternal dominion, then the mother must be at least a co-sharer in supreme authority, for "no body can deny but that the Woman hath an equal share, if not the greater, as nourishing the Child a long time in her own Body out of her own Substance" (1984: 180). Similarly, Filmer's "garbled" "half-quotation" of the second commandment as "Honour thy Father" surely proves that he is working from an apocryphal (Catholic) text or unreliable pseudepigraphic work that neglected the canonical "and thy mother" (1984: 161). This is not, of course, a premature attempt by Locke to extend notions of equality to women. Rather it is a strategy to render high paternal power ridiculous by making it at least half-female. Nothing has more power to make paternal power impotent and ludicrous than the appeal to the weakness of woman.

7. Conclusions; Legacies

Locke and Filmer's Bibles are related to the two versions of the Bible that were locked in combat during the Civil War – although not in any straightforward way. Filmer's Patriarchal/Monarchical Bible looks at first glance like the Deferential/Passive Bible. However, it is more like the Active Revolutionary/Republican Bible because it is less of a static icon and more of a gigantic vocabulary that seeks to connect itself, directly, at the level of detail, to the state. The Liberal Bible is a dilute version of the Active Revolutionary/Republican Bible. It is a reaction against the Active Revolutionary/Republican Bible as much as it is a reaction against the Patriarchal/Monarchical Bible. The Liberal Bible proved far more successful and enduring than its wilder predecessor because: (a) it stood for a far more moderate theological-politics; and (b) it turned the Bible into something more like a symbol and less like a set of divine speech acts demanding to be actualized in any direct, literal sense. Like the quietist, deferential, passive Bible, the Liberal Bible negates the literal application of the Bible to the polity. However, it does not achieve this by a blatant ban – a "Leave things to God and Caesar" – but by a more subtle and sophisticated act of theological-political negation. The kenotic creative moment at the start of the Liberal Bible is understood as a negation of direct theocratic power. The Liberal Bible can be best understood as a set of operational boundaries placed on valid interpretations of the Bible's theology and politics. It reduces the Bible to a few benign and vague axiomatic politico-theological principles that can be liberally applied (excuse the pun) thereafter.

The theories of secularization/democratization articulated by Bellah, Fukuyama, Gauchet and Berger are indebted to the Liberal Bible. The spirit of the Liberal Bible is faithfully expressed in the ideas that God, through his transcendence, granted the world proto-secular independence (Berger), or that the origins of "democracy" and "political equality" lie in the Christian doctrine of the "universal dignity of man" (Fukuyama). Its presence can equally be felt in the 2007 *Human Rights Reader* – not least when the Ten Commandments are read not as a manifesto of patriarchal powers (as in Filmer) but as a manifesto of equality and "morality, justice and mutual respect" (Ishay 2007: 31). Whatever their theological-political orientation, all the current, creative, appeals to the theological-political promise of the Bible and Christianity take place within the legacy of the Liberal Bible. They dance their giddy theological-poetic acrobatics above the safety net of the Liberal Bible. They can take such risks because they can safely invoke the Bible as the source of a few axiomatic politico-theological principles rather than (as in the Active Republican/Revolutionary Bible), the source of a detailed textual agenda for the state. Darker, theocratic Filmerian Bibles are forgotten. Detailed biblical agendas that would now appear as ludicrous or retrogressively fundamentalist are repressed. A very particular kind of Bible – a Bible with an inbuilt commitment to hands-off transcendentalism and an intrinsic allergy to monarchy/theocracy – is invoked in campaigns for more Bible/Christianity in the public square. Exhortations to return to Christian/biblical sources are located in the aftermath of the revised origin that the Liberal Bible represents.

Long before my attempts to name and "out" it, the Liberal Bible has clearly been present. It has exerted a forceful influence due to its highly palatable revisions of theological and biblical force. Because it appeals to the non-contingent power of the origin – the first moment of the creation – the Liberal Bible masks the contingency of its own formation. It occludes the distinctly modern (I deliberately do not say secular) edge of its formulation of justice. At a time when the self-evidently proto-democratic, benign force of the Bible is being assumed in contrast with other less progressive scriptures, it may well prove important to remember that the Liberal Bible does not date back to the Creation of the World (over six thousand years ago according to Ussher's calculations). Rather, it is of fairly recent vintage at just over three hundred years old.

I am not arguing that modern notions of justice come from Locke, not the Bible. I am not siding with Lilla and saying that redemption lies on the side of the secular. What is interesting (and worrying) to me is the way in which my argument might easily be misunderstood thus, precisely because this particular debate is habitually seen as a matter of taking one of two very distinct sides. *Why* are the options limited (and polarized to) Lilla versus Hauerwas and Wolterstorff; strident manifestos of a purely redemptive Bible versus rhetorical denunciations of the Bible/the Christian as the evil ghost of theocracy? (In these very public debates it never comes down to a frank discussion of good texts and bad texts, texts of redemption and "texts of terror", as it has done, of late in Biblical Studies. The arguments are purified, the counter-texts occluded, and there is a strenuous avoidance of the idea of the ambiguity of the biblical/divine. And do we really have to decide between a trajectory of progress and redemption the further we get from Christian origins, or, conversely, a story of decline and Fall as the Manichean dualities are mapped crudely on to time? One dominant story among Christian ethicists crudely merges selfishness and secularism. It reports how a catastrophic Fall, beginning with Ockham and nominalism and ending up in the mire of the "individualistic mentality of the

Enlightenment" represented a fatal contamination of the once purer Christian communitarian understanding of rights (Wolterstorff 2008: 44–45).[28] Here Christian origins – represented either by the Bible or the good medievals – represent the virginity of a story of beginnings prior to corruption/Fall. Origin is seen as a key to essence. Almost in a Filmerian sense the governing question becomes "Who is the Father (and is he Christian, or secular?)". The question "What good can come from a way of thinking about justice and rights whose parentage is late-medieval nominalism or Enlightenment political theory?" is assumed to make some kind of sense (Wolterstorff 2008: 44). Morality tales where Religion battles Secularism (or vice versa) make good headlines. But by stridently polarizing the religious and the secular and seeking to purify their beloved object from contamination, they intimate the fear that we are not really clear enough yet on what the two sides are and that they are not yet quite fully prised apart. A phenomenon like the Liberal Bible suggests why we still lack this perfect clarity and polarity. As a symptom of our founding fusions and confusions, it conjoins sources "secular" and "religious", "human" and "divine" as sponsors and foundations of the separation of "state" and "church", "politics" and "religion", "human" and "divine".

By arguing that the Liberal Bible is not original, I am not claiming that it is spurious, inauthentic, late: hence not True, not "in" the Bible as such. "Origins" are never created solely by the original text. Rather, as Ward Blanton astutely observes in his study of recent appeals to Christian origins, the origin is created in a "reflective play of mirrors" in which "the 'truth' of any given depiction of ancient Christianity emerges only in that same moment in which an audience recognises this depiction to be an exemplary embodiment of those distinctions in terms of which it desires to identify itself" (2007: 6). This is an important lesson for biblical scholars who tend to be literalists and historicists, disposed to thinking in reductive terms of what a text "is". We, of all people, are believers in origins. Hard-wired into our discipline is an inbuilt faith in the value of the original over the later addition or the distorting interpretation that comes after and covers over the original that seeks to be uncovered/revealed. But this idea of an original, static or historically circumscribed text is a professional's or literalist's dream. It attempts to pin down the spirit of volatility, inversion and transformation in/of the Bible that was so evident in the vernacular Active Republican/ Revolutionary Bible. (Like the Liberal Bible, professional biblical studies is a reaction against this interpretative chaos.) But it fails to do justice to how the Bible goes on being heard   as divine speech acts, desiring to do things in the world. Whatever our successes in creating internal rules for our discipline, biblical scholars will never have sufficient powers to police the performative success or failure of the biblical or ideas of "the Bible" that operate beyond the tether of a text. A Filmerian reading is no more or less "in" the original than a Lockeian one – and no more or less possible/impossible if the times and theo-political temperatures are right. When it comes to numinous things like possibilities and powers, the biblical text can never act as a single force determining or limiting: (a) projections of the true shape of Christian/biblical power(s); and (b) projections of the desired powers of the Christian/biblical in the state.

Notes

1. For an insightful discussion of the implications of Wolterstorff's appeal to the Bible, see Ward Blanton, "Wolterstorff's Bible-as-'frame'" *The Immanent Frame*, blog posted 1 April 2009 (http://www.ssrc.org/blogs/immanent_frame/2009/04/01/wolterstorff's-bible-as-frame/).
2. For example see Davis and Riches (2005: 22, 29–30) following Wright (2003); Desmond (2005: 175); Milbank (2003: 105). While denouncing the "anthropology of individual dominium" associated with figures like Locke, Milbank's argument builds on the legacy of the Liberal Bible, advocated by figures like Locke, and, lurking behind it, the more radical (republican) Bible. See the discussion below.
3. Academic authors, of course, are not always directly consulted about their book covers.
4. Found in the afterword to the reprint edition.
5. For trenchant critique of Gauchet, Asad (2008).
6. I am using "English" here because union between the two and three kingdoms was fluctuating and uncertain in the seventeenth century, and Britain was an anachronism in the 1680s.
7. This phrasing is used in anon. *The Political Catechism* (1643), here quoted from a later edition: *The True Portraiture of the Kings of England, Drawn from their Titles, Sucessions, Raigns and Ends ... To which is added the Political Catechism* (London: 1688).
8. See Pocock (1987).
9. On the battle for the One in Genesis, see Schwartz (1987).
10. Whigs and Tories were nascent parliamentary parties that first emerged in the late 1670s. Loosely speaking, the Tories were the court party, including Catholic supporters of the Stuart kings and Anglican churchmen. Whigs – or the country party, or liberal party – were MPs often in favour of non-conformism and a more active role for lawyers and parliament, who were generally at a greater distance from the court.
11. See, for example, Calamy [(1970: 11–80) preached 22 December 1641; published London: 1642]; McGiffert (1983: 1151–76), and Collinson (1991: 20–23).
12. Hauerwas identifies as a United Methodist but also worships at an Episcopalian church. Milbank is Anglo-Catholic.
13. For "eucharistic anarchism", see Milbank (2003: 105).

14. I'm referring to the series of no less than 16 novels by Tim Lahaye and Jerry B. Jenkins that have topped the best-seller list in the USA.
15. For one contemporary description of the laws of primogeniture as "drown[ing] all the kittens but one" see Kishlansky (1996: 12). For the famous statement about the "poorest he" and the radical idea of universal suffrage, see the speech of Colonel Rainsborough at the so-called Putney Debates (1647): "For really I think that the poorest he that is in England has a life to live, as the greatest he; and therefore, truly sir, I think it's clear, that every man that is to live under a government ought first by his own consent to put himself under that government; and I do think that the poorest man in England is not at all bound in the strict sense to that government that he has not had a voice to put himself under; and I am confident that when I have heard the reasons against it, something will be said to answer those reasons, inasmuch that I should doubt whether he was an Englishman or no, that should doubt of these things" (cit. Wootton, *Divine Right and Democracy*, pp. 285–317 [286]).
16. See Hill (1993: 117) citing Andrew Marvell's advice to Cromwell in "The First Anniversary of the Government under O.C.". In the parable of Judges 9, the humble bramble accepts the kingship declined by the rich olive, vine and fig, but declines all the pomp of kingship, offering instead that the people "come and take refuge in my shade" (Judg. 9:15). Despite modelling himself on the thorn-bush and describing himself as Lord-Protector, Cromwell held court like a king, had the burial of a king, and ended up a king "in all but name" [see Sherwood (1997) and MacLean (1990: 152–53)].
17. For the legislation passed by the Republic, see for example Hill (1993: 203, 231). The blasphemy act was passed in 1650. In 1656 Alexander Agnew was hanged for denying that the scriptures were the word of God. The adultery act of 1650 made adultery a capital offence. It resulted in the execution of four women and no men.
18. John Milton cited the precedent of Abraham, David, Gideon and Joash as justification for polygamy and divorce.
19. See for example Hos. 13:8 or Isa. 63:1–6. For the latter as a description of God as wine-stained tramp see Sawyer (1993: 72–82).
20. For discussion of this engraving see Knoppers (2000: 41–43).
21. See Laslett (1984: 62).
22. See Fuchs (1999: 127–40) and Jay (1992).
23. For Foucault's argument that biopolitics – the political obsession with biological life – shows how political power has contracted in the micro-unit of the family see Foucault (1984) and Foucault (1991).
24. For performative utterances, see Austin (1962).
25. In Wilson's quietist version of biblical history, the lesson of the Babylonian exile is similar: "nor was their condition much improved in Babylon, and yet they are commanded to offer Sacrifices, and pray to the life of the King, and of his Sons".
26. I'm sure this pun has been used before – and more than once. The only example I can recall is John Mullan's "How Divine Right Went Wrong" (2006) – a review of Tim Harris, *Revolution: The Crisis of the British Monarchy* and Edward Vallance, *The Glorious Revolution: Britain's Fight for Liberty*.
27. For a now classic statement see White (1967: 1203–07).
28. For a brief synopsis of this narrative of decline, see Wolterstorff (2008: 44–45).

Bibliography

Asad, Talal. 2008. "Reflections on Blasphemy and Secular Criticism." In *Religion: Beyond a Concept*, ed. Hent de Vries: 580–609. New York: Fordham University Press.

Atkyns, Robert. 1816. "An Enquiry into the Power of Dispensing with the Penal Statutes." In *Complete Collection of State Trials and Proceedings for High Treason and Other Crimes and Misdemeanours, from the Earliest Period to the Year 1783*, 34 vols., ed. T. B. Howell, Vol. 11: col. 1200–1247. London: Hansard.

Atwood, Margaret. 1987. *The Handmaid's Tale*. London: Virago.

Austin, J. L. 1962. *How to Do Things with Words*. Oxford: Clarendon Press.

Bellah, Robert. 1976. *Beyond Belief: Essays on Religion in a Post-Traditional World*. New York: Harper and Row.

Berger, John. 1967. *The Sacred Canopy: Elements of a Sociological Theory of Religion*. Garden City, New York: Doubleday.

Blanton, Ward. 2007. *Displacing Christian Origins: Philosophy, Secularity and the New Testament*. Chicago, IL: University of Chicago Press.

Calamy, Edmund. 1970. "England's Looking-Glasse." In *Fast Sermons to Parliament* (vol 3), ed. Robin Jeffs, 11–80. London: Cornmarket Press.

Collinson, Patrick. 1991. *The Birthpangs of Protestant England: Religious and Cultural Change in the Sixteenth and Seventeenth Centuries*. New York: Palgrave Macmillan.

Daly, Mary. 1973. *Beyond God the Father: Toward a Philosophy of Women's Liberation*. Boston, MA: Beacon.

Davis, Creston and Patrick Aaron Riches. 2005. "Metanoia: The Theological Praxis of Revolution." In *Theology and the Political: The New Debate*, eds Creston Davis, John Millbank and Slavoj Zizek, 22–51. Durham, NC and London: Duke University Press.

Debray, Régis. 2004. *God: An Itinerary* (trans. Jeffrey Mehlman). London and New York: Verso.

Derrida, Jacques. 1974. "White Mythology: Metaphor in the Text of Philosophy." *New Literary History* 6 (1): 5–74.

Desmond, William. 2003. "Neither Servility nor Sovereignty: Between Metaphysics and Politics." In *Theology and the Political: The New Debate*, eds Creston Davis, John Milbank and Slavoi Zizek, 153–82. Durham, NC and London: Duke University Press.

Figgis, J. Neville. 1896. *The Theory of the Divine Right of Kings*. Cambridge: Cambridge University Press.

Fitzgerald, Timothy. 2007. *Discourse on Civility and Barbarity: A Critical History of Religion and Related Categories*. Oxford: Oxford University Press.

Filmer, Sir Robert. 1884. *Patriarcha, or the Natural Power of Kings* (1680). In Henry Morley (ed.), John Locke *Two Treatises on Civil Government, preceded by Sir Robert Filmer's Patriarcha*: 11–73. London: George Routledge and Sons.

Foucault, Michel. 1984. "Nietzsche, Genealogy, History." In *The Foucault Reader*, ed. Paul Rabinow, 76–100. New York: Pantheon Books.

_____. 1991. "Governmentality." In *The Foucault Effect: Studies in Governmentality*, eds G. Burchell, C. Gordon and P. Miller, 87–104. Chicago, IL: University of Chicago Press.

Fuchs, Esther. 1999. "The Literary Characterization of Mothers and Sexual Politics in the Hebrew Bible." In *Women in the Hebrew Bible*, ed. Alice Bach. New York and London: Routledge: 127–140.

Fukuyama, Francis. 2006. *The End of History and the Last Man*. New York: Free Press.

Gauchet, Marcel. 1997. *The Disenchantment of the World: A Political History of Religion*. Princeton, NJ: Princeton University Press.

Hill, Christopher. 1993. *The English Bible and the Seventeenth Century Revolution*. London: Penguin/Allen Lane.

Ishay, Micheline R. (ed.). 2007. *The Human Rights Reader: Major Political Essays, Speeches, and Documents from Ancient Times to the Present*. New York and London: Routledge.

Jay, Nancy. 1992. *Throughout Your Generations Forever: Sacrifice, Religion and Paternity*. Chicago, IL and London: University of Chicago Press.

Johnston, Nathaniel. 1686. *The Excellency of Monarchial Government, Especially the English Monarchy ... In All Which the Principles and Practices of Our Late Commonwealths-Men Are Considered*. London.

Kishlansky, Mark. 1996. *A Monarchy Transformed: Britain 1603–1714*. London: Allen Lane/Penguin.

Knoppers, Laura Lunger. 2000. *Constructing Cromwell: Ceremony, Portrait and Print 1645–1661*. Cambridge: Cambridge University Press.

Laslett, Peter. 1984. "Introduction." In *Two Treatises of Government*, ed. Peter Laslett, 3–126. Cambridge: Cambridge University Press.

Lilla Mark D. 2007. *The Stillborn God: Religion, Politics and the Modern West*. New York: Knopf.

Locke, John. 1984a. "First Treatise." In *Two Treatises of Government*, ed. Peter Laslett, 135–263. Cambridge: Cambridge University Press.

_____. 1984b. "Second Treatise." In *Two Treatises of Government*, ed. Peter Laslett, 265–428. Cambridge: Cambridge University Press.

MacLean, Gerald. 1990. *Time's Witness: Historical Representation in English Poetry 1603–1660*. Madison, WI: University of Wisconsin Press.

McGiffert, Michael. 1983. "God's Controversy with Jacobean England." *American Historical Review* 88: 1151–76.

Milbank, John. 2003. *Being Reconciled*. New York: Routledge.

Moore, Roy. 2005. *So Help Me God: The Ten Commandments, Judicial Tyranny and the Battle for Religious Freedom*. Nashville, TN: Broadman and Holman.

Mullan, John. 2006. "How Divine Right Went Wrong." *The Guardian, Review*, 25 February.

Pocock, J. G. A. 1987. *The Ancient Constitution and the Feudal Law; A Study of English Historical Thought in the Seventeenth Century*. Cambridge: Cambridge University Press.

Sawyer, John. 1993. "Radical Images of Yahweh in Isaiah 63." In *Among the Prophets: Language, Image and Structure in the Prophetic Writings*, eds P. R. Davies and D. J. A. Clines, 72–82. (JSOTSup 144). Sheffield: JSOT Press.

Schwartz, Regina. 1997. *The Curse of Cain: The Violent Legacy of Monotheism*. Chicago, IL and London: Chicago University Press.

Sherwood, Roy. 1997. *Oliver Cromwell: King in All But Name*, Stroud, Gloucestershire: Sutton.

Shuger, Debora. 1990. *Habits of Thought in the English Renaissance: Religion, Politics, and the Dominant Culture.* Berkeley, CA: University of California Press.

Swift Report. 2005. "Most Americans Want to See Constitution Replaced by Ten Commandments." http://swiftreport.blogs.com/news/2005/11/most_americans_. html. [Accessed March 2007.]

Taylor, Charles. 1989. *Sources of the Self: The Making of the Modern Identity.* Cambridge: Cambridge University Press.

_____. 2008. "A World Consensus on Human Rights?" In *Human Rights* (Critical Concepts in Political Science), eds Richard Falk, Hilal Elver and Kisa Hajjar, 141–151. London and New York: Routledge.

Tierney, Brian. 1997. *The Idea of Natural Rights: Studies in Natural Rights, Natural Law and Church Law 1150–1625.* (Emory University Studies in Law and Religion.) Atlanta, GA: Scholars Press.

Wallis, Jim. 2005. *God's Politics: Why the Right Gets it Wrong and the Left Doesn't Get It.* New York: HarperOne.

White, Lynn Townsend, Jr. 1967. "The Historical Roots of our Ecologic Crisis." *Science* 155 (3767): 1203–07.

Wilson, John. 1684. *Discourse of Monarchy, more particularly, of the imperial crowns of England, Scotland and Ireland, as it relates to the succession of His Royal Highness, James Duke of York.* London.

Wolterstorff, Nicholas. 2008. *Justice: Rights and Wrongs.* Princeton, NJ and Oxford: Princeton University Press.

Wootton, Daniel (ed.). 2003 [1986]. *Divine Right and Democracy: An Anthology of Political Writing in Stuart England.* Indianapolis, IN: Hackett.

Wright, N. T. 2003. *Resurrection and the Son of God.* Minneapolis, MN: Fortress.

Rough Justice?

Philip Davies[a]

When we speak nowadays about ethics we consider it in terms of either philosophy or religion, and both disciplines claim the subject as their own. But each understands it in its in own way: one as a matter of rational analysis, the other as rooted in divine revelation. Rarely, since the Enlightenment, have these two discourses been combined. Indeed, they go back to different ancestors: Western philosophy, whether or not all "footnotes to Plato",[1] derives from its classical heritage; whereas we do not look to the Bible for philosophy. We do not look to the Bible for 'philosophy'.[2] On the other hand, the Western 'God' (whether the one we believe in or do not) is biblically defined: we no longer recognize the Greek or Roman gods. Does this mean that we cannot bring the Bible in a useful way into our philosophy of ethics? Should we, indeed, recognize Plato as a theologian, and a monotheistic one at that, and also consider that while the Bible does not do philosophy in the way we conventionally recognize, it can be read and debated in much the same way that we still read and debate Plato?

I will argue that we can, and that the biblical texts display their own kind of philosophical reasoning on many topics, including social justice. This reasoning involves a "canonical" approach that constructs a dialogue or dialectic between texts that sometimes may have little or not direct

[a] Philip Davies is an Emeritus Professor at the University of Sheffield, where he took a post after teaching in Ghana. Davis' areas of expertise include intertestamental and rabbinic literature, the Persian and Hellenistic periods, and the Dead Sea Scrolls. In addition to his work as an Executive Officer for the European Association of Biblical Studies and as an Editor of Equinox Publishing, Davies co-founded the *Journal for the Study of the Old Testament*. His long list of publications includes *The Damascus Covenant* (JSOT, 1983), *In Search of Ancient Israel* (JSOT, 1992), and *On the Origins of Judaism* (Equinox, 2009).

historical association, though quite often, as I hope to show, there is a conscious debate occurring.

Collective Punishment

The biblical dialectic of social justice is a thread that may be picked up at a number of points. I have found the easiest to be collective punishment. It falls under the rubric of what Hugh Pyper has called "rough justice" and is of course a widespread phenomenon. Two instances come to mind as I write: the collective reprisal effected on the population of Gaza ("disproportionate response", as the Israeli Prime Minister was willing to call it), and the global financial crisis, in which every single person on the planet is being punished for the excessive greed of bankers and other financial speculators. Neither of these seems fair on the large number of individuals who are personally innocent of fault. But is there nevertheless a defensible principle of collective justice?

The books of Kings portray divine punishment for the religious policies of the Israelite and Judean monarchs as being borne by the people as a whole. The entire "Deuteronomistic" corpus (Joshua to Kings) is a record of the guilt and punishment of a nation (or two nations), in which individual merit plays only an occasional and even incidental role. Even if the religious apostasy initiated by the guilty kings was followed by most people, incurring their individual responsibility, often enough there were righteous individuals in their midst. According to 1 Kgs 19:18, for instance, as many as 7000 in Israel did not worship Baal. In 2 Samuel 24, when David's census is punished by a plague upon the people, David appears to regard the offence as his alone, and protests (v. 17): "I alone have sinned, and I alone have behaved wickedly; but these sheep, what have they done? Please let your hand be against me and my family". Other details make this collective punishment even less palatable: David himself is not personally infected, and even his offence is provoked by Yahweh as a result of his anger (for no specific reason) against Israel and Judah.[3]

This is but one case in the Hebrew Bible where a human protests to Yahweh against his collective punishment. But there is little protest, ancient or modern, against the entire Deuteronomistic scheme whereby the nation as a whole is punished for offences committed by leaders that it did not necessarily choose nor follow. The book of Deuteronomy itself however, lays stress not upon the moral leadership of the king but on the people, both collectively and individually. This is done by addressing its commands to an alternating singular and plural "you" in a way that suggests to us that social behaviour is ultimately a collection of individual behaviours and that we are answerable for what others do in our society.[4] This does not amount to a doctrine of corporate personality[5] but rather to the fact that individually we cannot isolate ourselves from either the deeds of others or their consequences. This principle may not be as agreeable to our modern individualistic society as to one where kinship relations and social solidarity play a stronger role; and it is deserving of serious consideration.

Nevertheless, the dialogue does not end: it has much further to go. For the many biblical protests – apart from that put in David's mouth – against the punishment of innocent individuals shows that the idea of punishment on those individually innocent was an uneasy one. But before we follow the thread in that direction, we can consider the case of Achan (Joshua 7). Here, individual and collective punishment seem to operate together. Individual punishment – we might call it "smooth justice" – is certainly the object and the outcome of the story, but two different mechanisms of collective punishment are also operating. First, there is the military defeat of Israel, which is hardly a natural or automatic consequence of Achan's actions but a voluntary divine response that takes the form of a collective punishment. Achan's death does not *prevent* that punishment, but only brings it to an end. Second, Achan's punishment involves his whole family, regardless of any individual innocence on their part. Now, we might argue that Achan's treatment effectively brands him as a Canaanite, while Rahab's treatment welcomes her as an Israelite, so that ethnic affiliation is the real goal of the story. That interpretation, however, leads the issue of collective punishment in the direction of racial hatred and even genocide, and we shall not go there (though we might ask whether Achan's treachery was worse than Rahab's, whether in intent or consequence).

We might also ask what might have occurred if it had not been possible to identify the individual responsible. Deut. 21:1–9 deals with a case of murder by an unknown person. Here again corporate responsibility lies on the nearest community, and the elders must avert this by washing their hands over a heifer whose neck has been broken, asking for divine absolution and so avoiding "social justice" (In Mt. 27:24 Pontius Pilate famously recapitulates this gesture, though with the intention of diverting personal responsibility from himself to others.) The recourse to what is in effect a cultic remedy that results in no punishment on a 'guilty' party is, however, hardly typical of Deuteronomistic ethics, but fits quite well with the worldview of Leviticus, where we find the issues conceived in a quite different way.

The worldview of Leviticus construes sin almost entirely in corporate terms, since it is regarded as a defilement that affects the whole land, especially the sanctuary. Rather than attaching morally to its cause, uncleanness is not of itself a moral quality and it can be contagious. The priority therefore is removal rather than punishment, and this is a cultic matter. Acts of contrition, accompanied by the appropriate ritual of sacrifice and/or cleansing are not instances of *punishment* but of *effacement*, corresponding to the modern notion of retributive rather than punitive justice. In the Day of Atonement ritual (Leviticus 16) the High Priest sacrifices a bull as a sin-offering for himself and his household (v. 6), and one of two goats as a sin-offering for the people, whose sins would otherwise defile the sanctuary (vv. 15–16). They are, rather, gestures of acknowledgement and of reconciliation. On the Day of Atonement the collective guilt is accepted by the High Priest on behalf of all (v. 17), and in the well-known ceremony of the goats, effaced via two mechanisms. One is the goat of the sin-offering, the other is the transference of the uncleanness/ sin to the other goat that is sent into the wilderness. Collective guilt is thus transferred to an individual that has no guilt at all. Because the idea that an innocent individual should bear collective guilt is generally abhorred these days, the word "scapegoat" has a negative connotation – though paradoxically certain Christian doctrines of atonement (that highlight the "justice" of God) glorify one particular instance of it.

It is worth underlying the two different (Deuteronomi[sti]c and Priestly) views of sin by considering their respective mythologies. The Priestly myth, now lost from Genesis but disguised in 6:1–4 and rendered more accurately in the Enochic *Book of the Watchers* (1 Enoch 1–36) and the ritual of Leviticus 16 (see Davies 2006) regards sin as a supernatural force that entered the world from outside, and continues to generate pollution. The story of Adam, Eve and Cain, though not regarded as a Deuteronomistic one, nevertheless expresses a similar view: that sin enters the world through human disobedience and is dealt with by punishment, in this case individually tailored: Adam, Eve, the snake and Cain each receive their own different retribution. Yet even here we should not overlook the element of collective punishment in that the "curses" are inherited by their descendants. The story hardly justifies the Augustinian theory of an *inescapable*, transmitted, flaw of human nature ("original sin"), but it certainly acknowledges that children suffer for the sins of their parents – and no doubt implies that most humans, like Adam and Eve, will commit their own acts of disobedience and so justify their bequest. The Priestly myth concentrates on measures to atone for, "cover" and remove "sin" while the other emphasizes divine punishment as the response. The difference can also be seen in the two views of the Flood entwined in Genesis 6–9: on one view it is a punishment for collective human sin (from which Noah's exemption is purely matter of divine whim); the other sees it as a necessary means of cleansing an earth that has been polluted by humans, from which Noah is rescued by virtue of his personal rectitude (and in both cases the families are also saved).[6] The differences between these two positions is far from an antiquarian issue: there is a contemporary debate on whether punishment for crimes should be punitive, corrective or restorative – whether offenders should "serve their time" and restart with a slate from which the debts have been cleared, or "see the error of their ways", or if indeed much crime is the result of a social deprivation that should be removed as the most effective way of reducing crime. That they are not mutually exclusive seems to be indicated by the biblical treatment.

Biblical Opposition to Collective Punishment

We find within the Bible protests against the idea of collective punishment. We can take as an example whether children should be punished for the offences of their parents. The families of both Rahab and Achan were respectively rewarded and punished in this way. In the case of exiled Judeans, the penitential prayers of Nehemiah 9 and Daniel 9 or even Tobit 13 – all of these prayers spoken by individually righteous people – the continuing exile is a just punishment. Responsibility for previous sins is accepted. But some descendants of Judean deportees to Babylonia seem to have regarded themselves as *unjustly* suffering for offences committed by their parents (this is not the same as decimation, where the victims are not necessarily individually innocent). In both Jeremiah and Ezekiel we find a protest against inherited punishment:

> In those days they shall no longer say: "The parents have eaten sour grapes, and the children's teeth are set on edge". But all shall die for their own sins; the teeth of everyone who eats sour grapes shall be set on edge. (Jer. 31:29–30)

There is a much fuller statement in Ezekiel 18, which opens with the same proverb: "the parents have eaten sour grapes", etc. It continues (vv. 4–9):

> Know that all lives are mine; the life of the parent as well as the life of the child is mine: it is only the person who sins that shall die. If a man is righteous and does what is lawful and right – if he ... does not oppress anyone, but restores to the debtor his pledge, commits no robbery, gives his bread to the hungry

and covers the naked with a garment, does not take advance or accrued
interest, withholds his hand from iniquity, executes true justice between
contending parties ... such a one is righteous; he shall surely live.

Ezekiel's formulation shows that the issue is not purely about parents and
children but about all individuals (and that may be implied in the Jeremiah
text also). Whether or not dictated by specific instances, both texts offer a
definition of divine justice that individualistic moderns find much more
congenial. From a historical-critical point of view, it is natural to conclude
that an older corporate ethic has been replaced by a more "enlightened"
individual one, for which the most dramatic evidence is the introduction
of a belief in a resurrection, whether of the righteous alone, or of all. Indeed,
purely in respect of parents and children, these texts refute Exod. 34:6–7
(repeated almost verbatim in Num. 14.18):

> ... a god merciful and gracious,
> slow to anger, and abounding in steadfast love and faithfulness,
> keeping steadfast love for the thousandth generation,
> forgiving iniquity and transgression and sin,
> yet by no means clearing the guilty,
> but visiting the iniquity of the parents
> upon the children
> and the children's children,
> to the third and the fourth generation.

But let us note a major problem with this resolution. First, as the story of
the first humans shows, descendants cannot always be free of punishments
inflicted on ancestors; executed criminals leave widows and orphans. If
the nub of the matter is indeed the continued exile of deported ancestors,
moreover, the justice is still somewhat "rough" unless all the deportees
were guilty and all their descendants innocent. In other words, there
remains an element of collectivity. The expansion of the proverb in Ezekiel
suggests something more closely matched to individual virtue, beyond
the issue of *inherited* punishment. But here the problem is *how* such
individual allocation of justice is to be effected. The book as a whole gives
no hint of an answer: the vision of the revived bones has often been taken as
a hint of individual resurrection, but the majority scholarly opinion favours
a collective meaning. Indeed, Ezekiel's overriding concern for national
identity vastly overshadows its suggestion that ultimately individuals merit
their own individual recompense.

Is Collective Justice Possible? The Lesson of Sodom

A key episode in the biblical dialogue on collective punishment is the story of the destruction of Sodom (Genesis 18–19), a text much discussed elsewhere in this volume. The story of Sodom also contains a key philosophical interchange in which Abraham is interrogating Yahweh. The conversation can, at the level of plot analysis, be taken as a bargaining process in which Abraham ensures that Lot is not caught up in the coming destruction of Sodom (Davies 1995a, 1995b). But it is more usually read as a debate about divine justice, establishing that Yahweh will not inflict punishment on the innocent. But there is a deeper issue, surfacing in Abraham's statement (18:25):

> Far be it from you to do such a thing, to kill the righteous with the wicked, so that the righteous and the wicked are treated the same! Far be that from you! Does the judge of all the earth not do what is just?

This is generally taken to be a rhetorical question, an opening gambit establishing common ground. But its force is slightly diminished in translation. In Hebrew the cognates *shophet* and *mishpat* are more obvious than the cognates "judge" and "justice". Also, the Hebrew does not distinguish "can" or "should" from "does", leaving the translator the task of determining the precise meaning of the question. But all of the alternatives ultimately lead to the same point: if one is "*shophet* of all the world" then what does it mean to say that one does, should or can "do justice"? The logic of this statement, however, can lead in one of two directions, and each direction takes us back to a fundamental rift between a revealed religion and a humanistic philosophy. On the one hand, how could the supreme *shophet*, do anything else *but* justice? If he is the *source* of *mishpat*, he *defines mishpat* and to say that he is "unjust" would simply be a logical contradiction. This logic assumes that Yahweh is supremely sovereign, a premise consistent with the strict form of monarchic theism that the biblical texts on the whole affirm. In the ancient Near Eastern world, where the king is the ultimate source of justice, such a separation of "justice" from "royal will" is equally problematic. But monarchy sought to justify itself as a divine order, and a king could logically claim to operate in accordance with *divine* justice. On the other hand, if to say that the supreme judge does justice is not a tautology, then justice is an independent principle, and as such compromises divine sovereignty. It also means humans can be just independently of the divine will. And if humans believe that the supreme sovereign god *ought* to be just – if this god himself recognizes this as Abraham's challenge implies – then there is a moral principle higher than god himself.

There is one more twist to this. Both parties in the dialogue accept that punishing the guilty and the innocent equally is unjust. But *not* punishing the guilty and innocent equally is also unjust. Since the crime of the guilty then goes unpunished. Hence, if justice is a principle independent of Yahweh, he *cannot* exercise it by collective retribution. But neither can he by doing nothing. So it is quite permissible to ask *"can* the supreme judge do justice?" – that is to say, can he deliver to all individuals their just merits – "smooth justice"? All this philosophy is entailed in a single question.

"New Sodom"

The alternatives of divine autonomy and a principle of justice lead us to Sodom from Babylon and the descendants of Judean deportees. From Sodom they take us to Nineveh. Here we overhear another conversation about justice, though on this occasion the human protagonist, Jonah, is pleading for collective retribution. Significantly, Jonah does not define Yahweh as "just" but rather as "gracious and merciful, slow to anger and full of loyalty and inclined to relent where evil is concerned" (as he says in 4:2). Accordingly he is sending Jonah to warn the Ninevites so that they will repent and so avoid justice. Jonah's rebuke is little short of an accusation of *injustice*. He has a point, too: Yahweh usually only lets Israelites repent. Had the god behaved like this in Noah's time the Flood might never have come. Or indeed, Sodom might still be standing. But now Yahweh is apparently less interested in requiting.

Yet, the ship in which Jonah had travelled had been about to sink with all on board. Had it not been for Jonah's request, reluctantly granted, to be thrown into the sea (why didn't he just jump?) the entire crew and passengers would have been killed for the offence of one person. This seems blatant injustice to modern readers, and does not suggest that Yahweh has in any way revised his *modus operandi*. He is happy to have the entire shipload die with no chance to repent – and indeed, they have done nothing to repent of, except for not being exclusively devoted to his cult. As at Sodom, the issue of sovereignty will *versus* justice is made explicit (1:12–14):

> [Jonah] said to them, "Pick me up and throw me into the sea; then the sea will become calm for you; for I know it is because of me that this great storm has hit you". Nevertheless the crew rowed hard to pull the ship back to land, but they were unable to, for the sea became stormier against them. So then they

cried out to Yahweh, "Please, Yahweh, do not let us die for this man's life. Do not make us guilty of innocent blood; for you, Yhweh, have done as you saw fit."

Whereas at Sodom Abraham had appealed directly to Yahweh's capacity to be just, here the sailors more bluntly contrast a principle of justice (that they should survive) with Yahweh's own will (that they should die). Jonah suggests, however, that, like Achan, his own punishment would end that of the crew, since the divine will was really only that he should die. But, of course, he no more dies than do the sailors, or – within the confines of the story – the residents of Nineveh.

At the end of the story Yahweh gives to Jonah the answer he might have given to Abraham. Indeed, he is sovereign and not obliged to be just – or rather, not to be just all the time (on this see especially Bolin 1997). But does this strike a happy note, or deliver a final answer? Indeed not: the readers of the book can hardly have been expected to applaud the divine mercy to Nineveh. On the other hand, they knew that Nineveh, like Sodom, *had* been destroyed – both for their sins (as emphasized by Guillaume 2009). We seem to be hearing that we like the idea of justice, and the idea of mercy and the idea of a sovereign god. And that we cannot have all three. In any situation we may choose one or the other. And the biblical authors, collectively but not unreasonably, ascribe the same arbitrariness to their god.

Smooth Justice, or Law and Order

The previous discussion has several times paused on the brink of a resolution of divine sovereignty and divine justice, according to which every person receives exact retribution in accordance with the divine will, without any arbitrariness. We find such a resolution in the book of Proverbs, along with a new construction: not disobedience to the divine command (Deuteronomic) nor defilement (Priestly) but wisdom and its absence, folly.[7] There is, again, a corresponding myth, though the very briefest. The creator god fashioned the universe with the aid of a female companion called Wisdom, such that a moral order is inherent in the material world. In this way, without any direct ongoing intervention, the just creator ensures that individuals receive what they deserve in this life. Laziness brings hunger; deceit brings downfall, and the choice of the wrong woman ... disaster! Ostensibly the system claims that virtue brings earthly success, measured in terms of social respect, long life, large family and wealth.

This account is philosophically a satisfying one, but has other problems. One is that the equation can be expressed in reverse: people with these benefits are shown to be virtuous and those without lack either wisdom or virtue (this is one of the arguments that Job's friends use against him). Another objection is that there are also poor and deprived people who are apparently *not* deserving of their lot – such as widows and orphans. But some kind of justice is effected for them by the generosity of the wealthy, whose own well-being is dependent in part upon their charity to the deserving poor – a very direct application of enlightened self-interest. Whether such charity should extend to the remainder, who are poor because they are lazy and foolish, is not clear.

Moderns can add another objection: that often the poor are poor *because* the rich are rich. But the science of economics is a post-biblical discovery – and in any case, being rich is today one of the two most popular ambitions in the developed countries (the other is being famous), and wealth means nothing unless there is poverty. For some reason, many rich people perform acts of charity but try their hardest to avoid paying taxes, as if taxes were not performing, at least in part, the same function.

But the chief objection is, of course, an overwhelming lack of empirical verification. As with the case of collective punishment, we can find numerous protests against this view of the world within the Bible. Qoheleth asserts that the deity is not concerned with justice as a principle: rain falls on everyone and death comes to good and bad alike, human and animal. If God was really good, life would be worthwhile. It is generally not, and so we are therefore to be thankful for whatever good we receive and not calculate the balance of merit. But if the creator is not concerned that life in his world should be just, does Qoheleth nevertheless believe that *humans* should be? If so, from whence shall we derive the principle? In the book of Job, however, the unjust suffering of the innocent is a major preoccupation, and more than one answer emerges. The first, which closes the main, poetic section, is that ways of Yahweh – including divine justice – cannot be understood by humans. The implication is that the concept of justice is a human one – but is it also a futile one, or only so when applied to God? The second answer, conveyed in the prose, is that Job was right to insist that Yahweh really is just. Job himself had also acted justly, and in accordance with the divine will. The final restoration of all Job's possessions underlines his, and God's "justice". The book also addresses the problem of Satan's challenge to Yahweh that led to the wager and to Job's afflictions: that rewards are only justly given when just behaviour is not conditioned by an expectation of them. (Socrates, for whom justice was a virtue to be prized for its own sake, would have approved.)

Smooth Justice, but Postponed

Many of the faults in the scheme – especially the impossibility of "smooth" justice within human society – are corrected by theories that postpone the exercise of divine justice to a time and or place beyond the present world order. (It is not necessarily the case that "justice postponed is justice denied".) A corporate version of the revised scheme imagines an eschatological intervention to eliminate all evil in the world forever. Such an intervention entails a reward for either Israel as a whole (e.g. Ezekiel 38–39; Daniel 2; 7; various prophetic promises of a glorious future for the nation and doom for other nations) or, in one case in the Hebrew Bible, a degree of individual retribution that probably does not involve all humanity (Daniel 12). The New Testament also offers salvation to individual believers, but there is no scope in this chapter to address that corpus, except to observe that salvation is not offered as a matter of *justice*. But the notion of a post-mortem (or eschatological) individual *judgement* has become entrenched in Judaism, Christianity and Islam and so mitigates the problem of divinely-tolerated injustice in this world. But while it is permissible to consider such a belief as a solution to the problem of injustice in the everyday world, we should beware of imposing an evolutionary or chronological framework. Belief in post-mortem judgement has a long history in ancient Egyptian belief: one of the most famous images in the *Book of the Dead* is the weighing of the soul.

According to this doctrine, how is justice established on earth – and need it be? Both Judaism and Islam lay stress on the need for the believer to practise justice during their lives, and within Christianity there are those who would agree. As with the Proverbs scheme, disinterested goodness reaps reward. And the fact is that none of these religions requires divine justice, whether corporate or individual, to be exacted on earth except through human deeds. Commands about how to behave justly are given in the scriptures, but the regime is clearly one of self-regulation, until or unless a collective divine punishment on the society ensues. The danger here is only too obvious, however. Quite apart from the near-impossibility of disinterested justice – can one resist the temptation of a reward? – there is the wider danger of concentrating on an individual "justice" ("you're worth it" runs the slogan) at the expense of an obligation to society, whose improvement seems less attractive as a goal than eternal individual bliss.

And here the thread makes its loop and we are back at the beginning. Collective punishment concentrates the mind on collective responsibility, if nothing else. Rough justice may be better, in the long run, than the smooth variety.

Epilogue

The outcome of the foregoing walk through biblical philosophy has been buttressed in a recent study of the book of Jeremiah by Plant (2008). Reviewing how the Bible depicts Yahweh exercising judgement in Israel, he identifies three broad categories: selective, unselective and national – observing that some texts combine one or more of these. Specifically in Jeremiah, chs 1–20 pronounce judgement on all Judah, while chs 30–33 prophesy restoration for all those deported and chs 21–24 distinguish those remaining in Jerusalem from those who surrender (21:1–10), Israel's leaders from the rest of the population (23:1–8), and deportees from non-deportees (24:1–10). In chs 27–29 exiled and non-exiled communities are further differentiated, while chs 37–45 offer hope to those who surrender (38:1–3) or remain in the land (42:1–22).

Plant's verdict is that divine judgement is unpredictable and at times verging on the indiscriminate. He suggests that the differences in perspective are theologically significant and that each polarity offers a valid though incomplete lens through which to interpret God's judicial action. But perhaps we can go a little further than this? Perhaps either the ways of God are incomprehensible, or that, there being no god, our own sense of justice is compromised and subject to variation, and that we simply project on to this supernatural "supreme judge" the very confusion that we can see in ourselves.

It would be nice to finish on a positive note, nonetheless. Humans do feel a passion for justice, even if we do not agree about its application. Our Western culture is caught between justice as a private virtue and a social responsibility or between a divine quality and a matter of the balance between what we deserve and what we earn. We praise justice but we also praise mercy, and the two are not strictly compatible. The rabbis saw this and credited their god with two personalities: Elohim believed in justice but Yahweh was a god of mercy. In Christian tradition there have always been efforts to contrast the gods of the Old and New Testament (Marcion) or, less heretically, the just Father and the merciful Son. The Bible can help us in our efforts to understand the nature of justice, and especially social justice. But it cannot tell us what justice is or how we can exercise it. It can, however point us away from an excessive individualism, a privatization of the notion of merit, even while it recoils from a crude notion of collective retribution. For the notion that individuals can expect "smooth" justice is fallacious: chance, disease and accident all ignore such considerations. Our increasing instinct to "blame" someone or something for every misfortune is a forlorn attempt to turn every mishap into a crime and so seek a recompense – as if that were "justice".

With the Bible we have to take the rough with the smooth.

Notes

1. "The safest general characterization of the European philosophical tradition is that it consists of a series of footnotes to Plato", Whitehead (1979: 39).

2. Nevertheless, we should not forget that rabbinic halakhah developed a logical system of exegesis of Torah that, while not establishing foundational principles of justice, applied arguments, deductions, inferences and analogies in accordance with "rules". Despite its indebtedness to neo-Platonism, early Christianity does not present an equivalent technique. In the Middle Ages, of course, the integration of "revealed" and "natural" truths reach its highest point.

3. According to the parallel account in 1 Chronicles 21, it was the Satan who incited David (v. 1).

4. The British Prime Minister Margaret Thatcher, a great advocate of "personal responsibility" famously declared that "there is no such thing as society" (quoted in *Women's Own* magazine, 31 October 1987). To be fair to ourselves, let us acknowledge that this opinion is nearly always quoted unfavourably.

5. For a critique of this concept, see Rogerson 1970.

6. The story of the Flood was very probably interpreted in early Judaism as prototypical of the Babylonian deportation, as a punishment for collective sins (Kings) and also as a necessary removal of a source of pollution of the land (Leviticus, Chronicles). But there is disagreement between various biblical texts over whether the guilt attaches to those deported rather than those left behind. In several texts (Ezra, Nehemiah), while the sins of the ancestors are acknowledged, the "returnees" represent themselves as latter-day Noahs, rescued from a flood and now restored to a land (that nevertheless still contains unclean elements).

7. The two are presented as if they might actually be part of a dualistic scheme, but Yahweh is not credited with creating folly and it seems preferable to define it, rather as Aquinas defined evil, in terms of a lack. On this interpretation Wisdom can represent a lost divine consort. In Jewish texts of the late Second temple period, such as those from Qumran, a dualistic creation myth is presented or implied that arguably is developed from, or at least influenced by, the worldview of Proverbs. Here "wisdom" and "folly" appear as virtually synonymous opposites such as "truth" and "falsehood" or "light" and "darkness".

Bibliography

Bolin, Thomas. 1997. *Freedom Beyond Forgiveness: The Book of Jonah Re-examined.* Sheffield: Sheffield Academic Press.

Davies, Philip R. 1995a. "Abraham and Yahweh: A Case of Male Bonding." *Bible Review* 11 (4): 24–33, 44–45.

———. 1995b. "Male Bonding: A Tale of Two Buddies." In *Whose Bible Is It Anyway?,* ed. Philip R. Davies, 95–113. Sheffield: Sheffield Academic Press.

———. 2006. "And Enoch Was Not, for Genesis Took Him." In *Biblical Traditions in Transmission: Essays in Honour of Michael A. Knibb,* eds C. Hempel and J. M. Lieu, 97–107. Leiden: Brill.

Philippe Guillaume. 2009. "'Arguing Under the Qiqayon Tree: An Introduction to a Set of Articles on Jonah." *Journal of Hebrew Scriptures* 9, article 3. http://www.arts.ualberta.ca/JHS/Articles/article_105.pdf

Plant, R. J. R. 2008. *Good Figs, Bad Figs: Judicial Differentiation in the Book of Jeremiah.* London and New York: T&T Clark.

Rogerson, J. W. 1970. "The Hebrew Conception of Corporate Personality: A Re-Examination." *Journal of Theological Studies* XXI (1): 1–16.

Whitehead, Alfred North. 1979. *Process and Reality.* New York: Free Press (originally delivered as the Gifford Lectures 1927–28).

Is the Belief in Human Rights Either Biblical or Useful?

John Sandys-Wunsch[a]

In many intellectual pursuits there lurks a skeleton in the closet that some might well prefer to forget. In a glass enclosure in London University there is a real skeleton namely the preserved mortal remains of Jeremy Bentham, one of the moving forces in the founding of the University of London. Bentham is either famous or notorious for his attack on inalienable civil rights.

Where are civil or human rights to be found? Given the attention paid to them it is surprising how unclear is the foundation on which they rest. I will present three theses. The first is that the notion of inalienable rights was the product of debates in England about legitimate government in the seventeenth century. Second, the Bible properly understood provides motivation and examples but not exact guidance in social matters. Third, Bentham is worth revisiting and on investigation he may even have right on his side in some of his comments.

The Origin of Inalienable Rights

In the seventeenth century England was not altogether a failed state but the civil war had put many institutions in question, not least of all the monarchy, and some people at least felt uneasy about legitimacy in political

[a] John Sandys-Wunsch: Canadian born, university education: BA 1956 English and French University of British Columbia; BA 1958 Theology (Oxford); Doctorate subject pentateuchal criticism carried out at Oxford, Strasbourg, and Tübingen, D.Phil. (Oxford) 1961. Lectured at Memorial University of Newfoundland, Oxford, and Laurentian University Sudbury, Ontario. Six years as editor Studies in Religion/ Sciences Religieuses. Sandys-Wunsch is a member SOTS, Canadian Society for Biblical Studies (former president).

life. Even after the Restoration the position of the monarchy was challenged once again by the Great Revolution of 1688 when James II was in effect deposed. It is when things go wrong that we get interested in how they go right and the works of Thomas Hobbes, Sir Robert Filmer and John Locke have to be seen against the background of this political turmoil. For Hobbes the immediate issue was how to prevent states from reverting to primaeval chaos; for Filmer it was how to justify the divine right of kings; and for Locke it was how to justify dethroning a monarch whom God has been kind enough to give you. All three men began with myths – "myth" in the sense used by most biblical scholars as a story nominally about the past but legitimating present practice and giving guidance for the future. Because they appeal to our imaginations, myths are very powerful, but they do lack precision and leave the door open to unexpected interpretations. A further complication is that myths do not depend on historical accuracy.

Hobbes' myth of origins, which he probably derived from classical sources, describes how originally human beings in a state of nature were a singularly fractious group where everyone's hand was against everyone else. Cooperation, so necessary for human survival, was impossible and Hobbes described early human existence as "solitary, poor, nasty, brutish, and short". Given this summation of human character, Hobbes, who did not enjoy civil disorder, felt that what was required was a government that would maintain order and prevent a lapse into the original chaos that was always threatening. This pessimistic view about human nature was a major factor in the difference between Hobbes' view of the state and the more optimistic views to be found in Filmer and Locke.

In comparison to the literary success of Hobbes and Locke, Filmer's reputation has not endured very well, for his support of the divine right of kings is not taken seriously in the present day. But Filmer had a common-sense argument against Hobbes' myth; he pointed out that apart from not explaining how human beings existed in the first place, Hobbes describes a situation in which, since everyone was free to kill anybody else and often did, humans would not have survived long enough to found a state. So Filmer began with the Genesis myth of Adam and Eve as founders of the first family. Despite Cain's act of homicide, the family as an institution provided the means for human beings to live cooperatively and survive as united groups rather than as Hobbes's lawless savages. More important, Adam was the first king and the heads of families eventually became kings in their own right as the human population increased. Therefore, argued Filmer, kingship is part of the divine order passed down from the beginning of the world and no one has the right to depose a monarch.

Hard as we find it to take Filmer seriously today, his work had a great influence in his own time, a development probably made more convincing by the long-standing tradition in popular religious teaching of interpreting the commandment about honouring your father and mother as including respect for the monarchy as part of your filial duties. But while belief in the divine right of kings was fine for re-establishing a monarchy after Cromwell's death, how could one condone the Glorious Revolution that drove James II from the throne in 1688 and put William and Mary in his place? The answer for many people was that you could not justify such an affront to God's anointed. In fact, a considerable number of Englishmen refused to take the oath of allegiance to the new monarchs on religious grounds, including even Sancroft the Archbishop of Canterbury and some other bishops who had been put to the Tower of London by James II. The non-jurors so-called mark the first major schism in the Anglican Church and they continued to exist as a separate church for another century.

In this situation, John Locke's *Two Treatises on Government* was designed to refute his formidable adversaries, Filmer and Hobbes. So like his two opponents Locke begins with a myth of origins, which in his case was essentially a modified version of Hobbes. But instead of the original humanity being a collection of murderous thugs, Locke's original humans were much more like the sort of gentlemanly undergraduates to be found at Christ Church Oxford where Locke was a Fellow. In Locke's myth these ancient progenitors of our race were quite aware of the demands of natural law, which requires decent moral standards amongst human beings.

At this point it is critical to point out two different types of law as described in political theory, namely natural law and positive law. Put very simply, natural law is based on standards disclosed by reason which apply generally to all human beings because it is based upon objective, eternal norms. This embraces the sort of regulation which peoples everywhere ought to recognize as applying to them. Examples of this sort of natural law would be legal/moral prohibitions such as murder or theft which obviously destroy the structure of society. Hence Cicero's assertion that true law was right reason that was congruent with nature (*De Republica* 3.22). The important point of natural law is that it cannot be changed: putting forward a legislative change to a natural law would be as great a folly as revoking the law of gravity. Positive law, on the other hand, is law enacted in particular countries that may well not apply in other jurisdictions.

Here is how Locke described his version of the state of nature where human beings knew full well that they were bound by natural law:

> The state of nature has a law of nature to govern it, which obliges every one: and reason, which is that law, teaches all mankind, who will but consult it, that being all equal and independent, no one ought to harm another in his life, health, liberty, or possessions: for men being all the workmanship of one omnipotent, and infinitely wise maker; all the servants of one sovereign master, sent into the world by his order, and about his business; they are his property, whose workmanship they are, made to last during his, not one another's pleasure: and being furnished with like faculties, sharing all in one community of nature, there cannot be supposed any such subordination among us, that may authorize us to destroy one another, as if we were made for one another's uses, as the inferior ranks of creatures are for our's. (Locke 1960: 289)

In other words Locke's first humans were well aware of right and wrong. However, while each of them had the right by natural law to self-defence and property, the trouble was that individuals are not always able to muster enough force to personally fend off others who do not choose to obey the rules. So the state was founded as humans grouped together for mutual support and exchanged their natural right to act for themselves in return for the state's promise to enforce their rights for them. Nonetheless human beings had not given up their rights completely when they traded in their natural law rights: if the civil order – say a monarchy with James II in command – did not carry out its duties competently, the citizens were justified in invoking their remaining natural rights and changing the government.

> The power that every individual gave the society, when he entered into it, can never revert to the individuals again, as long as the society lasts, but will always remain in the community … But if they have set limits to the duration of their legislative, and made this supreme power in any person, or assembly, only temporary; or else, when by the miscarriages of those in authority, it is forfeited; upon the forfeiture, or at the determination of the time set, it reverts to the society, and the people have a right to act as supreme, and continue the legislative in themselves; or erect a new form, or under the old form place it in new hands, as they think good. (Locke 1956: 122)

The origin of inalienable rights is thus embedded in Locke's myth about the origins of human society. It is important to bear in mind that Locke's principle concern was to refute Filmer's argument for the divine right of kings, not to establish a varied system of natural and irrevocable rights adhering to every citizen. The only natural right needed was to get rid of an arbitrary monarch.

However, the notion of rights began to be expanded beyond Locke's basic position that one ought not to harm another in his life, health, liberty, or possessions. The United States' Declaration of Independence says:

> We hold these truths to be self-evident, that all men are created equal, that they are endowed by their creator with certain unalienable rights that among these are life, liberty and the pursuit of happiness. – That to secure these rights, governments are instituted among men, deriving their just powers from the consent of the governed, – that whenever any form of government becomes destructive of these ends, it is the right of the people to alter or to abolish it, and to institute new government, laying its foundation on such principles and organizing its powers in such form, as to them shall seem most likely to effect their safety and happiness ... when a long train of abuses and usurpations, pursuing invariably the same object evinces a design to reduce them under absolute despotism, it is their right, it is their duty, to throw off such government, and to provide new guards for their future security.

In 1791 a Bill of Rights was attached as an addition to the United States Constitution but it does not really distinguish between natural and legislative rights. There have indeed been changes made to constitutional rights but citizens tend to treat some rights as inalienable, not least of all the right to possess and bear arms.

In the development of the notion of human rights, the emphasis has shifted from legitimating government to legitimating claims that citizens could make on government. Certainly in the Declaration of Universal Human Rights, declared by the United Nations in 1948, the theme is not legitimate government but the right of citizens to expect decent treatment from their government. The experiences of the horrors of the Second World War looms large in matters such the right to fair trial, freedom of speech, the right to emigrate, while others are what one might call the staples of a decent society. But the growth of the number of rights continued with the *International Covenant on Civil and Political Rights* and the *International Covenant on Economic, Social and Cultural Rights* (the latter two adopted in 1966 and entered into force in 1976).

From this perspective, it would appear that the ontological foundation of inalienable human rights is a myth created by a seventeenth-century philosopher and developed by the revolting American colonists in the eighteenth century. The meaning of rights changed from privileges established by and subject to statute law into inalienable privileges derived from nature and independent of legal precess. For Bentham this was a serious mistake. I will argue that Bentham would agree with this perception.

The Bible and Justice

From the point of view of some modern biblical scholars the Bible is a collection of books written and rewritten over a period of up to 1200 years. Much of the material was first transmitted in oral form and a considerable amount of editing of the written form has taken place. There is a great deal of variation in the sort of writings in the Bible – myth, history, law, moral exhortation, while the influence of Greek philosophy is evident in some books of the Apocrypha and even more in the New Testament. The effect of modern scholarship is to wash away the interpretative glue that long held the biblical books together into a perceived uniform work. The result is that it is no longer possible to claim there is only one set of moral or legal injunctions in the Bible.

In any discussion of the Bible and justice, it is salutary to recognize first that we know very little about the social history of the Israelites. It is clear that various legal and moral requirements were laid down, but the context in which they were enforced – or not – is unknown. Who had the right to make laws, how and where criminal and civil cases were carried out, and more difficult still, how many changes in procedures may have taken place in a period of about 1200 years (plus or minus the odd century)? The biblical texts (legal, wisdom and prophetic) suggest that Israel took justice and fair dealing very seriously. Even the king was not immune: the story of Elijah and King Ahab in 1 Kings 21 suggests that kings could be rebuked even in public and with impunity. While there was no word for "natural rights" in the modern legal sense, some rights are granted, such as flight to a city of refuge in a manslaughter case (Num. 35:11–12), or gleaning grain left by harvesters (Ruth 2:8). Even non-Israelites had protections in law; for in Deut. 21:10–14 if a soldier brought home a captured woman from a foreign country, he could marry her, but if matters did not work out he was not allowed to sell her as a slave; he had to let her go free. What is interesting about such rulings – which seems generous for their times – is that people who had little status or power (widows, orphans, strangers) were given protection.

There are in fact hints in the Old Testament of a sense of what we would call natural law. In Amos 2:1–3 the prophet says that God will punish the kingdom of Moab because its forces desecrated the grave of the King of Edom, which was not an Israelite country – a clear sign that Amos thought of his God as taking an interest in the wrong doings done by one foreign country to another. Similarly in a much later book – admittedly in the Apocrypha – *Jesus ben Sirach* 1:1 claims that all wisdom comes from God in a way that might be translated into natural law in a Latin context, even as the *Wisdom of Solomon* 6:1–4 states that all the kings of the earth who seek after wisdom get their dominions from God. Hence while the history of human rights as traced earlier was found to centre on the question of the responsibilities of the monarch, one dominant biblical view is that behind the monarch (and justifying monarchy itself) is divine authority: it is God who commands, and ultimately guarantees, the rights of humans, or at least of Israelites.

Bentham's Criticism of Human Rights

Jeremy Bentham (1748–1832) combined humanity and common sense. For example, in his objection to the death sentence for homosexual acts, he offered a list of all the reasons why homosexuality was thought to be a threat to society and then systematically showed the weakness of each one. He was also an advocate for the humane treatment of animals. Eschewing abstract discussions about whether animals had souls, he simply asked whether they feel pain. "The question is not, can they reason? Nor can they talk? But can they suffer?" (Bentham 1948: 331). He was probably the first writer of any stature to attack the usefulness of human rights as the inalienable birthright of every human being.

Bentham's written style is not always clear, and the publication of his output complicated. His *Anarchical Fallacies* was written sometime about 1799 but it not printed in English until two years after his death, and the actual title was not his but one chosen by the editor of the edition. Furthermore, he left a huge legacy of unpublished papers. Currently the Bentham project under way at University College London is working on a collection of Bentham's unpublished papers that consists of around 60,000 folios, arranged into 174 boxes (see www.ucl.ac.uk/Bentham-Project).

In the published version of *Anarchical Fallacies* Bentham states that he is commenting on the *Declaration of Rights* published under the name of the French National Assembly in 1791. It has been pointed out that some of the contents Bentham criticizes are not found in the original document. However, they are included in another *Declaration of the Rights of Man and Citizen* attached to the Constitution of the Year I (1793). Hence it should probably be assumed Bentham was in fact referring to the later document. The *Anarchical Fallacies* does not display a carefully planned argument, possibly due to complications between the writing and the publication. Here, however, are what might be seen as the basic points –

though not in the order in which he treats them. First, Bentham objects to the universal claims of the document. He says:

> as often as the utility of a provision appeared (by reason of the wideness of its extent, for instance) of a doubtful nature, the way taken to clear the doubt was to assert it to be a provision fit to be made law for all men – for all Frenchmen and for all Englishmen, for example, into the bargain. (Bentham 1843: 497)

This shows an early awareness of one of the weaknesses of rights discourse – that it assumes all cultures wish to entertain what a particular culture sees as desirable. As Bernard Shaw said, "Do not do unto others as you would that they should do unto you. Their tastes may not be the same."

Second, Bentham observes:

> They know not of what they are talking under the name of natural rights, and yet they would have them imprescriptible – proof against all the power of the laws – pregnant with occasions summoning the members of the community to rise up in resistance against the laws. What, then, was their object in declaring the existence of imprescriptible rights, and without specifying a single one by any such mark as it could be known by? This and no other – to excite and keep up a spirit of resistance to all laws – a spirit of insurrection against all governments as often as the utility of a provision appeared (by reason of the wideness of its extent, for instance) of a doubtful nature, the way taken to clear the doubt was to assert it to be a provision fit to be made law for all men – for a Frenchmen – and for all Englishmen, for example, into the bargain. (Bentham 1843: 501)

The effect of making rights supreme is to destroy orderly government with the double error of failing to define clearly what rights are and by making the undefined rights supreme over normal, precise legislation.

Third, Bentham attacks the validity of Locke's theory of inalienable rights, making a frontal attack on essentially what Locke argued, though without mentioning Locke by name. He straightforwardly describes imprescriptible rights as "more confusion – more nonsense – and the nonsense, as usual, dangerous nonsense". He put forward three criticisms. First, he denies "That there are such things as rights anterior to the establishment of governments" (see, for example, Locke 1960: 373–81). This statement seems to refer to Locke's suggestion about the existence of natural law before governments were established. Second, he objects to the idea that "That these rights *can not* be abrogated by government: for *can not* is implied in the form of the word imprescriptible, and the sense it wears when so applied, is the cut-throat sense above explained" (Bentham 1843: 500). Third, he alludes to Locke's suggestion that government was founded to enforce the pre-existing natural law in the following terms: "That the governments that exist derive their origin from formal associations, or what are now called *conventions*: associations entered into by a partnership contract, with all the members for partners – entered into at a day prefixed, for a predetermined purpose, the formation of a new government where there was none before" (Bentham 1843: 500).

Fourth, Bentham argues that belief in rights can loosen the necessary constraints of civilized life:

> Society is held together only by the sacrifices that men can be induced to make of the gratifications they demand: to obtain these sacrifices is the great difficulty, the great task of government. What has been the object, the perpetual and palpable object, of this declaration of pretended rights? To add as much force as possible to these passions, already but too strong, to burst the cords that hold them in, to say to the selfish passions, there – everywhere – is your prey! – to the angry passions, there – everywhere – is your enemy. (Bentham 1843: 697)

In other words instead of rights being controls over how a government treats its citizens, it is now a case of demands by citizens on government.

Fifth, Bentham makes a point that what is needed for the improvement of society is not declarations but education:

> It is for education to do what can be done; and in education is, though unhappily the slowest, the surest as well as earliest resource. The recognition of the nothingness of the laws of nature and the rights of man that have been grounded on them, is a branch of knowledge of as much importance to an Englishman, though a negative one, as the most perfect acquaintance that can be formed with the existing laws of England. (Bentham 1843: 524)

Successors to Bentham

As a postscript to this exposition of Bentham's attack, it seems appropriate to mention three authors who, although not necessarily complete Benthamites, have made relevant observations. The first, Dominique Clémont, in *Canada's Rights Revolution* discusses the history and efficacy of various civil liberties and human rights groups in the past sixty or so years of Canadian history. Clémont describes how different civil/human rights groups saw their purpose and carried on their campaigns in different ways with varying degrees of success (Clement 2008). While Bentham is not mentioned, the nature and the weaknesses of these groups are discussed is similar ways. For those who want an entry into what has happened in Canada in the area of rights, this is a fine book. Anthony Harvey's *By What*

Authority deals with the British scene and points out that theologians have seldom addressed the basic question of whether human rights exist at all. The most penetrating discussion of the whole matter of human rights is presented in Chris Brown's, *Universal Rights: A Critique*. His discussion on the difference between legal and moral rights and legal positive and natural rights is very useful indeed. His argument is that the liberal position on rights is and always was incoherent and confused and that the undoubted success of liberal societies is not traceable to their individualistic rights-oriented features (Brown 1997: 48). He argues that, at times, entrenched rights can be a hindrance to good government. Brown gives the example of the right to bear and own weapons in the US Bill of Rights, which has made it very hard to control firearms even though roughly 30,000 Americans are killed, one way or another, by guns every year. He also makes the point that it is not the promulgation of rights so much as basic changes in the common beliefs of a society that can bring about change. It follows *a fortiori* that decontextualized human rights are unlikely to be successful as the solution to various global problems. Brown considers that the problem of the United States in particular is that "Americans have more and more rights and less and less of a society in which to exercise them" (Brown 1997: 52). It would be unfair to both men to suggest Brown is simply following Bentham, but Bentham would not have been displeased with Brown's arguments had he read them.

Bentham and the Bible

Given that Jeremy Bentham left behind a huge number of unpublished manuscripts, any discussion of many of his opinions, not least of all his attitude towards the Bible, should be prefaced with a warning that material yet to be published may throw a different light on what is suggested in this chapter.

Bentham's approach to the Bible has to be seen as a subset of his position on what he called fallacies, by which he meant traditional positions on various matters were to be treated as beyond criticism or revision. For Bentham such unchangeable positions are a threat that can hinder good government by preventing necessary changes in law and administration. This concern of Bentham's was caught neatly in John Stuart Mill's superb article on Bentham in which he called Bentham the great questioner of things established. It is not surprising then that Bentham included the Bible as something that should be subjected to critical examination. In fact he makes it clear in his *Not Paul but Jesus* that he derived his guidance on biblical matters from reading Conyers Middleton who argued that not everything in the Bible was the direct word of God and therefore provided the opening that Bentham needed. But if Bentham found the necessary freedom to examine the Bible without preconceived conclusions, this did not mean he emulated his older contemporary Voltaire who tended to see much of the Bible as plain silly. While Bentham probably was close to a moderate Deism in his own beliefs, his attitude to the Bible was that he saw important teachings in parts of the Bible. It was the teaching of Jesus that was to be taken seriously. This would account for the vigour of the criticism he brought down upon those who would misuse the Bible in order to preserve things as they were: "In vain would they answer, what has been so often answered, that neither Jesus nor his apostles ever meant what they said – that everything is to be explained and explained away. By answers of this sort those and those alone would be satisfied, whose satisfaction with everything that is established is immovable, and not susceptible of experiencing diminution from any objections, or increase from any answers" (Bentham 1843: 468). In fact Bentham praises Quakers and Methodists for being more consistent in obeying the Bible than the clergy of the Church of England.

There are two outstanding matters where Bentham shows his critical approach, namely in the contrast between Paul and Jesus and in his discussion of the morality of homosexuality. Necessity is the mother of invention and Bentham turned to necessity's maternal care to try to introduce some room for disagreement within the church. So he turned his hand to New Testament exegesis (and one should not forget that he had learned Greek at the age of three.)

In *Not Paul but Jesus*, published pseudonymously under the name Gamaliel Smith (Smith 1823), Bentham argued that one had to make a choice about which part of the New Testament one chose as important. Bentham drove a wedge between the teaching of Jesus and the far more rigid and legalistic opinions of St Paul. Bentham argues that in the course of his labours Paul's work was simply an attempt to gain power by rejecting the accounts of those who had actually known the historical Jesus, and by so doing Paul became the source of all the dissensions which have disfigured the Church ever since (Smith 1823: iii–xvii).

Bentham's manuscript on the matter of homosexuality was not published until 1978. Given that homosexual practices could be punished by death until the middle of the nineteenth century, one can appreciate Bentham's reluctance to publish. But that he was willing in the eighteenth century to extend his questioning of accepted ideas to a subject that only reached general discussion in the latter part of the twentieth century shows the extent of his willingness to challenge the reasonableness of yet another fallacy.

In his treatment of what Bentham called "offences against the person", Bentham treated matters such as homosexuality, masturbation and so on in a remarkably modern fashion. He discussed these issues from two standpoints. The first was the matter of whether these practices actually caused evil to society in general apart from biblical prohibitions. The second sort of issue was once again based on biblical exegesis. Here again he is applying his critique of fallacies where matters are not discussed rationally but are simply proclaimed on the basis of old beliefs that are not allowed to be challenged because they were thought to be beyond rebuke. For example in dealing with the story of Sodom and Gomorrah he points out that the reason for the punishment might not have been homosexuality as such but simply for failure to treat strangers properly. He also argues that if God chose to bring down fire on the two cities, then obviously there was nothing humans could do, but this did not necessarily give human beings the right to burn homosexuals at the stake. Bentham also made the perceptive comment often mentioned in modern exegesis that the sin of Sodom was lack of hospitality to strangers, not homosexuality as such.

Bentham also has a perceptive comment on the psychology of some biblical interpreters:

> We need not consider at any length [the length] to which the rigour of such philosophy may be carried when reinforced by notions of religion. Such as we are ourselves, such and in many respects worse it is common for us to make God to be: for fear blackens every object that it looks upon. It is almost as common for men to conceive of God as a being of worse than human malevolence in their hearts, as to stile [?] him a being of infinite benevolence with their lips. (Bentham 1978: 201)

One point Bentham made gives cause to wonder whether he was given to sly humour, for he suggested that if gay men refusing to marry caused an injustice to women who lost them as possible husbands, then such men should pay a special tax which would be used to provide dowries for poor women.

To sum up, Bentham's view of the Bible is not so far away from modern biblical exegesis and liberal opinion in both biblical interpretation and the solid discussion of social matters. His determination to deal with rigid fallacies enabled him to raise interesting problems for biblical scholarship as well as for political thought. There is no doubt that Bentham had many shortcomings, as John Stuart Mill pointed out, but if his arguments are not as broad or as nuanced as they should have been thanks to Bentham's preference for complete clarity before actual complexity, he set as high a standard in biblical investigation as he did with political.

Bibliography

Anderson, Frank Maloy. 1967. *The Constitutions and other Select Documents Illustrative of the History of France 1789–1907*, 2nd edn. New York: Russell & Russell.

Bedeau, Hugo Adam. 2000. "'Anarchical Fallacies': Bentham's Attack on Human Rights", *Human Rights Quarterly* 22 (1): 261–79.

Bentham, Jeremy. 1823. *Not Paul But Jesus*, London, John Hunt. Published anonymously under the name of Gamaliel Smith.

_____. 1843. *Anarchical Fallacies* (Bowering Edition of Works of Bentham, 2). Edinburgh: William Tate.

_____. 1948. *An Introduction to the Principals of Morals and Legislation.* New York: Hafner.

_____. 1978. "Pederasty: Offences Against Oneself", *Journal of Homosexuality* 3 (4): 389–405; continued in 4 (1) (1978).

Brown, Chris. 1997. 'Universal Rights: A Critique', *The International Journal of Human Rights*: 1 (2): 41–65.

Clément, Dominique. 2008. *Canada's Rights Revolution.* Vancouver: UBC Press.

Harvey, Anthony. 2001. *By What Authority: the Churches and Social Concern.* London: SCM Press.

Locke, John. 1956. *The Second Treatise of Government.* Oxford: Basil Blackwell.

_____. 1960. *Two Treatises of Government*, Cambridge: Cambridge University Press.

Jesus: The Justice of God[*]

Stanley Hauerwas[a]

Justice: A Theological Proposal

A gift that comes with growing old, at least for me, is the discovery that your students say better what you think, or should think, than you are able to say. I once chided Herbert McCabe for not writing the book on Aquinas many of us thought only he could write. Herbert responded noting he had learned that if you wait long enough your students will do it for you. I should have written more about justice, but now I do not need to do so because Dan Bell has said what I should have said. By calling attention to Dan's work I am not trying to be humble, but rather to do what justice requires, that is, to tell the truth.[1]

In the "Epilogue" in *Performing The Faith: Bonhoeffer and the Practice of Nonviolence*, I tried to respond to Stout's criticism of my alleged view that "justice is a bad idea" (Hauerwas 2004: 215–41). I pointed out that my suggestion that justice is a bad idea was meant to call into question abstract accounts of justice often associated with liberal political theory that assumes a just social order is possible without the people who constitute that order being just. My worry about appeals to justice in advanced capitalist societies

[a]   Stanley Hauerwas is an American theologian, ethicist, and a legal scholar. He is currently the Gilbert T. Rowe Professor of Theological Ethics at Duke Divinity School, with a joint appointment at the Duke University School of Law. Throughout his career, he has worked to emphasize the importance of virtue and character within the Christian Church and has been an outspoken Christian pacifist and promoter of non-violence. Some of his recent publications include *The State of the University: Academic Knowledges and the Knowledge of God* (Blackwell, 2007) and *Hannah's Child: A Theologian's Memoir* (Eerdmans, 2010).

has been that such appeals can blind us to the ways our lives may be implicated in fundamental forms of injustice.

However my deeper worry about appeals to justice has been theological. Reinhold Niebuhr, in the interest of making Christians politically responsible, argued that in matters political Jesus must be left behind. Jesus must be left behind because the political work necessary for the achievement of justice requires coercion and even violence. For Niebuhr, justice names the arrangements necessary to secure more equitable forms of life when we cannot love all neighbours equally. Good Barthian that I am I worry that justice so understood becomes more important than the justice of God found in the cross and resurrection of Christ (Hauerwas 2004: 230).[2]

I do not pretend that these brief remarks in response to Stout provide an adequate account of justice. More needs to be said, but the more that needs to be said has been said by Dan Bell. So I begin by introducing you to Bell's account of justice because as I suggested he says better what I think I should say than I have said. Bell, moreover, provides the basis for an engagement in the second part of this paper with Nicholas Wolterstorff's account of justice in his extremely impressive and important book, *Justice: Rights and Wrongs* (Wolterstorff 2008). Finally I will end by trying to show why, if as Bell argues Jesus is the justice of God, Christians cannot help but have a passion for justice.

Bell begins his article, "Jesus, the Jews, and the Politics of God's Justice", with the observation that though Christians disagree about much we are in agreement that God does justice and so should we. Yet he thinks such an agreement is part of the problem just to the extent that the Christian enthusiasm for justice distorts our reading of Scripture. He is particularly critical of an approach he characterizes as "social justice advocacy" for how those who identify with such a position approach Scripture.[3] For according to Bell, advocates of social justice read Scripture for values and principles they think crucial to motivate Christians, in Bell's words, "to get off their pews, leave the stained glass bliss of the congregation and its liturgy behind, and go out into the world to do justice" (Bell 2006: 9).

Bell notes that such an approach presents justice as an external standard to which Christianity is accountable. Indeed it is assumed that the credibility of the faith depends on the Christian support of secular accounts of justice. Accordingly it is assumed that justice can be understood apart from Christian theological convictions and practices. Human rights, for example, are defended in a manner that renders irrelevant what Christians believe or do not believe about God. Such a view of justice, as well as the approach to Scripture associated with justice so conceived, Bell argues is determined by the modern political context.[4]

That context, moreover, is one in which the church is assumed to be apolitical and, therefore, not relevant for determining knowing as well as the doing of justice. Accordingly such a view of justice reinforces the politics of modernity in which "the church is consigned to the role of cultural custodian of values tightly cordoned off from political practice, which finds its highest expression and guarantor in the nation-state" (Bell 2006: 90). Desperate to show the social relevance of the church Christians ironically underwrite in the name of justice an account of social relations that presumes a privatized account of Christian convictions and the church.

But if such a view of justice displaces the church it also results in a subtle displacement of Jesus. Jesus is relegated to being a motivator to encourage Christians to get involved in struggles for justice. Even if Jesus is thought to have practised justice in his ministry he is appealed to as a symbol or example. For what really matters is not Jesus but justice. In a manner not unlike how Jesus is displaced, such a view also displaces the Jews as crucial for determining what we mean by justice. Social justice advocates often direct attention to the call for justice made by the prophets, but the justice for which the prophets called is assumed to be universal in a manner that has no particular or intrinsic relation to the Jewish people.

The universalistic presumptions that inform such a call for justice is but a correlate of the political vision that assumes the task is to manage the inevitable conflict characteristic of societies in which people share no goods in common other than the necessity to pursue their subjective desires and interests.[5] It is a given that such a political order is pluralistic which means no goods in common can be discerned through the exercise of practical reason.[6] It is, therefore, not surprising that such a view of justice, whether it is utilitarian or contractarian, whether it is a libertarian or egalitarian vision of rights, whether it be capitalist or socialist ends up using scripture to underwrite a distributive vision of justice determined by the presumption that the best we can do is to secure a plethora of discordant private goods.

An alternative to this view of justice as social advocacy, an alternative that first seems more theologically determined, Bell identifies as "justice as justification". This approach recognizes the importance of social justice, but makes the achievement of social justice secondary to the individual entering into a saving relation with Jesus Christ. Such a view often presupposes satisfaction theories of the atonement in which Christ's death is thought to render due the debt incurred by our sin. Yet this understanding of justice is individualistic which makes it congruent with the politics of modernity.[7] As a result the church remains an apolitical space assumed to be "spiritual" in contrast to the world of politics.

This understanding of justice also displaces Jesus as God's justice because Jesus must be the victim of divine justice. As a result the justice that is assumed to require Jesus' death is not remarkably different than the justice presupposed by the social advocacy approach. For it is a justice derived from the *suum cuique* conception that assumes that we can know what justice means apart from Christian convictions.[8] The justice God must enforce turns out to be thoroughly secular and, in particular, retributive in a manner that reinforces modern statist forms of politics. Such a view not only continues the displacement of the Jews, who at best become representatives of the futility of attempting to fulfil the demands of divine justice, but also reinforce a vision of redemption analogous to modern political hopes that despair of a renewal of communion and seek rather for the state to provide defeat of one's enemies.[9]

In contrast to these views of justice Bell provides a christocentric rendering of justice that is, in his words, "robustly ecclesial and in the service to discipleship" (Bell 2006: 94). For according to Bell a proper theological reading of justice must be Christological in a manner that is forgetful neither of the Jews nor the canonical plot of redemption. He thinks such a view is exemplified by Paul, particularly in Romans, in which justice is displayed "as the divine redemptive solidarity that has as its end the restoration and renewal of the communion of all in God" (Bell 2006: 95). In contrast to worldly notions of justice that demand a strict rendering of what is due the justice of God that is Jesus requires the endurance of offence and the offer of forgiveness in the hope that the unjust has been made just by being gathered back into communion.

Thus at the heart of God's justice is God's fidelity to the promise to Abraham which requires from Gentile converts a recognition of their dependence on the promised people called Jews. Bell argues that Paul provides, therefore, a crucial turning point for how we are to understand justice. For the Gentiles would rightly be suspicious if Jesus was but a sacrificial victim to satisfy the demands of a pagan justice or if he were the establishment of a justice completely divorced from God's promises to the Jews. But in contrast Paul argues that Jesus is not the victim of God's justice, but the very embodiment of God's justice through his faithfulness and obedience manifesting God's unrelenting desire for reconciliation.

For Bell Jesus does not exemplify a justice that can be known apart from his life nor does he provide a motivation for us to underwrite some secular version of justice. "Rather, Jesus in his person *is* the justice of God" (Bell

2006: 97). Justice so understood obviously has significant implications for how Christians understand their place in the world. For Christians the work of justice first and foremost begins with their participation in Christ's work. The liturgy, particularly baptism and Eucharist, become the form justice takes because through those rites we are incorporated into Christ becoming God's justice for the world.[10] In Bell's language Jesus does "not justify individuals who then go do justice on their own; rather, Jesus justifies persons in communion. Jesus justifies his body, the church. Being made just and doing justice are a matter of being immersed in the life of the ecclesial community; to do justice is to be a part of the community whose life is centered in and ordered by Jesus, God's justice" (Bell 2006: 97).

Bell thinks such a perspective illumines Augustine's contention in *The City of God* that true justice is to be found in the Christian community. Augustine argues that true justice is to be found in the Christian community because there, in contrast to Rome, the one true God is rightly worshipped. Justice, according to Augustine, is "where God, the one supreme God, rules an obedient city according to his grace, forbidding sacrifice to any being save himself alone" (Augustine 1972: 19, 23). Augustine, Bell suggests, praises Christianity not because Christians are able to do more than the pagans, but because Christians are liturgically incorporated into Christ rendering praise and worship to the one alone worthy to be praised and worshipped.[11]

Bell draws on Aquinas' contention that charity is the form of all the virtues to suggest how his understanding of Jesus as the justice of God transforms what the actual operation of justice will look like. Aquinas certainly begins his account of justice with the classical notion that justice entails "rendering what is due", but what is due turns out to be shaped by the love that is Christ. Justice is, for Aquinas, a general virtue that nurtures solidarity in the shared loves that constitute the common good, but Aquinas locates the solidarity justice enacts within the divine order of charity. Accordingly justice is no longer a matter of rendering what is due, but rather has as its *telos* the establishment of our humanity by making us friends with God.[12]

Justice may, therefore, entail mercy and forgiveness by forgoing a strict accounting of what is due.[13] In Bell's words: "Justice and mercy are not opposing logics; rather they share a single end – the return of all love, the sociality of all desire, in God. Justice attains its end by enacting mercy to overcome sin" (Bell 2006: 99). Accordingly Bell thinks Aquinas provides expression to Paul's understanding of Christ's work, that is, Christ's sacrifice was perfectly just, not because it satisfied a debt, "but because it renewed the communion of humanity in God; it was an expression of the divine fidelity to the redemptive promise made to Abraham" (Bell 2006: 99).

To so understand justice as being ordered by and to charity, Bell argues, has the effect of reconnecting justice with its Jewish roots. It does so because justice in the Old Testament defies retributive accounts of justice as well as those that are shaped by a strict rendering of what is due. *Mispat* and *sedaqah*, the words we translate as justice or righteousness, rightly indicate that justice is a matter of judgement linked closely with righteousness.[14] Accordingly justice for Israel cannot be a procedural, but rather is orientated by the commitment to establish a right relation between people and God. Justice is not the impartial administration of laws, but rather imitates the divine partisanship on behalf of the poor, the widow, and the orphan. But it is equally important to remember that God's penchant for the poor, the widow, and the orphan is an expression of God's unrelenting desire to liberate us from sin (Bell 2006: 100).[15]

Bell acknowledges that his account of Jesus as the justice of God is not without its difficulties. It attempts to be at once particularistic and universal. Justice is tied to a particular people and a person yet seeks also the restoration of human communion. The latter is thought to be impossible without the former. Does that make this account sectarian? Does it mean that Christians must abandon the world if Jesus is our justice? Bell answers these challenges by directing attention to Jeremiah's admonition to seek the welfare of the city even when you are in exile.[16] I am deeply sympathetic with Bell's use of Jeremiah, but I want to test his account, an account that I take as my own, by trying to draw out the differences between Bell's and Wolterstorff's accounts of justice. I do so because I think the contrast will be extremely instructive since Wolterstorff, like Bell, claims his understanding of justice does justice to the Scriptural witness.

Justice: A Philosophical Proposal

Nicholas Wolterstorff's, *Justice: Rights and Wrongs* is a major attempt to develop an account of justice that is at once theologically and philosophically defensible. I have little doubt that his book will rightly set the terms for discussion of justice particularly among Christians for some time. Bell's account of Jesus as the justice of God sounds homiletical when compared with Wolterstorff's careful and intricate arguments. Yet it will be the burden of my remarks to show why Bell's account of justice is not only more Scriptural than Wolterstorff's account, but I will also argue that

Bell's understanding of justice helps illumine some of the limitations intrinsic to Wolterstorff's theory.

It may be objected that the attempt to put Bell and Wolterstorff into conversation is not unlike trying to compare apples and oranges. If nothing else Bell's position is to be found primarily in two articles and, therefore, lacks the detailed development Wolterstorff provides. Moreover Wolterstorff is primarily a philosopher and Bell is a theologian. They can be interpreted, therefore, as attempts to address different audiences making any comparison difficult. Though Wolterstorff is a philosopher he clearly is writing for Christians, so I think it not unjust to suggest that as a philosopher he might have something to learn from Bell the theologian.

Wolterstorff not only writes for Christians, but much to his credit he engages scriptural and theological issues in his book. To be sure he does so in an attempt to develop a theory of primary justice as inherent rights as an alternative to theories of justice as right order (Wolterstorff 2007: ix–x). I hope to show that the distinction between primary justice, which Wolterstorff claims deals with distributive and commutative issues, in contrast to rectifying justice, which consists in response to breakdowns in distributive and commutative justice, is scripturally problematic; but I need first to give an overview of Wolterstorff's argument.

The structure of *Justice: Rights and Wrongs* is determined by Wolterstorff's contention that rights language has been wrongly dismissed by the O'Donovans and MacIntyre on grounds that the notion of inherent rights is the result of the nominalist philosophical developments which resulted in the sheer assertion of subjective rights as ends in themselves. Thus the further contention by the O'Donovans and MacIntyre that inherent human rights are implicated in a perverse possessive individualism correlative of liberal and capitalist social orders which have no place for understanding justice as right order (Wolterstorff 2007: 30–33). In order to rebut this narrative Wolterstorff develops a counter-narrative in which he tries to show that a conception of justice as inherent rights was not born in the fourteenth or seventeenth centuries but rather goes back to the Hebrew and Christian scriptures (Wolterstorff 2007: xii).

Wolterstorff acknowledges that the need to provide this counter history means the *Justice: Rights and Wrongs* is a very different book than the one he set out to write. It is so because in order to make his case for an understanding of justice as inherent rights he has been forced to provide a historical counter-narrative to that of justice as right order. Therefore, on page 241 of this 400 page book he writes, "We now leave narrative behind and attend exclusively to theory". But the assumption that "theory" can be separated from the narrative, and I confess I remain unclear how Wolterstorff understands the status of his narrative for his theory, is exactly the kind of move that worries the O'Donovans and MacIntyre. If you are able to show that inherent human rights must be acknowledged to exist on philosophical grounds, why do you need to find them in Scripture?[17]

Wolterstorff does not argue that conceptions of justice as right order, a conception he thinks first articulated by Plato in the *Republic*, is without relevance for an account of justice. According to Wolterstorff, right-order theorists need not and should not deny the existence of natural rights in general just as inherent natural rights theorists should not deny the existence of natural laws of objective obligation (Wolterstorff 2007: 37).[18] Yet Wolterstorff's strong argument is that in contrast to justice as right-order theorists that argue for human rights rightly maintain that we possess some rights that are not conferred but are inherent to our "possessing of certain properties, standing in certain relationships, performing certain actions, each of us has a certain worth" (Wolterstorff 2007: 36).[19]

Wolterstorff does not deny that rights language may have been put to perverse uses, but misuse does not undermine the necessary priority of justice as inherent rights to justice as right order. Contrary to MacIntyre's claim that rights assume an asocial individualism, our natural rights "are not the rights one would have if one were not living in society" (Wolterstorff 2007: 33). Rather our sociality is built into rights because a right is a right *with regard* to someone who is usually someone other than oneself, though it is also the case that someone may be oneself. But the crucial point is that rights are normative bonds that are not, for the most part, generated by the exercise of will on one's part (Wolterstorff 2007: 4).

Drawing on the work of Charles Reid and Brian Tierney, Wolterstorff argues that such a view of justice as inherent rights can be found in developments in canon law as early as the twelfth century (Wolterstorff 2007: 53–59). He also argues that such a view of rights is incipient in church fathers such as John Chrysostom's sermon on Lazarus and the rich man, but his case turns primarily on this reading of the Old Testament. He acknowledges that you cannot find in the Scripture "meta-level" talk about how to think about justice or rights. Yet he argues that O'Donovan's claim that justice in the Old Testament, either in the form of judicial judgement or as the claim as a plaintiff before a judge, wrongly limits the work of justice in the Old Testament to rectifying justice rather than manifestations of a primary justice based in justice as inherent right (Wolterstorff 2007: 68–75).[20]

Wolterstorff observes that the striking feature of talk about justice in the Old Testament is how justice is connected to treatment of widows, orphans, resident aliens, and the poor. He observes that the prophets and psalmists do not argue the case for caring for the poor, but rather they assume it (Wolterstorff 2007: 76). That they do so, Wolterstorff suggests, requires no special insight why the writers of the Old Testament assumed the vulnerable to deserve particular attention. They saw quite clearly that the widow, the orphan, the resident alien, and the poor are not only often vulnerable to injustice but disproportionately actual victims of injustice (Wolterstorff 2007: 78–79).

Such a "seeing", Wolterstorff contends, derived from Israel's memory that she too had experienced what it means to be an alien in the land of Egypt (Lev. 19:33) as well as what it meant to be a slave (Deut. 24:21). Thus the assumption that "those with social power in Israel are to render justice to the vulnerable bottom ones *as a public remembrance, as a memorial*, of Yahweh's deliverance of Israel from Egypt ... Israel is to do justice as a memorial of its deliverance by God from the injustice of slavery", Deut. 24:21 (Wolterstorff 2007: 80). Israel's commitment to justice is but the way she must live if she is to imitate and know Yahweh. Moreover even though the law was given to Israel to make her a nation unlike other nations, a holy people, Israel's recognition of Yahweh's kingship meant all nations were held accountable to be just.

Wolterstorff acknowledges that though Israel's writers did not use the language of rights, just to the extent they assumed Yahweh holds humankind accountable for doing justice, they assumed there was a normative structure of rights and obligations. Moreover justice cannot be limited to God's commands, but rather we are held accountable to a "deep structure" that assumes justice as inherent rights based on the recognition of the worth of human persons and of human beings (Wolterstorff 2007: 91). Therefore the prohibition against murder found in Gen. 9:6.

> Whoever sheds the blood of a human,
> By a human shall that person's blood be shed;
> For in his own image
> God made humankind

is not grounded in God's law "but in the worth of the human being. All who bear God's image possess an inherent right not to be murdered" (Wolterstorff 2007: 95).

Wolterstorff argues that the narrative he has identified with the Old Testament is fundamentally continued in the New Testament.[21] The justice

Jesus preaches when he opens the scroll in Lk. 4:17–21 makes clear that Jesus identifies himself as God's anointed whose vocation is to proclaim to the poor, the blind, the captives, and the oppressed the good news of the inauguration of the year of the Lord that marks the time when justice shall reign (Wolterstorff 2007: 117). Crucial for understanding the significance of Jesus' reading of the scroll is the necessity to acknowledge that Jesus does not merely proclaim the coming of God's kingdom, but he is identified as the king of this kingdom (Wolterstorff 2007: 120).

The acknowledgement of Jesus' kingship for Wolterstorff is the basis for the New Testament expansion of the scope of justice. Because Jesus is king the justice he establishes goes beyond that envisioned in the Old Testament because now it is not enough that the powerful give to the poor what is their due. Jesus has the more radical view that a social inversion is required in which the lowly are lifted up and the high ones are cast down (Wolterstorff 2007: 122–23). This does not literally mean that beggars are to become kings, but rather that justice will only be possible when the rich and powerful are cured of their attachment to wealth and power. Jesus, therefore, expands the Old Testament understanding of the downtrodden to include all those excluded from full participation in society because they are defective, malformed, or seen as religiously inferior (Wolterstorff 2007: 126–27).

Jesus' expansion of those subject to injustice indicates recognition that human beings have inherent worth and that worth is to be grounded in how they are to be treated. Such a recognition of rights is clearly presumed when Jesus says: "Look at the birds of the air; they neither sow or reap nor gather into barns, and yet your heavenly Father feeds them. Are you not of more value than they?" (Mt. 6:26). Such statements imply that to be a human is to have worth. Though Jesus does not say what that worth is, Wolterstorff suggests that "it seems safe to infer" that Jesus presupposed the idea that the worth one has is that which comes from being *qua* human (Wolterstorff 2007: 130–31).

Such is Wolterstorff's defence of an inherent natural and human rights theory of justice on Scriptural and historical grounds. As I indicated, however, he does not seem to think the narrative he has provided is necessary for the justification of a natural rights view of justice. Indeed the last third of his book is a defence of rights to show how, as he puts it, they "emerge from a certain interweaving of life – and history – goods and evils on the one hand, and the worth of human beings on the other" (Wolterstorff 2007: 288). But then one must ask: if a rights based account of justice can be generated in such a fashion, why did he need to provide the account he does of the Scriptural basis of a rights based theory?

Put more contentiously, I think it is not at all clear why he assumes justice as inherent rights is a necessary implication of calls for justice in Scripture rather than a right order account. Indeed his suggestion that texts such as Leviticus and Deuteronomy cannot help but appear to us as "a bewildering mishmash of regulations concerning ritual cleanliness, instructions concerning cultic practices, and principles of justice" (Wolterstorff 2007: 83), betrays his desire to find in the Old Testament an account of justice that is not dependent on the practices of an actual people. The distinction between primary theories of justice and rectifying justice turns out to be a way to escape the historical particularity of the text.

The same problem is apparent in his treatment of Jesus. Jesus may initiate a more expansive understanding of justice, but that very way of putting the matter makes Jesus a representative of a theory of justice rather than, as Bell would have it, the very justice of God. I suspect Wolterstorff would find Bell's understanding of Jesus as the very justice of God "limiting" just to the extent such a view would imply that how Christians understand justice may well be in tension with the presumption that an account of justice, a theory of justice, is possible as such.

Wolterstorff wants to have it both ways; that is, he wants the viability of justice as inherent rights with and without his narrative. Late in his book he observes he has reversed the narrative of those who see natural rights born of individualistic and atomistic modes of thought that climax in the UN Universal Declaration of Human Rights. In contrast he has argued that not only did the moral vision of the writers of the Hebrew and Christian Scriptures implicitly recognize natural and human rights, but these rights were given explicit conceptualization by the canon lawyers in the twelfth century. He acknowledges that the recognition of such rights remained an "exceedingly slow and halting process, however, until, quite surprisingly, it burst forth after the horrors of World War II in the UN Declaration" (Wolterstorff 2007: 361). Scripture can now be used as a resource for grounding such rights, but to put the matter that way means Scripture now serves to sustain a politics in which God does not matter. Wolterstorff may be right that rights were discovered prior to the creation of the capitalist subject, but even if that is the case I do not see how it can be denied that the language of rights as used in the world in which we now find ourselves underwrites an individualism that is not only possessive but agonistic.

Wolterstorff would find such criticisms odd, I am sure, because he argues that a secular grounding of rights is deficient just to the extent it cannot account for respect for humans who do not possess the capacity for rational agency (Wolterstorff 2007: 333). According to Wolterstorff human rights require a theistic grounding because only by understanding ourselves as created in the image of God do we have sufficient reason for excluding no one from due respect. He observes that the biblical writers were well aware that some human beings were created by God who lacked the capacity to exercise dominion, but they still have a human nature sufficient to resemble God (Wolterstorff 2007: 350). I am sympathetic with Wolterstorff's concern to have those who seem to lack rational capacity not to be excluded from claims of justice, but I remain unconvinced that his account of what it means for us to be in God's image can be sustained without a more robust Trinitarian account than he provides.[22]

I think finally the fundamental issue between Bell and Wolterstorff is one of theological method. That it is so I think is clear from Wolterstorff's quite charitable account of my claim in *After Christendom?* that justice is a bad idea. He suggests I could not have meant what I said, but rather my point is that the vocabulary of justice and rights has been so corrupted by its use in the "larger social order" that the language cannot be redeemed. By contrast Wolterstorff argues that not only can language be redeemed, "it must be redeemed – because, for one thing, to reject the language and conceptuality of justice would be to render the New Testament unintelligible. Pull justice out and nothing much is left. Justice understood in such a way, however, that it is not God or justice but God *and* justice – the justice of God and the justice God enjoins" (Wolterstorff 2007: 98).

That seems to me to put my problem with Wolterstorff's account of justice about as clearly as it can be put. Wolterstorff is no foundationalist, but the move he makes here, a move that I think shapes the structure and form of his book, assumes that we must be able to secure an account of justice in and of itself if we are to make sense of Scripture. Some forms of right order theory could have the same result, but it is usually the case that justice as right order requires the naming of a history that makes unavoidable the existence of a concrete people for display of justice.[23] In other words, I am suggesting that there is at once a tendency to ignore the significance of history and politics by developing justice in terms of inherent rights.

Wolterstorff, for example, certainly has it right to suggest that Israel's understanding that the care of those most vulnerable is required if she is rightly to remember what God has done for her, but he fails to be able to develop that insight for how we should think about justice. That such a remembering is not constitutive of his understanding of justice as inherent rights is, I think, but a correlative of his attempt to develop an account of justice persuasive for anyone at any time. I worry that such an account of justice may put him closer to Rawls than he thinks. But then that may be where he desires to be.

I acknowledge that the difference between Bell and Wolterstorff cannot be settled by quoting this or that passage in the Scripture that explicitly uses the language of justice. Indeed I assume, as Bell suggests, that our understanding of justice will depend on passages of Scripture that make no mention of justice. Rather what is at stake is a construal of Scripture as a whole. I obviously think Bell is much closer to getting such a construal right just to the extent his account of the relation between the two testaments, as well as the status of and relation between Jews and Christians, are crucial for how justice is to be understood.

A Passion for Justice

At the heart of Wolterstorff's account is an admirable passion for justice grounded in what he calls the "ur-principle" of action: "one should never treat persons or human beings as if they had less worth than they do have; one should never treat them with under-respect, never demean them". This principle once articulated can be put in even more general terms "that one should never treat *anything whatsoever* as having less worth than it is" (Wolterstorff 2007: 370). Wolterstorff is intent to sustain such principles in order to support what he calls the "moral subculture of rights". He worries that in the absence of such a subculture the increasing secularism to which we may be subject will make appeals to justice as natural rights less compelling. If we lose the language of justice as natural rights, moreover, Wolterstorff thinks we cannot help but slide back into tribalism (Wolterstorff 2007: 393).

Like Wolterstorff, I too want those who suffer from Alzheimer's to have the care that befits their status as human beings. Such care I believe, moreover, is a matter of justice. But I do not think such care is more likely to be forthcoming or sustained by a natural right theory of justice. Rather, I think Bell rightly suggests that what is required is the recovery of communion made possible through the works of mercy. In particular, Bell argues that a text such as Mt. 25:31–45 makes clear that the works of mercy are not principles or values that then must be translated into a more universal or secular vision of justice. Rather they summons us to participate in God's redemption by feeding the hungry, giving drink to the thirsty, clothing the naked, harbouring the stranger, visiting the sick, ministering to prisoners, and burying the dead. Such is the way, Bell suggests, that we learn what it means for Jesus to be the justice of God (Bell 2006: 106).

I know of no book that exemplifies better Bell's understanding of Jesus as God's justice than Hans Reinders' *Receiving the Gift of Friendship: Profound Disability, Theological Anthropology, and Ethics.* Reinders observes that much good has been done in the name of disability-rights for creating new opportunities as well as institutional space for the disabled. But such an understanding of justice is not sufficient if we listen to the disabled. They do not seek to be tolerated or even respected because they have rights. Rather they seek to share their lives with us and they want us to want to share our lives with them. In short they want us to be claimed and to claim one another in friendship.

If you need an image for what it means for charity to be the form of the virtues and, in particular, justice, take this scene from Jennie Weiss Block's book, *Copious Hosting: A Theology of Access for People with Disabilities.* She tells the story of Jason, a 14-year-old boy with profound intellectual disabilities who was born with spina bifida. He has an enlarged head and, because his arms and legs have often been broken because of a bone disease, his limbs are twisted. He cannot feed himself and must be carefully bathed and diapered. He is cared for by Felicia Santos who is a professional caregiver. Weiss Block reports on a particular visit, a visit that she says changed her life, when she witnessed Felicia "leaning forward, talking softly to Jason. He was smiling. I stood for a few minutes before speaking and watched their interaction. What I witnessed between them was the purest love – the kind of love that asks for nothing in return' (Reinders 2008: 188).[24] That is what charity-formed justice looks like.[25]

Bell acknowledges that viewed through the lens of modernity's politics such a view of justice, justice shaped by the works of mercy, will be dismissed as "philanthropy". But that is exactly the perspective that must be rejected if the justice that is the church is not to be identified with the justice of the nation-state. Wolterstorff worries that if justice is identified by Bell's "Spirit-blown mobile community" we will lack the universality necessary to sustain appeals to justice as such. But no theory of justice will be sufficient to do that work. Rather than a theory, God has called into the world a people capable of transgressing the borders of the nation-state to seek the welfare of the downtrodden.[26]

What we need is not a theory of justice capable of universal application. Rather what we need is what we have. What we have is a people learning again to live in diaspora. Bell concludes his article by observing that the broader argument concerning the necessity of attending to political context for a theological reading of Scripture converges with the development of a more focused argument concerning the nature of justice in Scripture. That it does so is crucial for understanding the political form that God's restorative justice takes. For as it turned out, Israel's political vocation took the form of a politics of diaspora through which she becomes a blessing to all people. Bell suggests a similar political vocation has been given to the church insofar as she has been joined to Israel's Messiah, requiring her to be on pilgrimage to the ends of the world seeking reconciliation through the works of mercy. Such is the justice of God.

> Here is my servant, whom I uphold,
> My chosen, in whom my soul delights;
> I have put my spirit upon him;
> He will bring forth justice to the nations.
> He will not cry or lift up his voice,
> Or make it heard in the street;
> A bruised reed he will not break,
> And a dimly burning wick he will not quench;
> he will faithfully bring forth justice. (Isa. 42:1–4)[27]

Notes

* I stole this title, as well as most of what I have to say from Dan Bell's reflections on justice that are to be found in his articles: "Jesus, the Jews, and the Politics of God's Justice" (2006: 87–111) and "Deliberating: Justice and Liberation," in *The Blackwell Companion to Christian Ethics* (2004: 182–195).

1. MacIntyre observes that Aquinas' account of justice is not only at odds with the accounts of justice characteristic of liberal modernity but they also involved a challenge to the conventional standards of his own age. For example MacIntyre directs attention to Aquinas' views on truth-telling and lying which require that we never assert anything except what we believe to be true. We are not required to tell all that we know because it is rightfully a matter of prudence when to or not to speak in terms of the duties and obligations we may have. But Aquinas, from MacIntyre's perspective, rightly maintains that we may "never lie, not for profit, nor convenience, nor pleasure, nor to cause pain or trouble. Lying is evil, and lying with malice is a mortal sin" (S. T. IIa-IIae, 109 and 110). Alasdair MacIntyre, *Whose Justice? Which Rationality?* (1988: 203).

2. One of the reasons I suspect my rhetorical gestures concerning why justice or freedom are "bad ideas" is some, particularly those who think of themselves as "ethicists" rather than theologians, fail to see how these seemingly outrageous claims reflect fundamental theological commitments. Francesca Murphy gets it just right in her book, *God is Not a Story: Realism Revisited* (2007). Noting Barth's insistence that Anselm's was not trying to prove God's existence she asks

then why does Barth think what Anselm did was so important. She puts the matter this way: "To write a systematic theology about divine revelation, Christ, the Trinity, reconciliation, and creation, one needs to use an immense number of *words*, words like good, flesh, incarnation, generation, procession, sin, and human. But if everything we know about God comes from God, one cannot take those words in their ordinary usage, or as from their apparent human origin. One must assume that one is using them *not* only with the truth imparted to them by their correspondence to ordinary objects, but also and crucially with the truth imparted to them by God, the first Truth. Barth says that Anselm is not concerned with the *existence* of faith – bringing it into being by showing its objects exists – but with the *nature* of faith. What kind of *understanding*, or *intelligence* can use theological language appropriately? Only one according to Barth, which, through grace, attains a 'participation' 'in God's mode of Being'. In his discussion of Anselm's proof, Barth is looking for a divine anchor onto which to hook theological language. There are no philosophical or naturally known 'analogies' between creatures and God, according to Barth, only analogies made known by the Revealer: he called analogies known by the revelation of God in Christ the analogy of faith, the *analogia fideia* … Since he has chosen an eleventh-century Platonizing Benedictine monk as his paradigm, the *anaolgia fideia* is very much an *analogy of participation*, the 'truing' of the theologian's words about God through their participation in the first Truth" (2007: 114–15). Of course one of the words that must be subject to such a "truing" is justice.

3. You know something has gone wrong when the phrase "social justice" is used. What kind of justice would not be "social"? The very description "social justice" reproduces the public/private distinction characteristic of liberal political regimes. I also think the phrase "restorative justice" has the same problems as the locution "social justice". Justice is or must be restorative if it is to be justice.

4. Bell notes that it is not accidental that the historical-critical methods emerged simultaneously with the advent of modern politics as statecraft. "Jesus, the Jews, and the Politics of God's Justice" (Bell 2006: 88).

5. In his article, "Deliberating: Justice and Liberation", in the *Blackwell Companion to Christian Ethics*, Bell puts it this way: "Liberalism re-imagined society as a teeming mass of individuals, each with their own interests, ends, and conceptions of what constitutes the good life. Consequently, justice was reconfigured; in contemporary parlance, now the right was given priority over the good. What constitutes justice is arrived at apart from any substantive agreement about what constitutes the good or *telos* of humanity. Justice in modern liberal social orders becomes essentially procedural. Under the sign of modernity, justice is a matter of arriving at a procedure for securing effective cooperation between and security among discrete individuals pursuing irrepressibly diverse plethora of self-determined interests and private goods. In this situation, justice is no longer conceived as a unitive force. Indeed, with the arrival of modernity, the general virtue of justice in invariably reduced to "legal justice" and equated simply with following positive laws of the state, or it is discarded altogether" (Bell 2006: 183–84). Bell's analysis obviously reflects the influence of Alasdair MacIntyre and, in particular, his *Whose Justice? Which Rationality* (Notre Dame: University of Notre Dame Press, 1988).

6. Bell puts the matter more forcefully in "Justice and Liberation" noting that the loss of a robust sense of the common good with the concomitant elevation of the individual means that theological calls for justice reproduce an account of justice understood primarily as the institution of procedures by which the regulation and exchange of goods is understood as an aggregate of autonomous individuals. Bell observes "noteworthy is the absence of justice as a general virtue concerned with nurturing a community's solidarity in a shared love" (Bell 2006: 185).

7. In a letter responding to an earlier draft of this essay David Aers observed that justification only becomes "individualistic" when divorced from incorporation into the body of Christ made possible through the sacrament of penance and Eucharist.

8. Bell argues that though such a view is often attributed to Anselm's account of the atonement, he thinks such a reading of Anselm to be a mistake. According to Bell "Anselm describes how humanity is taken up into the communion of love that is the life of the blessed Trinity (*theosis*, deification). In other words, according to Anselm, God became human not in order to meet the demands of an implacable justice before which even God must bow, but so that humanity might be restored to the place of honor that God from the beginning intended for humanity, namely, participation in the divine life" (Bell 2006: 96).

9. For a quite different account of Paul on righteousness see A. Katherine Grieb, "'So That in Him We Might Become the Righteousness of God' (2 Cor. 5:21): Some Theological Reflections on the Church Becoming Justice," *Ex Auditu*, 22 (Grieb 2006: 58–80).

10. Nathan Mitchell has written a wonderful account of the importance of liturgy as constitutive of justice. Mitchell observes, "The solution to poverty isn't ugly art and sappy music in our worship". On the contrary, "the more striking [the] beauty and integrity and careful celebration of the Sunday liturgy, the deeper 'Rilke's rule' sinks in: *You must change your life*. We must change our lives – *together*. The solution to hunger, homelessness, oppression, racism, homophobia, and the host of other social evils that destroy lives isn't careless liturgy, it's repentance, it's *changing our lives*; it's the voluntary renunciation of those addictions – to power, money, and control – that continues to divide the world into 'haves' and 'have-nots'. We won't feed the world's hungry by neglecting the liturgy." Nathan Mitchell, "Being Beautiful, Being Just", in *Toward Ritual Transformation: Remembering Robert W. Hovda* (Mitchell 2003: 81). The internal quotes are from an article by Hovda.

11. Bell's account of Augustine may strike some who have learned to read Augustine through Rienhold Niebuhr quite problematic. But Robert Dodaro's account of Augustine in his book, *Christ and the Just Society in the Thought of Augustine* (Dodaro 2004) supports Bell's account. Dodaro says, "Augustine maintains that justice cannot be known except in Christ, and that, as founder (*conditor*) and ruler (*rector*) Christ forms the just society in himself. United with Christ, members of his body constitute the whole, just Christ (*Christus totus iustus*), which is the city of god, the true commonwealth, and the locus for the revelation of justice" (2004: 72). Later Dodaro argues that Augustine thought that the civic virtues must be transformed by the virtues of faith, hope, and love as otherwise the statesman will pursue a false peace and prosperity for the earthly city (2004: 209). The transformation of the virtues is required because the

virtues, if they are to be true, must lead the soul to adhere to God because only those who adhere to God can overcome the consequences of sin – suffering, temptation, toil, and death (2004: 210).

12. Though I think Bell is in general right about Thomas' understanding of justice, as I point out in *Performing the Faith*, Thomas does say that an act of justice can be thought to have "rectitude" "without taking into account the way in which it was done by the agent" (*Summa Theologica*, translated by the Fathers of the English Dominican Province, 1947: 2.2.57,1). Therefore the "Treatise on Prudence and Justice" deals with a wide range of issues that might be thought "institutional" in which the standards of evaluation derive from expectations not always directly determined by theological considerations. I assume that any account of justice will, like Thomas' account, draw on expectations and manners of a people that have been honed from their peculiar history. Crucial to Thomas' account of justice is his understanding of part to the whole. Thus he says "all who are included in a community, stand in relation to that community as parts to a whole; while a part, as such belongs to a whole, so that whatever is the good of a part can be directed to the good of the whole. It follows therefore that the good of any virtue, whether such virtue direct man in relation to himself, or in relation to certain other individual persons, is referable to the common good, to which justice directs; so that all acts of virtue can pertain to justice, in so far as it directs man to the common good" (ST, 2.2.58,5). This is the basis for Thomas' judgements that it is lawful to kill sinners if they threaten the health of the whole body. ST, 2.2.64,2.

13. In his article in *Blackwell Companion to Christian Ethics*, "Justice and Liberation", Bell develops this understanding of Thomas noting that Thomistic justice is not only a matter of protecting the rights of strangers in the absence of shared love, but is about the nurturing of communion of saints in a shared love. Accordingly the often Niebuhrian presumed contrast between justice and peace is a mistake from a Thomistic point of view. For from Thomas' perspective justice redeems and is therefore predicated on peace. In other words justice is not merely the regulation of conflict but rather presumes the priority of peace. "Thus the common canard is transposed: 'Without peace there is no justice'" (2004: 189). Such an understanding of justice and peace has obvious implications for how one understands the "justice" that governs war.

14. Bell's emphasis on the place of judgement for understanding the work of justice in the Old Testament is the heart of O'Donovan's understanding of justice in *The Desire of the Nations* (Cambridge: University of Cambridge Press, 1996) and, more recently, *The Ways of Judgment* (Grand Rapids, MI: Eerdmans, 2005). It would be an extraordinarily fruitful enterprise to explore the similarities between Bell's and O'Donovan's understandings of justice. I am thinking, in particular, of O'Donovan's account of praise in *Desire of the Nations* and his treatment of mercy in *Ways of Judgment*.

15. Bell argues that this understanding of justice is necessary for the right reading of Scripture because justice is inseparable from the scriptural drama of redemption. "We see that God is just precisely as God is faithful to that redemptive intent. We see, as Paul argues, Jesus is the climax of the covenant, the promise of redemption, the justice of God who in his person breaks down the wall of hostility and restores the communion of all in God. Thus, the call to justice is

the call to be joined to Christ and so to Christ's body, the church, whose life is just insofar as its life is centered in and ordered by Jesus who is the justice of God" (2006: 100).

16. See Jer. 29:7. Bell intentionally chooses Jer. 29:7 because it seems to suggest that justice cannot be as narrowly circumscribed, as Bell may seem to have done. Of course you need to ask what politics would suggest that Jesus as the justice of God should be described as "narrow".

17. Wolterstorff does not engage the work of John Rawls because he thinks Rawls simply assumes the existence of inherent natural rights and therefore he does not develop an account of such rights (2007: 15–17). I find it odd, however, that Wolterstorff ignores MacIntyre's argument in *Whose Justice? Which Rationality?* that conceptions of justice and practical reason are necessarily interrelated. To be sure Wolterstorff has an extended discussion of why eudaimonistic ethical positions cannot sustain a theory of rights, but his arguments dealing with that issue do not take up MacIntyre's defence of an ethic of the virtues. In fact Wolterstorff provides no account of justice as a virtue. He may not think he needs to do so because of his arguments concerning eudaimonism, but a more direct discussion of why he thinks the question of the justice as a virtue can be ignored would have been welcome. One of the reasons he does not treat justice as a virtue is his presumption "that the concept of a moral virtue is conceptually posterior to the concept of a morally admirable act" (2007: 289). His position on this involves complex questions philosophical psychology as well as how act descriptions work that he does not develop in this book. Needless to say I have quite a different understanding of the significance of the virtues than Wolterstorff.

    I confess I find Wolterstorff's account of Augustine, to say the very least, odd. He argues that Augustine finally came to the view that virtue is not sufficient for happiness and as a result came closer to an inherent right account of justice than good order (2007: 198). In the light of Bell's account above, particularly Augustine's understanding of why worship is crucial for understanding the nature of justice, such a view as Wolterstorff's fails to do justice to Augustine's understanding not only of justice but of the virtues in general.

18. Wolterstorff, however, notes that though right order theorists can and should concede the existence of natural rights such a concession does not change the fact that natural rights will have a different significance for the right order theorist than the natural right theorist. For the right order theorist the violation of someone's natural right is never in itself the treating of a human being with less than due respect. Rather it is an indication that some natural law has been disobeyed. For example the right order theorist may say that the rights of the poor are being violated, but that is simply to call attention from the right order theorist perspective to the fundamental fact that the powerful and will to do are not fulfilling their obligation. "It is not a way of calling attention to the fact that the worth of those human beings who are poor is not being respected. The worth of human beings does not enter into his (right order theorist) way of thinking about rights" (p. 43).

19. Wolterstorff distinguishes between inherent rights and human rights. A right may be inherent to a certain status and that status may be intrinsic to the human being that possesses that status but not to our nature as such. Thus the status

of being a parent does not belong to human nature because one can be a human without being a parent (2007: 317–19).

20. Wolterstorff appeals to texts such as Isa. 28:17; 42:1–4 as well as Pss. 106:3; 112:5 to argue that the rendering of juridical judgement presupposes an account of primary justice.

21. Wolterstorff also deals with the theme of forgiveness in which he develops an account that God too has rights because if God did not have rights God could not be wronged. Forgiveness requires that the one who is to forgive has been deprived of that to which they have a right. He argues against Nygren's account of *agape* exactly because it is "justice blind" just to the extent Nygren fails to see that forgiveness necessarily incorporates the presumption of being wronged. (2007: 105) But here, Wolterstorff argues, this is one of the places that Jesus goes beyond the Old Testament because he regards our willingness to forgive those who wrong us is a manifestation of the repentance God requires for his forgiveness of those who wrong him (2007: 130).

22. See for example Hans Reinders' account the image of God and the disabled in his, *Receiving the Gift of Friendship: Profound Disability, Theological Anthropology and Ethics* (2008: 227–75).

23. Though I am more sympathetic with justice understood as right order I hope it is clear that the account of justice articulated by Bell is not to be construed in terms of Wolterstorff's understanding of those two alternatives.

24. I am confident that Wolterstorff would claim that his account of justice would also identify Felicia care of Jason as justice, but I do not see how justice understood as inherent rights can have such communion constitutive of justice in the way Bell suggests it must be.

25. I am not "reading into" Reinders' account because Reinders provides a quite extensive treatment of Thomas' understanding of charity as the form of the virtues (2008: 297–311). In doing so, however, he draws on the work of Paul Wadell to emphasize the primacy of God's grace. We are only able to acquire the virtues to make us God's friends because God has first befriended us.

26. For an account of the radical implications of the works of mercy see Johnson's, *The Fear of Beggars: Stewardship and Poverty in Christian Ethics* (2007).

27. Wolterstorff also quotes this passage from Isaiah observing that Isaiah is not suggesting that the servant will establish a fair legal system, but rather that the Servant will bring about a general social condition in which there will be no need for a judicial system to vindicate those who have been treated unjustly (2007: 74). Wolterstorff does not explore the difference a Christological reading of this passage may make.

Bibliography

Augustine. 1972. *The City of God.* Harmondsworth: Penguin Books.

Block, Jennie Weiss. 2002. *Copious Hosting: A Theology of Access for People with Disabilities.* New York: Continuum.

Bell, Daniel. 2006. "Jesus, the Jews and the Politics of God's Justice." *Ex Auditu* 87–112.

Hauerwas, Stanley. 2004. *Performing the Faith: Bonhoeffer and the Practice of Nonviolence.* Grand Rapids, MI: Brazos Press.

Murphy, Francesca Aran. 2007. *God is not a Story: Realism Revisited.* Oxford: Oxford University Press.
Reinders, Hans. 2008. *Receiving the Gift of Friendship: Profound Disability, Anthropology, and Ethics*, Grand Rapids, MI: Eerdmans.
Wolterstorff, Nicholas. 2008. *Justice: Rights and Wrongs*, Princeton, NJ: Princeton University Press.

Part II

Uses and Approaches to Bible and Justice

Justice and Violence in the Priestly Utopia

Walter J. Houston[a]

Introduction

Perhaps the only developed and consistent theory of the relations between God, human beings and their environment in the Bible is that sketched by the so-called priestly writer (P) in Chapter 1 and parts of Chapters 6–9 of Genesis. This would account for the considerable amount of attention these chapters, especially the first, have attracted in the debate on the Bible, Christianity and the environment. In particular, discussion has focused on the blessing on human beings in Gen. 1:28 (with the corresponding divine statement of intention in v. 26). This reads, according to the Hebrew text: "Be fruitful and multiply, fill the earth and subdue it; and rule over [or 'govern'] the fish of the sea, the birds of the air, and every living thing that crawls [or 'moves'] upon the earth."[1]

In what must be one of the most influential short papers in the history of the humanities, the historian Lynn White Jr. argued over forty years ago that a large share of the responsibility for the already looming environmental disaster was borne by the way this text had been applied in the history of Western Christianity to justify the increasing exploitation of the earth and its creatures (White 1967). The Bible here had evidently authorized humankind to take control of the earth and its creatures and to use them for their own benefit; theologians argued that the earth had been created for the good of humankind, and farmers and engineers and industrialists

[a] Walter J. Houston is a minister of the United Reformed Church who holds the position of an Honorary Research Fellow in the Biblical Studies Centre at the University of Manchester. He is also an Emeritus Fellow of Mansfield College Oxford. His career was spent mainly in theological education, specializing in Old Testament studies, at colleges in Cambridge, Manchester and Oxford.

over the centuries acted on that presupposition, with increasingly damaging effects on the health of eco-systems and the diversity of species. From a different point of view, Norman Habel has argued more recently that the text on the creation of human beings in Gen. 1:26–30 is an interruption in the consistent and beautiful story of the emergence of "Earth" (he treats this word as a proper name, with a capital letter and no article), which violates its spirit by imposing upon Earth a hierarchical dominance which devalues Earth and its creatures (Habel 2000).

White's article stirred much criticism: see, for example, Barr (1972: 15–30) or Houston (1979). Biblical scholars in particular argued, and generally agree, that the text in question does not mean what it was taken to mean. As I argued thirty one years ago (Houston 1979: 166–67), Gen. 1:28 could not imply that human beings were being given permission to exploit the earth and its creatures, for two main reasons: first because the position they were being given was one of kingship, and the Old Testament never authorizes kings to use their positions to benefit themselves, and denounces them when they do so; rather they exist to benefit their subjects; and secondly because v. 29 indicates that human beings need special permission, over and above the grant of "dominion", even to use plant produce for food, let alone exploit the earth in any other way.

But about ten years ago Peter Harrison pointed out that these criticisms of White were misplaced (Harrison 1999). It did not matter what the text originally may have meant; what mattered, what influenced history, was "what the text was taken to mean at certain periods of history" and "how it was taken to sanction a particular attitude toward the natural world" (Harrison 1999: 89). However, he went on to show that this specific text, on human dominion, had not in fact been taken in that way in the Middle Ages, which White saw as the key turning point in the rise of exploitative doctrines and practices in Western Europe (Harrison 1999: 89–95). In the Fathers and the early medieval period it had been allegorized: the beasts to be kept under control were the human passions; later the point became one of intellectual mastery of the world. (Barr had made a similar point with a slightly different emphasis: Barr 1972: 23–24.) Only in the seventeenth century did the text begin to be taken literally, and used to legitimize agriculture, colonization, and the clearing of virgin land: activities understood as the restoration of the human dominion lost with Adam's fall (Harrison 1999: 96–103). But this reading of the text emerged just at the time that an anthropocentric view of the universe was being questioned (Harrison 1999: 103). Thus the reign of the literal sense of the text over doctrine and practice was quite limited, virtually confined to the seventeenth century, according to Harrison.

Today, few of the leaders of politics, commerce and industry, who have the greatest influence on the way in which human activity impacts on the environment, would think of justifying their activities by reference to this text, and any influence it may have over them is at most extremely indirect. For those who do read it, the question is not how the text has in fact influenced the thinking and activity of people in the past, but how, or whether, it ought to influence ours. The issue is not reception history, but hermeneutics. Thus the "original meaning" comes back into the frame. Those who read the text are bound to be interested in what it "really means"; but they also want to know how it should now be interpreted. The remainder of this paper thus falls into two parts: on exegesis and on hermeneutics.

Exegesis

Any attempt to apply Genesis 1 to life has to take into account the fact that the world which is declared "very good" in Gen. 1:31 is not the world which presently exists. I am putting it strongly, of course: no new creation is required after the flood, and most of the elements of that world continue to exist; but the relations between them are profoundly transformed, according to the priestly account. This is acknowledged, for example, by Terence Fretheim, who uses the heading "Genesis 9:1–11:26 – A New World Order" (Fretheim 2005: 83). In Gen. 1:29–30 God assigns food to humans and animals respectively. Humans are to eat seeds and fruit, animals are to have the green stuff of the plants. Nothing is said about animal food for either group. It is true that it is not specifically prohibited, and some have taken this as a loophole to argue that it is not excluded (e.g. Calvin 1965: 99–100; Dequeker 1977). But human beings are specifically permitted to eat flesh in Gen. 9:3, implying, as most agree, that it was previously out of bounds. (See e.g. Westermann 1984: 163–64; also Harland 1996: 150.)

Thus the world brought into being by God's word of creation and blessing is a world without predation and without violence – so von Rad in his commentary (1956: 59) and William P. Brown (1999: 46–52). Humanity carries out its function of "government" of the animals by natural authority, not by coercion: this is demonstrated by Noah, who models this function to perfection, as Peter Harland (1996: 197), Brown (1999: 55) and Fretheim (2005: 52) all suggest. The animals simply "come" to Noah (7:9), without, it seems, needing to be driven or enticed.

Violence enters this world and totally wrecks it: "The earth was wrecked before God; the earth was filled with violence; and God looked at the earth and saw that it was wrecked, because every living thing (literally 'all flesh') had wrecked its way on the earth" (Gen. 6:11–12).[2] I have translated *kol bāsār*, "all flesh" as "every living thing", although some influential commentators, including Westermann, think it only refers to humanity (Westermann 1984: 416, following Hulst 1958). However, this is not the majority view, and it should be noted that "all flesh" means "every living thing" at every one of the numerous times it occurs in the flood account which follows (Westermann 1984: 416; Gardner 2000: 121). "Violence" *ḥāmās*, the Hebrew word used in 6:11–13, has been defined as "criminal oppression of the unprotected by those mightier than they" (Gunkel 1997: 143). Animals therefore must have been preying on one another, and indeed attacking human beings, to follow the hint of 9:5, and human beings have also been practising violence: the sequel in 9:3–6 implies that this has included eating animal flesh and attacking each other (Gunkel 1997: 148). Gardner (2000: 121) interprets "have wrecked their way" by way of 1:28–30: each group has disregarded the divine commands given here.

The priestly writer does not himself say how this could have happened. On some views of the history of the Pentateuch, the priestly writer incorporated the so-called J (non-priestly) narrative into his own, and in that case the story of Cain and Abel (Gen. 4:1–16) would have indicated an origin for violence among human beings. Cain's violence is repeated and magnified in his descendant Lamech (Gen. 4:23–24). Bernhard Anderson (1984: 163–64) takes this line. But Anderson also describes the events in Gen. 3 and 6:1–4 as violence; both cases are rather dubious, certainly as regards the present text of Genesis.

An alternative, though more speculative, view has been put forward by Philip Davies (Davies 2006). He takes the J passages, following Blenkinsopp (1992: 93), to be a supplement to P in Genesis 1–11, rather than an earlier document, and believes that the J passage Gen. 6:1–4 as it now stands is a deliberate bowdlerization of an account of the descent of rebel "sons of God", or angels, much more like the story of the Watchers in the Book of Enoch, one of the most important extra-canonical apocalyptic books, which offers two variant versions of this evidently older story. Here we are told: "the women became pregnant and gave birth to great giants ... the giants turned against (the people) in order to eat them. And they began to sin against birds, wild beasts, reptiles and fish. And their flesh was devoured the one by the other, and they drank blood. And then the earth brought an accusation against the oppressors. And Azaz'el [one of the angels] taught the people (the art of) making swords and knives, and shields and breastplates ... And the people cried and their voice reached unto heaven' (1 Enoch 7:2, 4–6; 8:1: Isaac 1983: 16). According to Davies, P's original story of the irruption of violence into God's good creation was something similar to this, derived from the same source as the Enoch story, and it has been censored and reduced to unintelligibility by the author of J, in order to promote against this a view of sin as purely human in origin, as described in Genesis 2–4, and summarized in Gen. 6:5–7, J's explanation for the flood, where the word *'dM* (humankind) recurs four times.

Whatever the origin of this universal violence, it is the reason why, as God tells Noah (Gen. 6:18), "I am bringing the flood on the earth to destroy everything which has the breath of life from under the sky". Yet the fresh start thus given the world is not a start over again from the original point. The charge given to humans through Noah in 9:1–7 differs in significant ways from the original one in 1:28–30: "The fear of you and the dread of you shall be upon every beast of the earth ...: into your hands they are delivered. Every moving thing which lives may be food for you; along with the green herbs, I give you everything" (Gen. 9:2–3). They are to control animals by force and fear, not by their recognized authority. The last sentence is mistranslated in all the modern versions. God cannot be saying "as I *gave you* the green herbs, so I give you everything" (the words italicized are not in the Hebrew), because he did not give them the green herbs in the first place: they were for the animals (1:29–30; see Harland 1996: 150). The sense is that humans are given control over all food resources, including those on which the animals feed, as well as being permitted to eat them. It seems that the relations between people and animals have been permanently altered: the flood has enabled a new start, but not a restoration of the primeval world.

If the blessing in Genesis 9 may be said to reflect the world as it is, that in 1:28–30 could be said to express the divine intention for the world: it is the cosmos in the mind of God, the ideal, the priestly utopia. If P places it at the start of creation, the Isaianic tradition places it in the ideal future (Isa. 11:6–9). Here the rule of the shoot from the stump of Jesse, the ideal king, who rules in justice and destroys oppressors, is figured in the peace which reigns in the animal world: "The wolf will dwell with the lamb, and the leopard will lie down with the kid ... a lion will eat straw like cattle, and a baby will play over an adder's den ... they shall not hurt or destroy in all my holy mountain, for the land will be full of the knowledge of YHWH as the waters cover the sea." It is the authority of the Messianic king, as well as the knowledge of God, which creates this peaceful world.

I would suggest that the function that humanity is to discharge in relation to the animals in Gen. 1:28 can be understood, at least in part, along the same lines. They are told to "govern" the animals. The Hebrew verb *rādâ*, usually translated "rule" or "have dominion", has been mined for various connotations according to the attitude of the interpreter to the text as a whole. Some assert that it implies harsh control, on the basis of a supposed original meaning "tread down" (e.g. Westermann 1984: 158–59):[3] it refers to the use of slaves in Lev. 25:43, 46; others, quite the reverse: Norbert Lohfink (1994: 12) refers to another possible original meaning "lead to pasture", so that the command is to domesticate the animals; and Erich Zenger (1983: 96) develops this into the picture of the human being as "shepherd of the animals", "who is to lead and protect the 'house of life' pastorally and competently". But talk of "original meanings" should have been banished from exegetical discussion long ago (Barr 1961). The word in every case means "rule", "govern", "control", but not necessarily implying harsh control, which is expressed with qualifying words, as in Lev. 26:43, 46, 53; Ezek. 34:4. It is not distinctively applied to kings, but when it is, it appears usually to refer to rule over foreigners and enemies (1 Kgs 4:24 [Heb. 5:4]; Isa. 14:6; Ps. 72:8; 110:2); and as it also applies to the control of slaves and conscript labour, its connotations are far from pastoral, in the modern sense of that word. But there are features of the context that serve to exclude the implication that human beings are to exploit the earth and other creatures for their own purposes. Brown (1999: 45–46) has four points; I would select just two.

On the one hand, human beings are created in the image of God. The discussion of the meaning and implications of this assertion is ancient and extensive and seems impossible to resolve (Jónsson 1988; Garr 2003). It cannot be adequately summarized here. But Westermann has a useful wide-ranging survey (Westermann 1984: 147–58), from which two interpretations emerge as the frontrunners. Westermann himself adopts the interpretation that "God has created all people 'to correspond to him', that is so that something can happen between creator and creature" (1984: 158). This is along the same lines as Barth's view that the human creature's nature as the image and likeness of God means that a human being can be addressed by God as "you", and is an "I" who is responsible before God (Barth 1958: 182–85). This lays all the emphasis on the relation between humanity and God; yet in the text the statement that humanity was created as the image of God is most closely linked with the attribution to them of dominion over the earth. The only other place where the idea is given significance is in Gen. 9:6, where it is the motivation for the avenging of human blood. Human beings have a dignity in virtue of their creation in God's image that means they cannot be destroyed with impunity.

The other view interprets humanity made in the image of God as representing God to the earthly creation. This view was developed by Wildberger (1965) and Schmidt (1964: 127–48) on the basis of Egyptian and Mesopotamian evidence, and also referred to by von Rad (1956: 56–58). In these ancient Near Eastern cultures kings are referred to as "the image of" such-and-such a god to their people, representing the god to them". In the same way, humanity as the image of God in Genesis 1 represents the majesty of God to the earth and its creatures. Westermann objects to this. Humans are not an individual like a king, and it is hard to see how they can be a representative. The idea does not fit with the theology of P, which emphasizes that God is transcendent and revealed only in defined holy places. "He could not possibly think of a human being as standing in the place of God on earth" (Westermann 1984: 153). And since there are some ancient Near Eastern passages speaking, like Genesis, of the creation of humans in the image of God, the proper comparison is with these, and not with the texts about kings. The first of these three objections is not strong. It might equally well apply to the notion of humans "ruling" the earth (like a king); but that is obviously in the text. The second is, I believe, based on a misunderstanding. The suggestion is not that God is actually present or revealed in human beings, but that human beings take God's place for this particular purpose. The third has some weight, but cannot be decisive.

I would take the view that the creation of humanity in the image and likeness of God entails the consequence that human beings are able to govern the earthly creation, and implies that in so governing, humanity functions to represent God. This does not in any way exclude the implication that humanity is the counterpart and conversation partner of God – a view which is obviously supported by the Bible as a whole. But following up the former implication, we should deduce that therefore people, exercising the divine prerogative, must be intended to supervise and care for creatures rather than exploiting them (compare von Rad 1956: 56–58; Brown 1999: 45–46).

The other feature of the context that needs to be taken into account has already been referred to: that the needs of human beings are met by a specific divine grant (Gen. 1:29), not by the freely chosen use of their power; and this grant does not include any use of animals for food or any other purpose. But if the object of the power granted is not for human beings to satisfy their needs (or wants), what is it?

A central function of government in the Hebrew conception is to check oppression. See, e.g., Ps 72:12–14, as well as Isa. 11:4: "He shall vindicate the poor with justice, and decide with equity for the wretched of the land; he shall strike the tyrant with the rod of his mouth, and slay the unjust with the breath of his mouth." Now "violence" – *ḥāmās* – is one of the ways in which oppression is conceived in the Hebrew Bible (Houston 2008: 67–68, 90, 142). Therefore I suggest that the authority of the human governors exists, among other things, to repress violence among the animals. Lohfink may, however, be right that this is to be done by peaceably taming them: or rather, in this primordial world they are tame to start with (1994: 12).

But once humans have taken to violence themselves, they are no longer able to prevent it from breaking out among the animals, especially if they are themselves wreaking it on them by killing and eating them. (Gardner 2000: 126; cf. Anderson 1984: 163–64). This connection is made explicit in the passage from 1 Enoch we looked at above. Thus they have lost their governing authority. The "fear and dread" inspired in the animals by human beings following Gen. 9:2 maintains their government, but is a poor substitute for the charismatic authority bestowed on them by the original blessing. On this conception the permission granted them to eat the flesh of any living thing is a means to enforce their authority. Interpreters in the critical period do not seem to have recognized that Gen. 9:2 implies a weakening rather than a strengthening of humanity's original authority; but Calvin, for example, speaks of "this dominion, which, although greatly diminished, is nevertheless not entirely abolished" (Calvin 1965: 291). I think this is a correct perception. Even with the post-flood blessing, humanity is unable to repress violence among the animals; they can only protect themselves and use the animals for their own needs. Gen. 9:5 makes it clear that one of the objects of this dispensation is to protect human beings from the attacks of wild animals.

So the differences between Gen. 1:28–30 and Gen. 9:1–7 arise from the difference between the ideal and the real, or in theological terms "fallen", worlds. Zenger characterizes the images of humanity presented by them each in the terms of ancient Near Eastern iconography as respectively the "shepherd of the animals" (cf. Barr 1972: 22) and the "lord of the animals", but he also tries to minimize the difference, speaking of the original blessing being "supplemented and extended" in Genesis 9 (Zenger 1983: 90–96; 118; 116). Most interpreters (e.g. Westermann 1984: 462) recognize the language of warfare in the phrases "the fear of you and the dread of you" and "into your hands they are delivered". Zenger attempts to avoid this implication by arguing that texts like Deut. 2:25 and 11.25, where the

Israelites are assured that fear and dread will grip their enemies, have to do with YHWH's clearing away of the nations before them without their needing to fight (Zenger 1983: 118). I do not find this convincing even in the context of Deuteronomy; the panic spread among the enemies may make it unnecessary to fight, but is a panic *in* war, not *to forestall* war. On Zenger's own showing (Zenger 1983: 122), wild beasts were always regarded as a threat to human life in the world of the Hebrew Bible, hence they needed to be fought; and his iconographic examples of the "lord of the animals" theme include the reliefs of the king of Assyria hunting lions from his chariot. If this is not war, what is?

But the dispensation also includes a measure to protect animals from wanton and uncontrolled attacks by human beings. Gerhard Liedke speaks of "reciprocal measures of protection" (*wechselseitige Schutzmaßnahmen*: Liedke 1979: 145). Verse 4 warns that flesh may not be eaten with its blood. The mode of expression is unclear, but the practical meaning is not, since it is a statement, the first in the Bible, of the basic rule of kosher slaughter. What is more difficult to see is its significance in the context, except that it appears to be saying that we may consume animals' flesh, but not their life. Odil Hannes Steck (1997) argues that, taken together with the fact that the eating of flesh is by divine permission (v. 3), this takes the killing of animals out of the realm of *ḥāmās*. It is the regulated exercise of a divinely granted liberty, not the private satiation of greed. The later dietary laws given to Israel (primarily in Leviticus 11) place this licence further under divine regulation (Houston 1993: 253–58).

As our theme is justice, we need to ask whether and how the priestly author would have seen these two successive dispensations as examples of justice. This cannot be simply answered from what the writer says elsewhere, as justice is not a topos in P. But it seems certain that the dispensation of Genesis 1 would have been seen as expressing the justice of the world order (cf. Schmid 1984). The author would have been baffled by Habel's criticism. Earth's perfection would have been seen to depend on a government representing the authority of God and ensuring the justice of God. Concepts of justice in the Hebrew Bible, indeed the ancient world as a whole, are rooted in structured relationships (Houston 2008). That the mere existence of authority should "devalue", in Habel's word (Habel 2000: 47–48), those subject to it would have been found a puzzling idea, especially if the intention of authority is to maintain just relationships among the creatures. So far from speaking "from the perspective of Earth", Habel appears to speak from the perspective of an extreme modern liberalism which is unable to swallow any concept of authority.

The dispensation in Genesis 9 is a more ambiguous matter. But it exists under the sign of God's covenant (Gen. 9:8–17), which guarantees its permanence, and may be seen to express God's justice. But from what we have seen, it is certain that justice would now be seen to be absent in the animal world. There is an interesting parallel in Greek literature, in Hesiod, *Works and Days*, lines 277–78: Zeus has decreed "that fish and beasts and winged birds should eat one another, since justice is not with them" (Hesiod 2006: 108–11). What we mean by "the law of the jungle" is the antithesis of justice. However, it seems that the rules in Gen. 9:4–6 are intended to ensure that human beings' relationships to each other and to the animal world are governed by law, not by the unregulated greed and exploitation which constitute violence. The rules are minimal, or even symbolic, and are likely to be thought inadequate to constitute justice; but evidently the writer believed this was the nearest approach to justice which was attainable among God's creatures in the world as it is.

Hermeneutics

It will now be clear how problematic any application of these texts must be for us today. On the one hand, the dispensation of Genesis 1 involves a conception of natural life that is wholly mythical. The relationship of creatures to each other in ecology as scientifically understood inevitably includes predation, otherwise the herbivores would destroy all vegetation; and the idea that human beings could control this by the force of their divine blessing seems to invoke magical ideas. The associated "subduing of the earth" probably refers primarily to agriculture (Brown 1999: 44),[4] and while this is a more realistic idea, it probably implies that the earth is improved by tillage, the draining of swamps, and so forth, as seventeenth-century interpreters thought (see Harrison 1999: 103); any idea that this (however organic the technology) reduces biodiversity and therefore the "goodness" of a world created with a variety of species, could only emerge in our own day. Still less is the idea of violence having been introduced by fallen angels, if that was indeed P's original idea, acceptable within the modern world-view.

On the other hand, while Gen. 9:1–7 is more realistic ecologically, the vast increase in human power enabled by scientific knowledge has, as Liedke puts it, pushed to an extreme the asymmetry of the conflict between nature and the human race in a way that the writer, for whom wild beasts continued to be a serious danger to human beings, was unable to conceive (Liedke 1979: 173). The sixth mass extinction of species in geological history has begun, but this is one is our responsibility: it demands effective rather than symbolic measures for the protection of nature.

If the literal application of these texts is an impossibility, it is equally impossible for us to use allegory like their early Christian interpreters. It is, however, possible to draw out their theological or ethical significance, and here I wish to concentrate on the ethical: using them as tools to reflect on the choices available to the human race at this time in our relation to other creatures of the earth.

Two factual points have been thoroughly and realistically grasped by the priestly author. One is the inescapable dominance of the human race over the earth. This is simply a fact, which cannot be wished away. The massive brain of our species, its possession of speech, its capacity for innovation and organization, make it inevitable that its will should prevail in relation to the natural world. The ethical conclusion from this is surely not to entertain fantasies of a world without such dominance, but to accept the responsibility which that entails, of making conscious reflective decisions about any action affecting other living creatures and earth systems.

The other is the ingrained violence of the natural world, the incessant competition for space and resources, often expressed in predation and exploitation, which forms the essential backdrop to Darwin's theory of natural selection. Too often environmentalists appear to give a sentimental picture of the perfect harmony and balance in the natural world which would exist if only it were not for human greed and meddling. If there is balance in natural ecosystems, it is not harmony, but an equilibrium of competitive efforts; and no balance is ever stable, but constantly changing as species rise and decline. The ethical question is how humans as the overwhelming victors in the evolutionary conflict, having upset all balances, should use their victory.

The ethical stance of the priestly text is against violence in the sense it bears in Genesis 6: the greedy and brutal violation of another's rights, integrity or life. The objection does not extend to the use of coercion by lawful authority: to describe P as "pacifist", as Zenger does (1983: 117), is problematic. The positive value the text promotes is better described as justice than as non-violence.

Now, the present activity of the human race towards the earth and its creatures is one of sustained, extreme and progressively destructive violence. We are using our victory to plunder and destroy. Given our capacity for conscious reflection and decision, it is possible for us to turn away from this inborn violence as other forms of life cannot. The mythical reign of divine justice sketched in Genesis 1 is in a sense attainable through us, the responsible representatives of the Creator, provided that we embrace the way marked out for us there. Years ago, Liedke coined the slogan "solidarity with creation in the conflict between humanity and creation", to be expressed by "lessening its suffering, relieving its need, reducing violence, and thereby giving it new hope" (Liedke 1979: 178). That task has yet to be seriously undertaken.

Notes

1. Verse 26 has "and the beasts and all the earth" after "birds of the air", and the LXX adds this in v. 28. The beasts are needed to complete the picture, but not "all the earth", which has already been mentioned.
2. Anne Gardner (Gardner 2000: 119–20) uses "destroy" for *šḥt* instead of the traditional "corrupt", to emphasize the verbal link with v. 13 and the sense of physical damage; I think "wreck" works better.
3. But as Lohfink points out (1994: 11), its alleged use in Joel 4.13 of treading the winepress is quite uncertain: *rĕdû* may just as well be derived from *yārad*, "go down". As this would otherwise be the only place where *rādâ* had this meaning, this seems more likely.
4. But Lohfink (1994: 9–11) thinks it simply means "take possession".

Bibliography

Anderson, Bernhard W. 1984. 'Creation and Ecology', in Anderson (ed.) 1984: 152–171.
Anderson, Bernhard W. (ed.). 1984. *Creation in the Old Testament*. London: SPCK.
Barr, James. 1961. *The Semantics of Biblical Language*. Oxford: Oxford University Press.
_____. 1972. "Man and Nature: The Ecological Controversy and the Old Testament", *Bulletin of the John Rylands University Library of Manchester* 55: 9–32.
Barth, Karl. 1958. *Church Dogmatics*, vol. III, part 1. Edinburgh: T & T Clark; tr. of *Kirchliche Dogmatik* III/1, 1945.
Blenkinsopp, Joseph. 1992. *The Pentateuch: An Introduction to the First Five Books of the Bible*. London: SCM Press.
Brown, William P. 1999. *The Ethos of the Cosmos*. Grand Rapids, MI: Eerdmans.
Calvin, John. 1965. *A Commentary on Genesis*. London: Banner of Truth, repr. of 1847; original 1554.
Davies, Philip J. 2006. "And Enoch Was Not, for Genesis Took Him". In *Biblical Traditions in Transmission: Essays in Honour of Michael A. Knibb*, eds C. Hempel and J. M. Lieu, 97–107. Leiden: Brill.
Dequeker, Luc. 1977. "'Green Herbage and Trees Bearing Fruit' (Gen. 1:28–30; 9:1–3)", *Bijdragen* 38: 118–27.
Fretheim, Terence E. 2005. *God and the World in the Old Testament* (Nashville, TN: Abingdon Press).

Gardner, Anne. 2000. "Ecojustice: A Study of Genesis 6.11–13". In Habel (ed.) 2000: 117–29.

Garr, W. Randall. 2003. *In His Own Image and Likeness: Humanity, Divinity and Monotheism*. Leiden: Brill.

Gunkel, Hermann. 1997. *Genesis Translated and Interpreted*. Macon, GA: Mercer Press [original 5th edn 1922].

Habel, Norman. 2000. "Geophany: The Earth Story in Genesis 1." In Habel (ed.) 2000: 34–48.

Habel, Norman (ed.). 2000. *The Earth Story in Genesis*. Sheffield: Sheffield Academic Press.

Harland, P. J. 1996. *The Value of Human Life: A Study of the Story of the Flood (Genesis 6–9)*. SVT 64; Leiden, Brill.

Harrison, Peter. 1999. "Subduing the Earth: Genesis 1, Early Modern Science and the Exploitation of Nature", *The Journal of Religion*, 79: 86–109.

Hesiod. 2006. *Theogony, Works and Days, Testimonia* (ed. and tr.) Glenn W. Most. LCL; Cambridge, MA: Harvard University Press.

Houston, Walter J. 1979. "'And let them have dominion ...': Biblical Views of Man in Relation to the Environmental Crisis." In *Studia Biblica* I, 161–84. JSOTS 11; Sheffield: JSOT Press.

_____. 1993. *Purity and Monotheism*. JSOTS 140; Sheffield: Sheffield Academic Press.

_____. 2008. *Contending for Justice*, 2nd edn. London: T & T Clark International.

Hulst, A. R. 1958. "Kol Basar in der priesterlichen Fluterzählung." *OTS* 12: 28–68.

Isaac, E. 1983. "1 (Ethiopic Apocalypse of) Enoch: A New Translation and Introduction." In James H. Charlesworth (ed.), *The Old Testament Pseudepigrapha*, vol. 1: Apocalyptic Literature and Testaments, 5–90. London: Darton. Longman and Todd.

Jónsson, Gunnlaugur A. 1988. *The Image of God: Genesis 1.26–28 in a Century of Old Testament Research*. Lund: Gleerup.

Liedke, Gerhard. 1979. *Im Bauch des Fisches: Ökologische Theologie*. Stuttgart: Kreuz Verlag.

Lohfink, Norbert. 1994. "'Subdue the Earth?' (Genesis 1:28)." In *Theology of the Pentateuch: Themes of the Priestly Narrative and Deuteronomy*, ed. Walter Brueggemann, 1–17. Edinburgh: T & T Clark.

Rad, Gerhard von. 1956. *Genesis: A Commentary*. London: SCM Press [original 1949].

Schmid, H. H. 1984. "Creation, Righteousness and Salvation: 'Creation Theology' as the Broad Horizon of Biblical Theology." In Anderson (ed.) 1984: 102–117.

Schmidt, Werner H. 1964. *Die Schöpfungsgeschichte der Priesterschrift*. WMANT 17; Neukirchen-Vluyn: Neukirchener Verlag.

Steck, Odil Hannes. 1997. "Der Mensch und der Todesstrafe in Gen 9,6a." *ThZ* 53: 118–30.

Westermann, Claus. 1984. *Genesis 1–11: A Commentary*. London: SPCK [original 1974].

White, Lynn Jr. 1967. "The Historic Roots of our Ecological Crisis." *Science* 155 (10, March), 1203–07 [reprinted many times].

Wildberger, Hans. 1965. "Das Abbild Gottes, Gen 1:26–30." *ThZ* 21: 245–59, 481–501.

Zenger, Erich. 1983. *Gottes Bogen in der Wolken: Untersuchungen zu Komposition und Theologie der priesterlichen Urgeschichte*. SBS 112; Stuttgart: Verlag Katholisches Bibelwerk.

A Signs Source: Approaching Deaf Biblical Interpretation[*]

Louise J. Lawrence[a]

As I sat down to write this essay, I was surely not alone in sardonically thinking to myself that the "Bible and Injustice" would perhaps have been a more appropriate title for this volume. In recent years reader-orientated perspectives of all stripes have exposed how various forms of oppression have been sustained by biblical texts. Such interpretations have not only unmasked repressive aspects of the "world that created the bible" but more broadly, tyrannical aspects of the world that the bible itself has played a part in creating (see Yarchin 2004: xxix). Just as advocacy interpreters have critically revisited biblical texts and their interpretations in relation to race, gender, class and sexuality, here my *sense*-itivities will be heightened through interaction with another marginalized group, the Deaf community.[1]

In recent years a move to incorporate bodily discourses within biblical interpretation has raised interpreters' awareness of the means by which particular socio-religious frameworks conceptualize the "able" or "normal" in contradistinction to the "disabled" or "abnormal".[2] With these developments have come increased sensitivity to how biblical images of disability "provide a window into a dynamic interchange between culture, author, text and audience" (Avalos *et al.* 2007: 5). Hector Avalos for example has developed "sensory criticism" (Avalos 2007: 51) to plot the extent to

[a] Dr Louise Lawrence is Lecturer in New Testament Studies at the University of Exeter. She is author of *An Ethnography of the Gospel of Matthew* (Mohr Siebeck, 2003), *Reading with Anthropology: Exhibiting Aspects of New Testament Religion* (Paternoster, 2005) and *The Word in Place: Reading the New Testament in Contemporary Contexts* (SPCK, 2009).

which biblical texts evaluate senses and how these may contribute to various ideological standpoints forwarded by them. Such perspectives allow biblical interpreters "to gain a better appreciation of how biblical authors conceptualise and treat human embodiment" (Avalos 2007: 58). Senses are entwined with social, literary, political and theological agendas[3] and accordingly in his study Avalos concludes that the Deuteronomic history promotes a sustained "sonic theology" perhaps because convenants in the ancient Near East were usually "heard". Yahweh is accordingly "heard" by the people, but not seen. In contrast the Book of Job is identified by Avalos as "visiocentric", metaphors of sight and blindness pepper the text and the extraordinary declaration in Job 42:5 of the primacy of visual encounters over auditory ones is summed up in the statement: "I had heard of you by the hearing of the ear, but now my eyes see you." Avalos rightly argues that critics should be dissuaded from using "sensory criticism" to identify "any particular view of the senses in biblical authors as 'normative' [for] today" (Avalos 2007: 59).

Of course, like any advocacy perspectives (feminism; postcolonialism; ecological readings) disability perspectives centred on the senses have started to approach biblical texts with both reading strategies of resistance (suspicion of the power or social structures that label one as "disabled" within the text) and reading strategies of recovery which seek to apologetically rehabilitate and rescue positive images of disability from the text (see especially John Hull's study on blindness, 2001). Even a cursory look at the New Testament in reference to "sonic" themes reveals a cacophony of "aural" imagery and thus a suspicion that the text "disables" the full participation of the Deaf community within its discourses. Hearing a person's voice involves establishing a personal connection with them (the sheep know their own shepherd's voice in Jn. 10:16). Moreover the Johannine "Word" declares "Everyone who is of the truth hears my voice" (Jn. 18:37). Similarly God's revelations are primarily auditory as at the baptism (Mk. 1:11; Mt. 3:17; Lk. 3:22), transfiguration (Mk. 9:7; Mt. 17:5; Lk. 9:35) and Paul's dramatic conversion (Acts 9:4). The faculty of hearing and the organ of the ear also becomes a synecdoche for cognition and insight: "true hearing involves listening and understanding", thus "to have deaf, heavy, or uncircumcised ears is to reject what is heard" (Ryken *et al.* 1998: 223). As such "deafness" also becomes one of the primary ways in which the rejection of Jesus' message is portrayed: "This is why I speak to them in parables, because seeing they do not see, and hearing they do not hear, nor do they understand" (Mt. 13:13).

Strategies of Deaf recovery could identify the fact that symbolic healing of blindness (and the concomitant spiritual "enlightenment" that is often presupposed in the narration of such healings) takes a greater role within the Gospels than the healing of deafness. Indeed we only encounter one extended narrative of a healing of a deaf man in Mk. 7:32–37.[4] In this episode Jesus puts his fingers in the man's ears, spits and touches his tongue and looking up to heaven demands that his ears be opened. Resistant readers could legitimately declare that this narrative follows a familiar "oppressive" pattern of portraying characters with sensory impairment as nothing more than sites of divine action, "objectified beneficiaries of divine healing" (Fontaine cited in Donaldson 2005: 101), or more starkly in Nancy Eiesland's terms "defiled evildoer[s]" (1994: 70) in need of physical and spiritual wholeness. Readings of a recovery bent, however, could possibly point to the fact that the "Deaf" man had not been "Deaf" all his life, for Mark tells us that when his "ears are opened, his tongue released, *he spoke plainly*" (Mk. 7:35) [a person Deaf from birth, would be without "plain" speech, having never heard it].[5] Recovery readings may also focus on positive images of "light" (Mt. 4:16) and "face" within the biblical tradition (Num. 6:25), for signing is a face-to-face performance and cannot be "seen in the dark".

Undoubtedly resisting oppressive ideologies of the senses and reconstructing biblical texts more positively in sensory terms is an important part of liberating "disability" readings. Generally though, it is true to say that "sensory" surveys of biblical texts, especially when disability is used metaphorically for social commentary and critique,[6] do not really focus on the real "lived experience of disability" (Schipper 2007: 103). It is this oversight that I will seek to address here by engaging with contemporary Deaf readers. This paper is divided into two main parts. First, I am going to introduce what could be termed the "colonization" of the Deaf community by the hearing in educational, religious and academic contexts. In many ways this process parallels the "colonization" of other countries and the missionary enterprise to impose the Bible (in a foreign tongue) on indigenous peoples; for "if an *ethnos* is defined as a culturally similar group sharing a common language, then the Deaf conceivably fit that category" (Davis 1995: 77). There is no doubt that the Deaf community have suffered oppression and marginalization within society in general, and churches in particular, on account of lack of access to texts and communication in their own British Sign Language (BSL). Thus akin to postcolonial and "global" biblical interpretations that have increasingly sought to comment on, and in some instances reclaim, the biblical tradition by producing readings in local tongues, worldviews and experiences the second part of my paper will document a contextual bible study I conducted amongst a Deaf group in Bristol. Contextual readings at grass-roots levels in communities, akin to those initiated by Gerald West in Africa (see West 2007) are central for a biblical interpretation "that is true and relevant for Deaf people" (Lewis 2007: 6). Hannah Lewis in her recent steps towards the construction of *Deaf Liberation Theology* (2007) brings out the importance of contextual readings by the Deaf quite forcefully when she openly states: "I am not really interested in what hearing people, however involved with Deaf people they might be, have said about what Deaf people think and what a theology of the Deaf would look like!" (Lewis 2007: 6). The import of her claim is that the "hearing" foreigners need to take careful notice of what the Deaf community's "signs source" on its own terms has to teach us.

"Colonization" of the Deaf

Nearly 9 million people in the UK have hearing impairments (Lees 2007: 166), however not all of those people would consider themselves Deaf with a capital "D". It is important at the outset to clarify what we mean when we talk about the Deaf. This inevitably impedes on different models of "deafness" held within discourse. The "medical" model sees the inability to hear as impairment and one that can be overcome to some degree by the use of hearing aids or implants. Disability Studies however have set out to question essentialist categorizations of disability and redefined it as a "form of social oppression, inequality and exclusion" (see Hutchinson 2006: 2). The alternative "socio-cultural" perspective they reveal sees the physical or social environment in which the person lives as "disabling". It is the third model however, that encapsulates Deaf with a capital "D" most appropriately, namely the cultural perspective. This sees the Deaf as a language minority group rather than a people who cannot hear properly and it is this understanding that informed Kyle and Woll's definition of the Deaf community in their celebrated volume on *Sign Language* (1988):

> It involves a shared language; it involves hearing loss; it involves social interaction and politics ... but all of these interrelate and interact with attitudes towards other Deaf people. The choice to communicate and share information with other people must be seen as a primary feature, and because of the language used by members of the community this communication will generally be restricted to other Deaf people. (Kyle and Woll 1988: 5)

Lewis reveals that historical instances of the disempowerment of the Deaf (particularly in reference to their own language) are analogous to political colonization defined as "a process of physical subjugation, imprisonment of an alien language, culture and mores and the regulation of education on behalf of colonial goals" (Lewis 2007: 32). Following this line of thinking Roger Hitching (2003: 16) pinpoints a significant date for such colonization, within the field of Deaf education, as the 1880 Milan Congress where in his words, "a small group of paternalistic hearing instructors opposed to the use of sign language decided that it would be in the best interests of deaf people if teachers adopted oralism" (Hitching 2003: 16). Oralism, which espoused oral methods of education and valued lip-reading as central, in fact dominated educational praxis of the Deaf until fairly recently. The Milan congress has since been identified in much of the literature as the single most important event for driving sign language underground and limiting not only the education and literacy of many Deaf children but also the decline of Deaf culture itself. Only in the 1960s was there a revision of Deaf education that sought to rehabilitate the use of sign language (even in mainstream education), and it was not until 1975 that the first interpreter was formally qualified. Since then interpreters have worked with a variety of Deaf students in schools, colleges and universities.

The educational context was not alone in promoting colonization of Deaf culture. Missions to Deaf people founded in the late nineteenth century likewise oppressed and vetoed the use of sign language. It was also a mission carried out by hearing "foreigners". Missioners tried to educate with a strong dose of patriarchal paternalism. In Hitching's opinion "they seemed to be carrying out a form of cultural imperialism as much as they were spreading the gospel" (Hitching 2003: 23). The paternalistic rhetoric evident in both the educational and missionary contexts constructed Deaf people as passive and dependent. Due to the centrality of communication through sign language, Davis and others have drawn comparisons between racial stigmatization and Deaf stigmatization as "outsiders" (see Davis 1995: 78). The accessibility (or rather inaccessibility) of texts within BSL has undoubtedly perpetuated this "outsider" status. Whilst the works of Shakespeare are in part now available in BSL, the Bible still is not (although a BSL version is currently being produced and this will ease the situation considerably).[7] One member of the group I worked with stated, "Deaf people have no access to the Bible. It's very hard, even in a Deaf church, to read the Bible at the same time that someone is signing it. One big advantage of technology is that in the future we will have access to the Bible in BSL straight to our I-pods that will mean that Deaf people will feel more confident because they will have already seen the Bible in sign." However, there is a tension here, for DVD/video "texts" assume a certain level of financial and technological sophistication which could exclude those not living in modern, urban, capitalist, technologically-developed societies.[8] Nevertheless without some form of open access to the Bible in their "mother tongue" it is no surprise that Deaf theology is often seen by the mainstream as marginal.[9] The sentiments contained in the 1997 Church of England report, *The Church Among Deaf People*, could well have been written by one of those paternalistic Victorian missionaries that Hitchings finds so objectionable. It condescendingly states:

> Their (the Deaf's) relationship with God, and his with them, is often untrammelled by detail or the complexities of knowledge and understanding. Often their faith is direct, clear and simple, but very powerful because it feels, to those who knew them, like the faith Jesus calls for, the faith that is childlike in its openness and trust. (Church of England 1997: 60–61)

The 1970s witnessed the rise of the Deaf Pride movement. More accessibility to television programmes and more Deaf representation on television helped this initiative. Deaf Pride involved a recovery of lost (literally silenced) moments of Deaf history, and British Sign Language was at last recognized as a discrete language with its own structure, grammar and regional variations (see Lewis 2007: 26). This led to the development of "Deaf World" and "Deaf Way" where through sign communication was freely available (Lewis 2007: 22). The colonized were at last openly resisting the oppressive structures that had previously "silenced" them.

Contextual Bible Study with the Deaf

One of the ways in which oppressed groups can resist the missionary/ imperialist forces imposed on them is to re-construct and re-member the Bible in reference to their own indigenous worldviews and experiences. Contextual bible study takes as primary the "community consciousness" of the interpreters and allows groups of "extra-ordinary"[10] readers free access to inhabit texts from their own cultural perspectives. I had the privilege to observe a Deaf group in Bristol interpret two biblical stories drawn from the Gospel of Luke, "The Stilling of The Storm" (Lk. 8:22–25) and "The Parable of the Lost Son" (Lk. 15:11–23) in this way.[11] Throughout the session, as will be seen, many of the participants concretely pictured Deaf culture in the biblical narratives they encountered and essentially produced a "postcolonial" recovery reading of these texts.

It was important at the outset that the group was allowed open access to all materials in BSL and that an appropriate "Deaf Space" was created. As with other cultural minorities who do not have a Bible openly accessible to them in their own language, even introducing the text to the group involved complex considerations. I was advised against using Sign Supported English (SSE), which follows English word order and finger spells some of the terms, as this is actually quite hard to understand in reference to biblical stories: "SSE translations are fraught with conflicts, aberrations and ambivalences, usually unintelligible and onerous to the majority of Deaf people" (Lewis 2007: 115). It was suggested that it would be better to give the texts in English (for the benefit of those members who could read) but also that a group member should tell the story in BSL (for the benefit of *all*, both readers and non-readers within the group). Telling stories in BSL, the Deaf heart language, as I learned was to engage with an oral and collective culture that envisaged the group not primarily as "readers" but "retellers" (Lees 2007: 166). "Remembered bible" is a term that West has used in reference to communal conceptions of a story (West in Lees 2007: 163) as opposed to literalistic renderings and this seems to have resonance with the BSL readings offered in my study. All participants in their diverse retellings highlighted for me the redundancies and gaps within the English translations of the biblical stories, which BSL, as a primarily oral, visual, spatial and performative language "filled in".[12] Each retelling, even if broadly based on the English text, involved some additional details that fleshed out the story "visually" in the mind's eye. One participant's signing of the "Stilling of the Storm" illustrates just this. Translated from BSL, it reads as follows:

> Jesus had been preaching and teaching and now wanted to rest. He decided they should go back to the other side of the lake so he asked Peter to do him a favour and take him across the lake in the boat. Peter called his other friends to set to work and they all got into the boat. They hoisted the sail and pushed off from the shore. Very soon, Jesus fell fast asleep because he was so tired. The disciples hard at work in the boat noticed that he was asleep and agreed to leave him since he was so tired. They continued their sail across the lake. A little later the water became choppy and the boat started to toss. The weather got worse and worse until the waves were huge and the little boat was in danger of being swamped. Meanwhile Jesus was still fast asleep (and snoring) in the back of the boat. The disciples really wanted to wake him up but they felt they shouldn't. They discussed it among themselves. They said that the wind was so bad and the waves so high there was real danger so he should wake up. How could they get out of danger? The disciples argued about who should wake up Jesus since none of them wanted to. One said, "I can't reach him – I'm too busy trying to steer a straight course." One of the men was too scared to touch Jesus. Eventually one person woke him up and said that all the crew were frightened of drowning because it was so rough. Jesus stood up in the boat and told the wind and waves to calm down. The

water immediately calmed down. All the disciples were utterly amazed. "That's fantastic", they said, "How did he do that?" "Ah well," said another, "He is Jesus after all – that's God!" Jesus said to them all, "Where's your faith?" Immediately they started defending themselves and blaming each other for their fear. In the end they said, "How did he do that? He really is God's Son."

The journey being conceived as a journey "back" across the Lake (rather than to alien territory on the other side); the disciples leaving Jesus alone because he was tired; the hoisting of the sail; their hard work; Jesus' snoring; the disciples' arguments about who was going to wake Jesus up; the question about *how* Jesus accomplished the stilling of the water (as opposed to Luke's identity question of "Who then is this that even the winds and waves obey him?") all visually enriched, and in parts changed, the depiction of the story. That "sign language seeks to involve the person being signed to in the re-living of the story, which is the container for the information being conveyed" (Hitching 2003: 43) certainly seems to have been corroborated here.[13] The group imagined themselves as crew on the boat and pictured the chaotic sea as the government's policies on Deaf education literally "rocking the boat" of their community. One participant noted "we know today that a lot of Deaf schools are closing and we understand that one of the reasons is that it's too expensive for Local Authorities to send Deaf children to residential Deaf schools, but the expense is nothing compared to the wealth the children gain as they experience language and community. We share community experience in the same way that God wants us to share his community experience and his love." Another imagined the journey to the other side of the lake as a Federation for Deaf People rally, sailing together to London to campaign for the recognition of BSL as a language in its own right.

To take another example in their reading of the parable of the Lost Son, the group first interpreted the characters within the story as Deaf, the younger son however wanted to leave the Deaf community and interact with the hearing world. As conversation went on, another interpretation was offered: the youngest son was a [hearing] CODA (child of deaf adults). He had grown up within a family and acted as interpreter for his parents. In a sense, he felt abused, his own goals and ambitions could not be realized due to his interpreting responsibilities and as a result he decided to leave home. The father's welcome home therefore was not to a wayward son, but rather to someone that had resisted oppressive forces imposed upon him and also someone that had eventually come to accept his basic identity and acknowledge his home place, though hearing, within Deaf culture. This spurned yet another reading: the younger son could be the deaf child of hearing parents who decided to leave his family to go to the Deaf community. This raised some interesting observations on the power assumptions inherent within the text itself that labelled the "Deaf" world as a place of dissolute living, impurity and famine (Lk. 13–14). The punch line of the story however involves the Deaf child returning to his hearing family and the family as a result making a great effort to learn sign language (exemplified by the killing of the fatted calf and ring and sandals) so the child would feel "in place".

Yet another reading saw the younger son being given a second chance. He represented in one participant's words, "Deaf people at school who are educated through a variety of methods including oralism, when they grow up and leave school they often shun the Deaf community. They immerse themselves in the hearing world, form relationships and even marry hearing people but all the time something is missing inside themselves. The language and culture of the community is what's missing. When the Deaf community accepts them back it's like a second chance – like the son who was 'dead' and now is alive." Related to this, another participant thought that Deaf people (imaged in the lost son) may think that the world of the hearing have everything, money and wealth. They may go in search of this world, but actually in the end find it wanting – "They may look rich but do they hold language and culture dear to their hearts?" – and have to return home to the Deaf space where community is central. In one participant's view, "whereas here in the Deaf world we may look poor, we are so rich because of our language and culture, so to my mind it goes back to values – the values we have, the riches we hold are those that will last – more like the values of heaven".

There were instances however where tensions between concepts inherent within the story and the visual translation into sign language surfaced. One particularly insightful example of this by one participant, involved reflection on the signing of the word "forgive" which the BSL version of the story presented to the group had used. The sign for "forgive" involves a movement resembling making the slate clean. Accordingly the participant stated:

> There's a lot of debate about how we should translate that word into Sign Language. There's an idea that it should be a fixed sign – forgive – as in wiping away all sin. I don't think it should be. The elder brother clearly didn't want his brother back, but the father accepted him back and was prepared to move on. This is forgiveness. The signs we use should show acceptance and moving on. He accepted that the son was back and he was prepared to move

on. But the older son had the old idea of forgiveness – of wiping the slate clean and he wouldn't do it. That's the problem today – a lot of people have that idea about forgiveness. But really it means that you can say to a person, "OK I know you did things in the past that were wrong. I accept that, and we're ready to move on. I won't look back, we'll move on!"

In the written story we are told that the father did not literally "forgive" (though his actions could perhaps be legitimately interpreted in that way) but rather was filled with "compassion" or "pity". His actions – seeing, holding and kissing – illustrate the acceptance and moving on of which the participant spoke. The elder son by contrast does seem to, as the Deaf interpreter suggests, work more with the idea of forgiveness as "wiping the slate clean" which he, in the end, cannot bring himself to do: "but it is possible that, out of love and respect for his father, he will [eventually] be persuaded by his father's words" (Tannehill 1996: 244). In effect this Deaf reader had touched upon the central crux of the parable: "the story of the prodigal supports the remarkable connection in Luke between repentance and joy ... the sign of repentance is not fasting and mourning but joy demonstrated in communal celebration. In the prodigal son this celebration is preceded by the son's return home and confession" (Tannehill 1996: 242). Now having briefly surveyed some of the ways in which the Deaf group interpreted these stories, two main contributions have emerged as pointers for what I have termed a "Signs Source" – a Deaf mode of biblical interpretation, first "Resistance to the Hegemony of Written Texts" and second, "Midrashic Techniques" of applying biblical texts to contemporary communities.

Resistance to the Hegemony of Written Texts
Lewis reveals that one factor in the "muting" of deaf experience within the academy has been the bias for written texts (Lewis 2007: 7). Biblical studies, itself an industry of the book, has promoted a hegemonic "textual' discourse that has kept the Deaf and their language on the margins. One of the great contributions of postmodernism has been to acknowledge and celebrate diverse forms and mediums of knowledge. To give just one example, reading with subalterns in India (Dalit peoples, etc.) Sathianathan Clarke has commended a 'multimodal' approach that encourages oppressed groups to "perform" transformation in response to biblical narrative and images. In oral cultures interpretations are "corporately weaved together" (Clarke 2002: 262) and frequently represented in "media other than writing" (Clarke 2002: 263); the Dalits, for instance, use drumming, dancing, spinning, weaving, painting, and carving in their hermeneutics. Clarke urges

mainstream biblical studies to literally "come to its senses" and acknowledge the great contribution that cultures that speak with their hands, rather than words and written texts can offer:

> It is pertinent to register the point that communities that work with their hands and are intimately related to the products they create do not have a need to separate reflective activity from the material activity they are involved with. Thus production, reflection and communication are connected and integrated into a human way of living. Praxis is a way of life. (Clarke 2002: 264)[14]

In a similar vein the post-colonial feminist, Musa Dube, initiates contextual interpretations of biblical stories among African readers and revels in the dictum offered by one participant that "God never opened the Bible". This graphically illustrates the fact that God was active and dynamic, not contained in, or contained by particular written directives in printed texts. Dube accordingly celebrates those, like the Deaf community who "retell and weave their own stories of healing and empowerment" (Dube 2000: 195). In relation to Deaf biblical interpretation sign language as a medium needs to be valued, not only for the great contribution it makes in visualizing the biblical texts – how was the sail hoisted on boats in first century Galilee?[15] – but also as a representative language of an oral culture. Sign language in itself is a mode of communication in a collective culture and as such may be nearer the earliest Palestinian "oral" modes of transmission of "gospel" traditions. As such a "Signs Source" is pregnant with potential promise for even the most historically minded biblical scholar to consider.

Midrashic Techniques

Oral and performative cultures are collective as opposed to individualistic and, as such, "oral hermeneutics" often reappropriates a text to a cultural context shared by others: "Sometimes the story is framed in a new context, or the ending changed, or variants suggested alongside the original story" (Lewis 2007: 120). Peter McDonough has investigated issues of translation of Gospel stories into sign language; he found that what the Deaf community and the hearing community valued as good translations differed significantly. For the Deaf, the most important criteria were that translations were "embodied in its own culture and colloquial idiom" (McDonough cited in Lewis 2007: 118). In contrast for the hearing the most important element was a "direct and true translation of biblical texts" (McDonough discussed in Lewis 2007: 118). With this in mind, it is not unreasonable to draw a parallel with modern (hearing) and post-modern

(Deaf) approaches, or to couch it in more biblical studies terms, modern historical readings (hearing) as opposed to Jewish "Midrashic" approaches (Deaf) that likewise attempt to fill in gaps "both within the biblical text and between the biblical text and contemporary culture" (Sherwood 2000: 100). The myriad readings of the parable of the Lost Son and the very strong emphasis on weaving Deaf culture into the fabric of both this parable and the Stilling of the Storm, corroborates the association with Midrash which Daniel Boyarin has recently identified as involving "interpreting and completing the text in accordance with the codes of his or her culture" (Boyarin 1990: 14). Paddy Ladd's claim that story telling is central to Deaf identity likewise gives credence to viewing their mode of interpretation as Midrashic (Ladd 2003).[16] He submits "storytelling is a form of oral transmission of text, it is a traditional art in many cultures, including Deaf culture, and in the hands of a skilled practitioner accurately transmits what is seen as the essence of the narrative" (Ladd discussed in Lewis 2007: 118). Unlike in Luke's original version of the "Stilling of the Storm" narrative where the characters remain bemused about Jesus' identity ("Who then is this that the winds and the waves obey him?") in Derek's "performance" of the story the end becomes a "gestic" declaration of faith to the community: "How did he do that?" "Ah well," said another, "He is Jesus after all – that's God!" In "Midrashic" interpretation, likewise, the attitudes of the characters and the storyteller become important parts of the reading. In Hitching's terms such interpretations are not merely giving the meaning "but also the speaker's attitude to his listeners and to what he is saying" (Hitching 2003: 70) within the performance. Such interpretations liberate the personal and collective stories of readers from the straitjacket of dispassionate, "modern" modes of reading. Stephen Moore applauds such developments when he rejoices in the liberation from "the boredom of conventional and impersonal reading of the Bible, from separating a person from the scholar, from suppression of innermost desire of what a critic wants to say" (Moore cited in Nelavala 2006: 65).[17]

"Approaching" Deaf Biblical Interpretation

Whilst it is possible to revisit "sensory" images within biblical texts to recover or resist certain portrayals, here by reading with the Deaf community, I have sought to engage with the "lived experience" of Deafness. I have proposed that a Deaf biblical interpretation constitutes a challenge to the hegemony of written texts and in common with other subaltern readings, advocates multimodal forms of interpretation. To use Hitching's particularly evocative image, Deaf hermeneutics "moves away from a purely wordy God to one in terms of vision and touch ... A God who gives visions and dreams" (Hitching 2003: 21). In order to challenge textual hegemony one must, as Lennard Davis in his study *Enforcing Normalcy: Disability, Deafness and the Body* (1995) contends, not only make "Deafness" more "mainstream", but also reconstruct the centre to become more "Deaf-stream". In his words, "one of the tasks for a developing consciousness of disability issues is the attempt, then, to reverse the hegemony of the normal and to institute alternative ways of thinking about the abnormal" (Davis 1995: 49).

I have also wagered that a Deaf biblical interpretation has commonalities with Jewish Midrash that revels in myriad interpretations, which stretch, realign and shape a malleable text into contemporary relevance. The results may have been very different if the texts used within this study were those in which metaphors of sensory impairment played a more prominent role (for instance in the "social association of disability and moral laxity", Melcher 2007: 129). Perhaps the group would not so easily have translated their Deaf experience and culture into the fabric of "texts of Deaf terror", or maybe in contrast they would have subversively constructed resistant *midrashim* which ideologically "took sacred elements of rabbinic thought and then inverted them against their sacred origins" (Handelman in Sherwood 2000: 100) more contextual readings of this sort undoubtedly need to be pursued.

One last point, the use of the term "*Approaching* Deaf Biblical Interpretation" within the title of this paper is used advisedly. I am well aware of my status as a hearing "foreigner" or "dis-abled" in Deaf space. However, in initiating a contextual biblical study with a Deaf group I have attempted to *approach* the "lived experience of Deafness" in response to biblical stories. Contextual studies of this sort could be just the start of a remembrance of not only Deaf history in the Bible but also a challenge to those hearing scholars that as yet "do not have ears to hear" the potential contribution of Deaf modes of biblical interpretation in the academy.

Notes

* This essay is a revised version of Chapter 7 "Reading Among the Deaf" pp. 91–104 in L. J. Lawrence, *The Word in Place: Reading the New Testament in Contemporary Contexts* (Paternoster 2009).
1. On language: "Deaf with capital D refers to culturally deaf people"; "deaf with lower-case d refers to anyone with significant hearing loss". "Deaf mute is no longer acceptable, rather d/Deaf people without speech" is preferred (see Lewis 2007: x). Hereafter I will capitalise Deaf to denote the cultural model of deafness.

2. In 1995 there was an SBL "Religion and Disability Studies Consultation". In 2003 the SBL hosted a further session entitled "The Blind, The Deaf and the Lame: Biblical Representations of Disability". A recent *Semeia* volume entitled, *This Abled Body: Rethinking Disability in Biblical Studies* (Avalos *et al.* 2007) continues research in this area.

3. John Hull (2001) reads the text as blind persons, sensitive to both positive and negative images but also where the text assumed sightedness as the norm and he as blind reader feels alienated as result.

4. In Mt. 12:22–32 the discourse focuses less on the healing of the deaf person without speech and more on the power by which Jesus performs the miracle, hence the passage is often referred to as the Beelzebub controversy.

5. I am grateful to Gill Behenna for sharing this Deaf interpretation with a group at the South West Ministry Training Course, Easter School (March 2008). I am also indebted to Gill for facilitating my work with the Deaf community and for arranging Rosemary Macro to help her work in the group and transcribe group discussions for me. I am also hugely grateful to the Deaf group participants for giving up a whole Saturday to engage with the material so whole-heartedly and give such stimulating and thoughtful responses to the questions posed.

6. For example "blindness may represent the incapacity of humanity to see into the future, lameness can designate the crippling effects of social ideologies" (Schipper 2007: 103).

7. See Signs of God website: http://www.bslbible.org.uk/news.php

8. I am grateful to Susannah Cornwall for making this point in her response to my paper.

9. Participants in the Deaf group also commented on the inaccessibility of mainstream worship to the Deaf community. Church pews disallowed face-to-face encounter (so central to sign language). Lighting, hymns, not to mention oppressive lyrics (e.g. "open our ears Lord"!) were also viewed as "disabling" for the Deaf community.

10. West has identified the "ordinary reader" to refer to those at the margins of society in general and scholarly discourse in particular. Some have voiced dissension about the term and West's most recent work has actually identified "extra-ordinary" African agency in some contextual readings (2007: 29–47). Stephen Jennings whilst voicing misgivings about the prejudicial connotations involved in the term "ordinary reader" nevertheless chooses to retain it within his work. In his words, "Though the term is not without its problems, not least because it tends to elide various categories of persons who are not necessarily the same, and whose interpretations could be radically different from one another, it is connotatively powerful in conveying the sense that one's social location influences one's interpretation and application of anything, the Bible included" (Jennings 2007: 49).

11. This is part of a larger project entitled "Texts of Land, Sea and Hope" (sponsored by the South West Ministry Training Course) in which I am reading selected narratives from the Gospel of Luke in a variety of groups across the South West.

12. Hitching's reveals how the "storytelling approach in Scripture is mirrored in sign language and how both describe relationships and convey attitudes and intension by appealing to visual and spatial imagery" (Hitching 2003: 39).

13. Lees similarly states, "using remembered texts could mean inviting participants to remember stories about sensory experiences" (Lees 2007: 167)
14. Lewis similarly claims, "the growth of oral hermeneutics and visual ways of presenting the text are part of this process of freeing the readers of the Bible from the tyranny of a written text that claims it is the only authoritative work of God" (Lewis 2007: 123).
15. Or to give another example Lewis reveals that a shepherd envisaged in our context is a sheep chaser or herder, however akin to the shepherd in ancient Israel the sign is not "sheepherder", but rather "sheep leader" (Lewis 2007: 119).
16. Similarly Hitching writes, "Storytelling is intrinsic to Deaf culture. Deaf people use it to pass on information and to help them cope with life. In their stories they include self-mocking elements and make fun of interactions with hearing people. Storytelling also influences how they conceptualize reality and create their worldview. In Deaf culture the storytelling mode, the dialectical nature of encounters and the greater experience of immediacy create differences in the backdrop against which reality is interpreted" (Hitching 2003: 69)
17. Of course there is tension here. Susannah Cornwall pointed out to me in discussion that the gaps in English translation which BSL fills in are only "gaps" if an "original" text, in our case the written versions of the Bible in original languages (which are themselves a calcification of the traditions as orally transmitted) are viewed as canonical and legitimate. Linked to this, is the problem that the freezing of the story in a DVD/video version may stifle the fluid and dynamic nature of traditional BSL performances.

Bibliography

Avalos, H. 2007. "Introducing Sensory Criticism in Biblical Studies: Audiocentricity and Visiocentricity." In *This Abled Body: Rethinking Disabilities in Biblical Studies*, eds H. Avalos, S. Melcher, J. and Schipper, 31–46. Atlanta, GA: Society of Biblical Literature.

Avalos, H., Melcher, S. and Schipper, J. 2007. *This Abled Body: Rethinking Disabilities in Biblical Studies.* Atlanta, GA: Society of Biblical Literature.

Boyarin, D. 1990. *Intertextuality and the Reading of Midrash.* Indianapolis, IN: Indiana University Press.

Bishop, M. E. (ed.). 1995. *Religion and Disability: Essays in Scripture, Theology and Ethics.* Kansas: Sheed and Ward.

Church of England. 1993. *The Church Amongst Deaf People.* London: Church House Publishing.

Clark, S. 2002. "Viewing the Bible Through the Eyes and Ears of Subalterns in India." *Biblical Interpretation* 10: 245–266.

Davis, L. 1995. *Enforcing Normalcy: Disability, Deafness and the Body,* London: Verso.

Donaldson, L. E. 2005. "Gospel Hauntings: The Postcolonial Demons of New Testament Criticism." In *Postcolonial Biblical Criticism: Interdisciplinary Intersections*, eds S. Moore and F. Segovia, 97–113. London: T&T Clark.

Dube, M. 2005. *Postcolonial Feminist Interpretation of the Bible.* Missouri: Chalice Press.

Eiesland, N. L. 1994. *The Disabled God: Towards a Liberatory Theology of Disability.* Nashville, TN: Abingdon Press.

Hitching, P. 2003. *The Church and Deaf People.* Milton Keynes: Paternoster Press.

Hutchinson, N. 2006. "Disabling Beliefs? Impaired Embodiment in the Religious Tradition of the West." *Body and Society,* 12 (4): 365–81.

Hull, J. 2001. *In the Beginning There Was Darkness: A Blind Person's Conversations with the Bible.* London: SCM Press.

Jennings, S. 2007. "Ordinary Reading in Extraordinary Times: A Jamaican Love Story." In *Reading Other-Wise: Socially Engaged Biblical Scholars Reading with Their Local Communities,* ed. G. West, 49–62. Atlanta, GA: SBL.

Kyle, J. G. and Woll, B. 1988. *Sign Language: The Study of Deaf People and Their Language.* Cambridge: Cambridge University Press.

Melcher, S. J. 2007. "With Whom Do the Disabled Associate? Metaphorical Interplay in the Latter Prophets." In *This Abled Body: Rethinking Disabilities in Biblical Studies,* eds H. Avalos, S. Melcher, and J. Schipper, 115–130. Atlanta, GA: Society of Biblical Literature.

Nelavala, S. 2006. "Smart Syrophoenician Woman: A Dalit Feminist Reading of Mark 7:24–31." *Expository Times* 1: 18: 64–69.

Ladd, P. 2003. *Understanding Deaf Culture.* Clevedon: Multilingual Matters.

Lees, J. 2007. "Remembering the Bible as a Critical Pedagogy of the Oppressed." In *Reading Other-Wise: Socially Engaged Biblical Scholars Reading with Their Local Communities,* ed. G. West, 73–86. Atlanta, GA: SBL.

Lewis, H. 2007. *Deaf Liberation Theology.* Farnham: Ashgate Publishing.

Ryken, L., Wilhoit, J. C. and Longmann, T. (eds). 1998. *Dictionary of Biblical Imagery.* Downers Grove, IL: InterVarsity Press.

Schipper, J. 2007. "Disabling Israelite Leadership: 2 Samuel 6:23 and Other Images of Disability in the Deuteronomistic History." In *This Abled Body: Rethinking Disabilities in Biblical Studies,* eds H. Avalos, S. Melcher and J. Schipper, 103–114. Atlanta, GA: Society of Biblical Literature.

Sherwood, Y. 2000. *A Biblical Text and its Afterlives: The Survival of Jonah in Western Culture.* Cambridge: Cambridge University Press.

Sugirtharajah, S. (ed.). 2006. *The Postcolonial Biblical Reader.* Oxford: Blackwell.

Tannehill, R. C. 1996. *Luke.* Nashville, TN: Abingdon Press.

West, G. (ed.). 2007. "(Ac)Claiming the (Extra)ordinary Reader of the Bible." In *Reading Other-Wise: Socially Engaged Biblical Scholars Reading with Their Local Communities,* ed. G. West, 29–48. Atlanta, GA: SBL.

Yarchin, W. 2004 *History of Biblical Interpretation: A Reader.* Peabody, MA: Hendrickson Publishers.

From a Reconstruction and Development Programme (RDP) of the Economy to the RDP of the Soul: Public Realm Biblical Appropriation in Postcolonial South Africa

Gerald West[a]

The African National Congress (ANC) led tripartite alliance (including the Congress of South African Trade Unions (Cosatu) and the South African Communist Party (SACP) came into political power in 1994 with a clear mandate from the South African masses to transform South African society, especially its neo-liberal racial capitalist economy. The structural mechanism for this socio-economic transformation was the Reconstruction and Development Programme (RDP), which included strong state intervention and an African socialist orientation. The RDP was a broadly canvassed and mandated policy. However, in 1996, with almost no consultation, even within the tripartite alliance, the RDP was dropped and the Growth, Employment and Redistribution (GEAR) socio-economic policy replaced it. Its orientation was neo-liberal capitalist with a non-interventionist "managers of capital" government.

In 1994 the RDP was, in the words of former president, Thabo Mbeki, "the core" of the ANC's election manifesto. In the midst of a commitment to the economically transformative agenda of the RDP, South Africa's first democratically elected president, Nelson Mandela, reminded the nation

[a] Gerald West teaches Old Testament/Hebrew Bible and African Biblical Hermeneutics in the School of Religion and Theology, University of KwaZulu-Natal, South Africa. He is also Director of the Ujamaa Centre for Community Development and Research, a project in which socially engaged biblical scholars and ordinary African readers of the Bible from poor, working-class, and marginalized communities collaborate for social transformation.

that not only did their economy need a RDP, so did the soul of the nation. Little attention was paid to this call for "an RDP of the soul" until recently. In 2007 Thabo Mbeki recovered this call, reminding the nation in his Nelson Mandela Lecture of the call, and devoting most of his lecture to an elaboration of Mandela's inaugural call.

What was most amazing, to a biblical scholar, was that the primary resource Mbeki drew on to make his argument for "an RDP of the soul" – the Bible. In an extended engagement with various biblical texts Mbeki managed to shift the focus from an RDP of the economy to the RDP of the soul. The final shift of RDP from economy to morality took place some months after Mbeki's address, in the one of the 13 discussion documents debated at the ANC's policy conference, entitled quite simply, "RDP of the soul". The transformation is complete, what was a programme to transform the South African economy has become morality. And the Bible, back in the public realm after some years in the wilderness, has been one of the mechanisms in this transformation. This paper analyses this shift in detail and reflects on the return of the Bible to the public realm in post-apartheid, postcolonial South Africa.

Introduction

The history of South Africa over the past three-and-a-half centuries has been "a history of inequality". In his economic analysis of South Africa from 1652–2002 under this title, Sampie Terreblanche provides a detailed account of the systemic relationship between power, land and labour in South Africa (Terreblanche 2002). He identifies a number of successive systemic periods in South African history, beginning with "the mercantilistic and feudal system institutionalised by Dutch colonialism during the second half of the 17th and most of the 18th century (1652–1795)" (Terreblanche 2002: 14). This was followed by the system of British colonial and racial capitalism (1795–1890) and a related system of British colonial and mineral capitalism (1890–1948) (Terreblanche 2002: 15). Unfree labour patterns were intensified when the Afrikaner-oriented National Party won the general election of 1948, and although they "did not drastically transform the economic system of racial capitalism institutionalised by the English establishment, it used its political and ideological power to institutionalise a new version of it" (Terreblanche 2002: 15). "Since 1990", continues Terreblanche, "we have experienced a transition from the politico-economic system of white political domination and racial capitalism to a new system of democratic capitalism"

(Terreblanche 2002: 15). South Africa's economic system has moved, Terreblanche argues, "over the past 30 years from one of colonial and racial capitalism to a neo-liberal, first-world, capitalist enclave that is disengaging itself from a large part of the black labour force" (Terreblanche 2002: 422). This transformation, though it has "coincided with the introduction of a system of representative democracy which is effectively controlled by a black, predominantly African, elite", still exhibits "an ominous systemic character" (Terreblanche 2002: 422–23).

> In the new politico-economic system, individual members of the upper classes (comprising one third of the population) profit handsomely from mainstream economic activity, while the mainly black lumpenproletariat (comprising 50 per cent of the population) is increasingly pauperised. Ironically, individual members of the black and white upper class in the new system seem as unconcerned about its dysfunctionality as individual members of the white elite were about that of the old. The common denominator between the old and the new systems is that part of society was/is systemically and undeservedly enriched, while the majority of the population were/are systemically and undeservedly impoverished – in the old system through *systemic exploitation*, and in the new system through *systemic neglect*. (Terreblanche 2002: 423)

If, as Margaret Legum has argued, "It doesn't have to be like this!" (Legum 2002), the title of her book on alternatives to the Washington Consensus, how then has our socialist-leaning liberation struggle brought us to this socio-economic state? While it may seem a bold claim, it is not that surprising that in South Africa the Bible has had something to do with this state of affairs!

From Conversion to Capitalism

The long association of nineteenth-century mission and colonialism with capitalism is well documented. While the primary objective of the missionaries who went to Southern Africa from the late 1700s was to awaken the dormant intellect of the African through the direct power of the Word (Comaroff and Comaroff 1991: 230), Africans were always more interested in the other items the missionaries brought with them, including items such as guns, tobacco and candles, but most of all access to the chain of trade the missionaries provided between the interior and the emerging European colony on the coast (West 2004). Given, therefore, the lack of interest in the Word, missionaries were forced "to take a more circuitous route via the laborious reform of habit" (Comaroff and Comaroff 1991: 230). In the words of the Rev. John Philip, the London Missionary Society Superintendent at the Cape in the early 1800s,

The elevation of a people from a state of barbarism to a high pitch of civilization supposes a revolution in the habits of that people, which it requires much time, and the operation of many causes to effect. By the preaching of the gospel, individuals ... may be suddenly elevated to a surprising height in the scale of improvement, and the influence of such a person, on a savage tribe, must be great; but those on whom the power of divine truth operates in a direct manner, bear but a small proportion to the numbers who are only the subjects of an indirect or reflected influence. ... [The] mass of people ... are but slightly affected with divine truth. (Comaroff and Comaroff 1991: 230; see Philip 1828: 2, 355)

Because of this conviction concerning the need to revolutionize the habits of Africans, missionaries were particular about performing "the mundane signs and practices of European modernity", accompanied by preaching and praying, conversation and exhortation, in the firm hope that the childlike Africans would not only learn by imitation (following Eph. 5:1) but also benefit from the temporal benefits of civilization (Comaroff and Comaroff 1997: 120). Hard work and the material benefits that it produced were central to the missionary vision; "commerce" was an alternative and antidote to both slavery and primitive African communism (Comaroff and Comaroff 1991: 79–80), and the missionaries were determined to save the African from both.

The missionaries took it for granted that, "tied together by the mechanism of the market, they were indissolubly bound up in the workings of advanced capitalist economy and society" (Comaroff and Comaroff 1997: 120), and so for Africans to gain entry into the Christian commonwealth, they must be inducted into God's economic order. The entry into the sacred economic order was via a transformation of African agriculture. The missionary John Campell, on his second journey to the missions in South Africa on behalf of the London Missionary Society, argued that "Till the present system [of agrarian production] shall undergo a complete revolution, such a population can never abound in grain, nor can it become an article of trade" (Campbell 1822: 2, 60). The missionary emphasis on a revolution in African agriculture "owed much to the close ties, both sociological and imaginative, that bound the missionaries to the displaced peasantry at home". "But, even more fundamentally", argue John and Jean Comaroff, "the Christians were from a world in which cultivation and salvation were explicitly linked – and joined together, more often than not, in a tangled mesh of horticultural imagery, much of it biblical in origin" (Comaroff and Comaroff 1997: 121).

In their effort to transform African agriculture, the missionaries "spoke of reclaiming the prodigal soul along with the wasted garden". As the

Comaroffs go on to argue, "[t]he idiom of improvidence was neither accidental nor incidental. Saving the savage meant teaching the savage to save" (Comaroff and Comaroff 1997: 166). Africans must be taught to turn away from their inefficient mode of production so that, using God's talents, they might bring forth the greatest possible abundance. "Only then would black communities be animated by the spirit of commerce that – along with the Gospel of Christ – promoted exchange on a worldwide scale. Only then might they be part of the sacred economy of civilized society" (Comaroff and Comaroff 1997: 166). For the missionary the political economy was a form of "secular theology" (Comaroff and Comaroff 1997: 166), and so the missionaries set out to establish economic reform with religious zeal, persuading with word and deed the Africans "to accept the currency of salvation, a task involving the introduction, along with the gospel, of market exchange, wage work, sometimes even a specially minted coinage" (Comaroff and Comaroff 1997: 168).

This transformation of the African economy did not always proceed as planned, nor did it always match the imagination of the missionaries, but over the course of the nineteenth century, the majority of southern Africans were "drawn into the net cast by the commodity form: all came to partake of relations and transactions involving money and manufactures, whether as wage earners, as consumers, as the sellers of produce, as taxpayers" (Comaroff and Comaroff 1997: 216). And the Bible, as we have witnessed, played a part in this alteration.

From Racial Capitalism to Reconstruction and Development

How fitting then that after more than a century and a half of racial capitalism, the first macro-economic policy of a liberated South Africa, the Reconstruction and Development Programme (RDP), should be declared to have an "almost biblical character" by the then Deputy President Thabo Mbeki (Mbeki 1995: 1).

The RDP originally emanated from the Congress of South African Trade Unions (COSATU), and particularly its most powerful affiliate, the National Union of Mineworkers (NUM), and was envisaged as "a set of socio-economic benchmarks against which the performance of a new democratically elected government would be judged" (Terreblanche 2002: 108). Driven by COSATU, many members of the democratic movement made contributions, including the African National Congress, though the bulk of the work was done by members of the Mass Democratic Movement (MDM) (Terreblanche 2002: 108).

The RDP stated that "the democratic government must play a leading and enabling role in guiding the economy and the market towards reconstruction and development" (cited in Terreblanche 2002: 108), and warned that policies concentrating primarily on promoting economic growth "would accentuate existing inequalities, perpetuate mass poverty, and soon stifle economic growth". Thus the government was tasked with actively integrating economic growth with economic reconstruction and social development, being ever mindful of the distortions and injustices that had become endemic during racial capitalism and white political domination (Terreblanche 2002: 108–09).

Swept to power in the 1994 election, with the RDP as its election manifesto, the ANC and now national President Nelson Mandela declared the RDP to be "the cornerstone on which the ... GNU (Government of National Unity) is based", and "the centerpiece of its socio-economic policy" (cited in Terreblanche 2002: 109). As Sampie Terreblanche argues, "Its symbolic importance and consensus it created cannot be overemphasised, because it formed an important part of the nation-building and healing process after centuries of deep divisions and conflict" (Terreblanche 2002: 109). The RDP provided a "bold new social democratic vision", based on a state which would take the lead in promoting major structural adjustment towards a high-wage, high-productivity economy, while at the same time providing "basic welfare rights", including "the right to basic needs such as shelter, food, health care, work opportunities, income security and all those aspects that promote the physical, social and emotional wellbeing of all people in our country, with special provision made for those who are unable to provide for themselves because of special problems" (cited in Seekings and Nattrass 2006: 347).

Driven to a considerable degree by the trade unions and civic organizations, the RDP emphasized that central to the new government's planning process must be "both the meeting of the populace's basic needs and the active empowerment of that populace in driving its own development process" (Saul 2005: 206). In macro-economic terms the RDP put forward non-market mechanisms for the provision of basic goods and services, advocated a process of decommodification by turning exchange-values back into use-values, and set about democratizing access to economic resources (Legassik 2007: 456–57). And even though its central chapters were compromised "in the direction of free-market premises" (Saul 2005: 206), it was hailed by left intellectuals as posing "challenges to the commanding heights of capitalism, racism and patriarchy", by proposing "structural reforms" which would start the building of socialism under capitalism and lead inexorably to a socialist transition (Legassik 2007: 457). Notwithstanding its weaknesses, the RDP was, wrote John Saul at the time, "less what it is, than what it might become" in the context of further class struggles (Saul 2005: 206–07).

Is this, then, what Thabo Mbeki meant when he said, in 1995, that the RDP had an "almost biblical character"? Unfortunately not, if we replace this phrase in its context. Mbeki acknowledges that the RDP had "established a unique national consensus on the need for prosperity, democracy, human development and the removal of poverty". "However", he goes on to say, "despite its almost biblical character, the RDP Base Document did not provide us with all the answers". This is because, he continues, "We have always known that its many many priorities and programmes need to be distilled into a series of realistic steps, guided by a long term vision and our resource constraints" (Mbeki 1995: 1). What Mbeki seems to be saying here is that the prophetic vision of the RDP, like the prophetic vision of the Bible, is not really realistic.

Within two years of its adoption, the RDP was replaced, with almost no consultation – the hallmark of alliance liberation politics up to this point – by a new, pro-capitalist, macroeconomic policy, GEAR (Growth, Employment and Redistribution). Indeed, writes Martin Legassik, though the name of the RDP continued to be invoked by the ANC up to the 1999 election campaign and even later, "the economic leadership of the ANC had from the start no intention of implementing the RDP where it clashed with their pro-business aims of export-orientation, trade liberalisation, fiscal austerity or privatisation" (Legassik 2007: 457). Swept to power under the flag of the RDP, the ANC government began, within days, to dismantle the RDP's African socialist potential (Legassik 2007: 458). The "objective" political factors which led to this include the following two factors, according to the analysis of the South African Communist Party (SACP): a negotiated transition to democracy in the late-1980s and early-1990s which brought together the apartheid regime, unable any longer to rule, and the ANC-led alliance, yet to decisively defeat the apartheid state; and the emergence of a "bonapartist state" in which "the bourgeois class had already lost, and the working class not yet gained the ability to govern the nation", resolved, if only temporarily, by a form of state in which a great heroic personality stands above the contending forces (SACP 2006: 19–21). The iconic status of Nelson Mandela and the power of the office of the presidency were used by the ANC to enforce "acceptance" of GEAR, even though Mandela later regretted the way in which it was done (SACP 2006: 21), for there had been no discussion of the shift away from the RDP even within the ANC National Executive Committee, nor had there been any consultation with the Tripartite Alliance partners, COSATU and the SACP (Legassik 2007: 458).

In the analysis of the SACP, "the GEAR process needs essentially to be understood as the first decisive step in the launching of a new state/presidential project under the effective direction not of Mandela, but of his successor, then deputy president, Thabo Mbeki" (SACP 2006: 21). This does not mean, the SACP goes on to acknowledge, that there were not "objective" economic factors that shaped the character and evolution of the post-Mandela presidency and its adoption of GEAR (SACP 2006: 22). However, to argue that there is a certain "objectivity" about the South African presidency and its macroeconomic policy is not to argue, says the SACP, that their particular trajectories were or are inevitable. Clearly global and national realities impose real constraints, which the South African left need to appreciate, but "national realities would have allowed (and still do allow) different, much more transformative outcomes" (SACP 2006: 22).

While I agree with the SACP that "the key features of the 1996 [GEAR] class project are not merely the result of a particular person with particular subjective traits (the kind of argument that sometimes dominates William Mervyn Gumede's biography [(Gumede 2007)], and is also to be found in much of the anti-Mbeki pro-Zuma mobilisation at present)" (SACP 2006: 22), Thabo Mbeki is responsible for using the Bible to legitimate the move from the RDP to GEAR. So at this point in my paper I turn from the political and economic factors that characterized this shift and focuses on the use Mbeki made of the Bible, in the public realm, to lend legitimacy to the shift. But I before I do, it is important to note the cost of retaining the rhetoric of the RDP while rejecting its economic vision.

While the ANC had already shut down the RDP in March 1996, the ANC nevertheless used it as their election manifesto in 1999, declaring that the RDP "was the only relevant detailed programme to carry South Africa to freedom and social justice" (cited in Terreblanche 2002: 112). By sustaining the rhetoric of the RDP, with its people-centred and utopian project, but abandoning its socialist macro-economic policies, the ANC "started to put into the heads of ordinary South Africans the idea of 'empty promises', which resounded so loudly in the delivery protests of 2004 onwards" (Legassik 2007: 457), and continues to echo in the waves of xenophobic violence wracking our country at present.

From Body to Soul

Thabo Mbeki has shown a rather ambiguous attitude to the Bible in his public speeches. His Mfengu (or Fingo) missionary-Christian education in the East Cape and his love for classic literature would have made Mbeki thoroughly familiar with the Bible, but his upbringing in the staunchly African Marxist home of Govan and Epainette Mbeki and his expulsion from his missionary-Christian school, Lovedale College, in his matric year for his active involvement in the African Students' Organisation would have made him deeply aware of the Bible's ambiguity. And yet an analysis of his public speeches over the past ten years or so shows a more regular use of the Bible and a more positive appropriation of some of its strands (West forthcoming).

The most marked use of the Bible by Mbeki was in the 4th Annual Nelson Mandela Lecture (Mbeki 2006a). What makes this occasion so significant is not only the substantial use he makes of the Bible, but how he uses it to shift the focus of the RDP from a programme about economic renewal to a metaphor about moral renewal. So extensive is his use of the Bible in this lecture that he felt the need to point out in the oral presentation of the lecture (though it is not included in the published version) that his extensive reference to the Bible did not mean that he was "about to become a priest" (to which this audience responded with laughter) (Mbeki 2006b). Embarrassed by his constant reference to the Bible before his immediate audience of the educated, somewhat liberal, elite, Mbeki nevertheless crafts a lecture deeply dependent on the Bible, mindful, I have argued (West forthcoming), of the masses watching television or listening to the radio, for whom the Bible is a significant and sacred resource in their daily struggles.

He begins the lecture by invoking the masses, saying, "I believe I know this as a matter of fact, that the great masses of our country everyday pray that the new South Africa that is being born will be a good, a moral, a humane and a caring South Africa which as it matures will progressively guarantee the happiness of all its citizens". For this to happen, Mbeki continues, we must "infuse the values of Ubuntu into our very being as a people" (Mbeki 2006a: 1).

"But what", he goes on to ask, "is it that constitutes Ubuntu beyond the standard and yet correct rendition 'Motho ke motho ka motho yo mongoe: Umuntu ngumuntu ngabantu'?! [A person is a person because of other people]." Remarkably, giving precedence to the Bible, granting it the prerogative to interpret the indigenous African concept "ubuntu", he then turns, immediately, to the Bible, beginning a detailed exposition of Proverbs:

The Book of Proverbs in the Holy Bible contains some injunctions that
capture a number of elements of what I believe constitute important features
of the Spirit of Ubuntu, which we should strive to implant in the very bosom
of the new South Africa that is being born, the food of the soul that would
inspire all our people to say that they are proud to be South African![1]

The Proverbs say: [Prov. 3:27–31] Withhold not good from them to
whom it is due, when it is in the power of thine hand to do it. [28] Say not
unto thy neighbour, Go, and come again, and to morrow I will give; when
thou hast it by thee. [29] Devise not evil against thy neighbour, seeing he
dwelleth securely by thee. [30] Strive not with a man without cause, if he have
done thee no harm. [31] Envy thou not the oppressor, and choose none of
his ways. (Mbeki 2006a: 1–2).[2]

Having quoted the text, he then goes on to appropriate it, making the
point that "The Book of Proverbs assumes that as human beings, we have
the human capacity to do as it says, not to withhold the good from them to
whom it is due, when it is in the power of our hand to do it" (Mbeki 2006a:
2). Adopting an African-American type preaching cadence, Mbeki
elaborates on what Proverbs might be understood to assume of us in our
current context: "It assumes we can be encouraged not to devise evil against
our neighbours", "It assumes that … we should not declare war against
anybody without cause", and "It urges that in our actions, we should not
seek to emulate the demeanour of our oppressors, nor adopt their evil
practices" (Mbeki 2006a: 2).

Mbeki acknowledges "the cynics" might say that such behaviour is
only what "we would expect and demand of angels", and, unfortunately,
he concedes, there are very few "such angels in our country". Indeed, he
continues, it is easier to identify "evil-doers" than those "we can honestly
describe as good people" (Mbeki 2006a: 2). To illustrate what he is saying,
Mbeki then turns to another classic text, Shakespeare's Richard III, in
which the Duke of Gloucester "unashamedly declares his evil intentions"
in the "Now is the winter of our discontent …" speech, in which the Duke
of Gloucester conspires to set his brother and the king "In deadly hate the
one against the other" (Mbeki 2006a: 2–3). This "open proclamation of evil
intent", Mbeki continues, "stands in direct opposition to the directive in
the Proverbs which says, 'Devise not evil against thy neighbour ….'"; and
Mbeki returns to Proverbs 3, quoting verse 30 (Mbeki 2006a: 3).

By juxtaposing these texts Mbeki makes the point that "the intention to
do good, however noble in its purposes, does not guarantee that such good
will be done". Nevertheless, he continues, the presence of "many Richards"
in our midst should not mean that we should "avoid setting ourselves the
goal [set by the Bible] to do good!" (Mbeki 2006a: 3). What is needed,

therefore, says Mbeki, is what Nelson Mandela called the need for an "RDP of the soul" (Mbeki 2006a: 3).

Mbeki admits that the RDP "was eminently about changing the material conditions of the lives of our people", and that "It made no reference to matters of the soul, except indirectly" (Mbeki 2006a: 3). He then assures his audience, quoting extracts from the original RDP document, that its concerns "were and remain critically important and eminently correct objectives that we must continue to pursue" (Mbeki 2006a: 3). However, he goes on, deftly, to argue that the RDP's intention to improve the human condition implies a spiritual dimension. Human fulfilment, he says, consists of more than the access to "modern and effective services" promised by the RDP.[3] "As distinct from other species of the animal world, human beings also have spiritual needs"; thus, he continues, "all of us and not merely the religious leaders speak of the intangible element that is immanent in all human beings – the soul!" What is more, he adds, "all human societies also have a soul!" (Mbeki 2006a: 4)

He then returns to the contrast between Proverbs and Richard III, and argues that "the construction of a humane and caring society ... entails a struggle rather than any self-evident and inevitable victory of good over evil' (Mbeki 2006a: 4). As in many of his speeches, Mbeki's rhetoric often exceeds the logic of his argument; but it is reasonably clear that what Mbeki is arguing here is that a substantial part of what we must do to succeed in our purpose of bringing about the good is to participate, both as individuals and as a society, in the RDP of the soul.

In the next part of his speech he elaborates on what the nation needs to do "to accomplish the RDP of its soul" (Mbeki 2006a: 5). The background of the struggle facing us, Mbeki argues, is racial capitalism and its "well-entrenched value system that placed individual acquisition of wealth at the very centre of the value system of our society as a whole" (Mbeki 2006a: 6). Such a value system also "assumed a tolerant or permissive attitude towards such crimes as theft and corruption" (Mbeki 2006a: 6). The next few pages of his speech elaborate on how the capitalist system displaced the values of human solidarity with the values of individual profit maximization (Mbeki 2006a: 6–8). This value system, Mbeki asserts, is what we have "inherited" (Mbeki 2006a: 6), resulting in a society today in which for many "personal success and fulfilment means personal enrichment and striking public display of that wealth" (Mbeki 2006a: 8). Such values and attitudes "cannot but negate social cohesion and mutually beneficial human solidarity", and bring about "the destruction of human society". But, continues Mbeki, we must defeat "the tendency in our society towards the deification of personal wealth as the distinguishing feature of the new citizen of the new South Africa" (Mbeki 2006a: 9).

As he develops his argument for an RDP of the soul, Mbeki, now midway through his speech, returns again to Proverbs, this time to Prov. 6:6. The literary context in which he quotes the latter is worth indicating at some length:

> With some trepidation, advisedly assuming that there is the allotted proportion of hardened cynics present here this evening,[4] I will nevertheless make bold to quote an ancient text which reads, in Old English:
>
> [Prov. 6:6-11] Go to the ant, thou sluggard; consider her ways, and be wise: [7] Which having no guide, overseer, or ruler, [8] Provideth her meat in the summer, and gathereth her food in the harvest. [9] How long wilt thou sleep, O sluggard? when wilt thou arise out of thy sleep? [10] Yet a little sleep, a little slumber, a little folding of the hands to sleep: [11] So shall thy poverty come as one that travelleth, and thy want as an armed man.
>
> I know that given the level of education of our audience this evening,[5] the overwhelming majority among us will know that I have extracted the passages I have quoted from the Book of Proverbs contained in the St James' edition of the Holy Bible.
>
> It may be that the scepticism of our age has dulled our collective and individual sensitivity to the messages of this Book of Faith and all the messages that it seeks to convey to us.
>
> In this regard, I know that I have not served the purposes of this Book well, by exploiting the possibility it provides to say to you and everybody else who might be listening, "Go to the ant, thou sluggard; consider her ways and be wise". (Mbeki 2006a: 10)

This is a truly remarkable shift from Mbeki's earlier back-handed appropriations of the Bible. He not only engages with the text in detail, he distances himself from the educated, elitist, liberal and sceptical attitudes that may dismiss his references to the Bible. He even deprecates his own grasp of the text. Though there is some coyness, embarrassment and humour here, as is evident in the oral presentation, Mbeki is also deeply serious.

He realizes that citing "from the Book of Proverbs will, at best, evoke literary interest and at worst a minor theological controversy", but his "own view is that the Proverbs raise important issues that bear on what our nation is trying to do to define the soul of the new South Africa" (Mbeki 2006a: 10).

> I believe they communicate a challenging message about how we should respond to the situation immanent in our society concerning the adulation of personal wealth and the attendant tendency to pay little practical regard to what each one of us might do to assist our neighbour to achieve the goal of a better life. (Mbeki 2006a: 10)

Mbeki invokes the hardworking and communal ant of Proverbs in order to argue that the nation "must develop the wisdom that will ensure the survival and cohesion of human society" (Mbeki 2006a: 10).

He realizes that "many among us might very well think" that he is indulging in wishful thinking in "trying to wish away the waves of self-aggrandisement that might be characteristic of global human society" (Mbeki 2006a: 10), so he strengthens his argument – by quoting another biblical text. The text he chooses is from the book of Genesis, and again he states explicitly that he is quoting from "the Holy Bible". The Genesis text he quotes is 3:19, and on this occasion the reference is given:

> "In the sweat of thy face shalt thou eat bread, till thou return unto the ground; for out of it wast thou taken: for dust thou art, and unto dust shalt thou return" (Gen. 3:19). (Mbeki 2006a: 10)

"This biblical text suggests", argues Mbeki, "that of critical importance to every South African is consideration of the material conditions of life and therefore the attendant pursuit of personal wealth" (Mbeki 2006a: 11). The point he seems to be making here, though again the logic is not that clear, is that immediate material means are important, perhaps even foundational. He supports this biblical claim by a fairly extensive appropriation of the materialist philosophy of Friedrich Engels, Karl Marx and Vladimir Lenin, citing from their work.[6] However, he then immediately juxtaposes "materialism" with "idealism" in order to make the related point that materialist concerns cannot be allowed to be our only concerns. "In the context of our own challenges, this 'idealism' must serve to focus our attention on issues other than the tasks of the production and distribution of material wealth" (Mbeki 2006a: 11).

What Mbeki does through this intertextual exchange is to inaugurate a discussion of the relationship between materialism and idealism. This discussion is not that easy to follow, but he seems to be saying that though Marx and the Genesis text are legitimately concerned about material considerations, we must not abandon aspects of idealism, which, as we might now suspect, he also finds in the Bible, this time citing John's gospel: "[Jn 1:1] In the beginning was the Word" (Mbeki 2006a: 12). Our preoccupation, Mbeki seems to be arguing, has been with Marx's "Man must eat before he can think!", whereas we should also be considering Rene Descartes' "I think, therefore I am" (Mbeki 2006a: 11). The Bible is useful in exploring this tension because it acknowledges the need for both bread and soul, body and mind/Word.

Mbeki interrupts his argument at this stage in his speech to deal overtly with his prolific use of the Bible: "I am certain that many in this auditorium have been asking themselves the question why I have referred so insistently on the Christian Holy Scriptures. Let me explain" (Mbeki 2006a: 12).[7] The crux of his explanation is that in the context of our country's daily economic deliberations, the debate itself "must tell us that human life is about more than the economy and therefore material considerations". This is important, Mbeki continues, because

> I believe that as a nation we must make a special effort to understand and act on this because of what I have said already, that personal pursuit of material gain, as the beginning and end of life purpose, is already beginning to corrode our social and national cohesion. (Mbeki 2006a: 12)

What this means, Mbeki goes on to state, is "that when we talk of a better life for all, within the context of a shared sense of national unity and national reconciliation, we must look beyond the undoubtedly correct economic objectives our nation has set itself" (Mbeki 2006a: 12). It is not GEAR, the government's neo-liberal capitalist macro-economic policy, Mbeki is arguing, that is to blame for the personal pursuit of material gain. It is some moral failing that requires an RDP of the soul. The RDP as a macro-economic policy has been rhetorically replaced by an RDP of the soul.

The speech now makes a somewhat abrupt digression from South African concerns to the situation in the Middle East, though he hangs on to his economic thread, implying that the crisis in the Middle East is economically induced (Mbeki 2006a: 12). Drawing on the poetry of William Butler Yeats, "The Second Coming", Mbeki appeals to his audience not to allow a "monstrous beast" to be born from South Africa's new Jerusalem (Mbeki 2006a: 13). He continues, alluding perhaps to the novel by Chinua Achebe (Achebe 1958), by saying "that for us to ensure that things do not fall apart, we must in the first instance, never allow that the market should be the principal determinant of the nature of our society" (Mbeki 2006a: 14). Instead of placing the market at the centre, a centre which cannot hold, we must place social cohesion and human solidarity, in a word, ubuntu (Mbeki 2006a: 14).

Continuing his critique of the market, but without saying anything about the place of the market in his government's macro-economic policy, Mbeki returns to the Bible as a resource for resisting "the demons that W. B. Yeats saw slouching towards Bethlehem to be born":

> We must therefore say that the Biblical injunction is surely correct, that "Man cannot live by bread alone" [Mt. 4:4/Lk. 4:4] and therefore that the

mere pursuit of individual wealth can never satisfy the need immanent in all
human beings to lead lives of happiness. (Mbeki 2006a: 14)

This is Mbeki's final reference to the Bible. He shifts his attention in the
final few pages of his speech to emphasizing our need for a "cohesive human
society" (Mbeki 2006a: 15), praising our nation's gains and the dangers that
persist from our past. But we are fortunate, he concludes, because "we had
a Nelson Mandela who made bold to give us the task to attend to the 'RDP
of the soul'" (Mbeki 2006a: 16).

From Rhetoric to Policy

The Nelson Mandela Lecture prepared the ground rhetorically for a shift
from an RDP of the economy to an RDP of the soul. The ANC policy
document, "The RDP of the Soul" (ANC 2007), turns rhetoric into policy.
Accepted at the ANC's National Conference in Polekwane in December
2007, this document became official ANC policy for both the incumbent
Mbeki government and the elections in 2009.

The preamble to the policy document "The RDP of the Soul" makes the
link to this lecture clear, following the document's statement of intent
with a quotation from the lecture:

> This document reviews the problems we found in Liberation, analyses them,
> and sets out the way of Transformation through the reconstruction and
> development of the nation's spirit. For it is the spirit of South Africans that
> drives our political, economic and social processes.
>
> "The question must therefore arise – for those of us who believe that we
> represent the good – what must we do to succeed in our purposes? ... We
> must strive to understand the social conditions that would help to determine
> whether we succeed or fail. What I have said relates directly to what needs to
> be done to achieve the objective that Nelson Mandela set the nation, to
> accomplish the RDP of the Soul." Thabo Mbeki. (ANC 2007: 1)

The first part of the policy document, headed "Liberation brought us a
packet of problems", analyses the "packet of problems" liberation brought
the ANC, including a lack of experience in government, an underestimation
of the actual population statistics, the ongoing global dictatorship of capital,
a persistent Western imperialist project, an inherited and infecting culture
of corruption, crime caused by "need, greed or violence", and negative
attitudes towards transformation in the media (ANC 2007: 1–3). Though
the first part of the document immediately invokes the RDP, reminding
members of its six basic principles, the "packet of problems" analysed after
this invocation seem to suggest that the RDP is no longer workable, without

explicitly saying this – except that it is implied that the RDP was flawed because it was based on incorrect population estimates (ANC 2007: 1). The RDP is not mentioned again until the fourth and final part of the policy document, though it is alluded to in the third part of the document.

The third part of the policy document returns to the problems that "inhibit the progress from Liberation to Transformation", and is headed "Analysing the answers". The preamble to this part notes that to the list of problems discussed under part one, part two has added another, namely "conservative religion" (ANC 2007: 5). But the focus of the third part is on the positive factors which are a resource for transformation, the problems notwithstanding. The first positive factor is that oppressive empires eventually collapse, and that there are already signs that the dreaded oppressive US Empire is collapsing from within (ANC 2007: 5). The second factor is "a new economic system", where the policy document finally lays an RDP of the economy to rest, without it being explicitly mentioned. The "recovery of soul in the secular world moves us onward", the policy document argues somewhat obscurely, from thinking of economics "in terms of a conflict between earlier capitalist and socialist systems" (ANC 2007: 5). The "ongoing evolution of human society" and the "political wisdom which led us to liberation without ongoing violence, is directing our economic wisdom to discover a new role for capital in a new concept of socialism" (ANC 2007: 5). Socialism has not been abandoned, but reconceptualized. The new economic relationship between

> the national democratic state and private capital is one of unity and struggle. On the one hand, the democratic state has to create an environment conducive for private investments from which investors can make reasonable returns, and through which employment and technological progress can be derived. On the other hand, through effective regulation, taxation and other means, the state seeks to ensure redistribution of income, to direct investments into areas which help national development, and broadly to ensure social responsibility. (ANC 2007: 5)

In the words of the SACP, the ANC have become "managers of capital", and this policy document seems to accept that role.

The fourth and final part of the policy document charts "the way of transformation". Returning to the economic RDP for the last time, the policy document draws on the centrality of the notion of "struggle" in the RDP document. Though "The RDP of Soul" policy document does not acknowledge that the root struggle discussed in the RDP document is the economy, it takes up the language of "the struggle" to urge all South Africans to join the struggle, which in this case "demands a struggle to evolve a new society through compassion, cooperation and commitment, which includes an economy designed for people not for profit, and the release of spiritual values into secular life" (ANC 2007: 7).

From Morality to Economy

Spiritual values, the concern of Mbeki's Nelson Mandela Lecture and the ANC policy document, "The RDP of the Soul", are very important in the now stuttering "new" South Africa. That religion should receive such a prominent place in an ANC policy document in post-apartheid/postcolonial South Africa is significant, recognizing as it does the deeply religious reality of South African society and the dangers of ignoring religion in its social transformation. Given how Christianity was used to institute South Africa's "colonialism of a special kind" (de Kock 1993: 65) there was an understandable hesitation after liberation to foreground religion. Nelson Mandela, the iconic representation of South Africa's national potential, has been scrupulous in his avoidance of almost any reference to religion. But as a number of commentators have noted (West 2006c: 164–166), including the "The RDP of the Soul" policy document (ANC 2007: 3), this reticence to engage with religion in the public realm has simply allowed conservative, what *The Kairos Document* called "Church Theology" (Theologians 1986), forms of religion to proliferate uncontested. As the "The RDP of the Soul" policy document notes in its analysis, the "separate development [i.e. apartheid] of Religious Institutions is as strongly entrenched as it was in the apartheid era", with the basic problem being that religious leaders are "too busy running their inherited separate activities to work out united strategies for transformation" (ANC 2007: 3). Fortunately, "The RDP of the Soul" policy document points out, there are "progressive prophets" in all sectors of South African society "promoting progressive movements in religion and politics, economics and academia, schools and colleges, unions an businesses, medicine and the media" (ANC 2007: 5).

However, it could be argued that by consigning religion and spirituality to its own policy document – for religion is only mentioned once in the other 12 ANC policy documents, in connection with Islam in the international arena – reinforces the idea that religion has its own separate sphere. Furthermore, by so overtly removing reconstruction and development from the economic sphere and reassigning it to the spiritual sphere, which both Mbeki and the "The RDP of the Soul" policy document so adeptly do, the idea that economics is the domain of the state and the soul the domain of religion is reinforced.

"The RDP of the Soul" policy document insists that government may and should remind the religious sector of their responsibilities, stating that "the ANC has a major responsibility to spell out the dangers when [religious] people promote organisations which are opposed to the spiritual or material development of our people, whatever religious credentials they may claim" (ANC 2007: 7). But, I would ask, may and should the "prophetic prophets", particularly those promoting progressive economic policy, spell out the dangers to the ANC government when they promote economic policies which are opposed to the spiritual or material development of the people, whatever economic credentials they may claim?

From the Bible to Marxism (and back)

When the progressive religious sector in South Africa does try to engage with the state around economic matters, the usual refrain is that we do not really understand the complexities of the global economic situation. We should stick to doing what we do best, namely care for the soul, and leave the state to take care of the economy. Even when we follow the advice of the South African Communist Party that "the left needs to re-connect with those located in the commanding heights of the state apparatus" (SACP 2006: 29), many of whom have deep religious affiliations, we are met with a condescending "if only you knew what we knew about the global economic reality you would know better than to advocate for unworkable African socialist economic options". So how are we – and my focus in what follows will foreground the socially engaged biblical scholar – to go about "disrupting the political elite/capital axis" (SACP 2006: 29) that characterizes the ANC government's macro-economic policy?

Invoking the comment by South African theologian Takatso Mofokeng, that in the absence of a people ready to embrace Marxism, the Bible is the most "easily accessible ideological silo" for the masses of South Africans in their struggle for liberation (Mofokeng 1988: 40), David Jobling reflects on how the Bible/Christianity (and this slashed formulation is his) might forge an alliance with Marxism as part of a project of social transformation (Jobling 2005).

Jobling notes, correctly, that Mofokeng is making a temporal and strategic point, namely that the Bible/Christianity is only more useful than Marxism because the masses are not yet ready for Marxism. So while the Bible/Christianity is more serviceable for now, Marxism may be more serviceable

at a later stage in the struggle (Jobling 2005: 188). Both the Bible/
Christianity and Marxism have globalizing tendencies, but, argues Jobling,
this is what makes them so serviceable to local situations, for "to maintain
their energy and to expand their options, [local situations] need some sort
of organized view of the outside world which confronts them" (Jobling
2005: 189).

> Local struggles need structures of mediation capable of linking them together,
> of keeping in touch with a whole "globe" of local struggles. The universality
> of the worldwide church and of international socialism offer such mediating
> possibilities. (Jobling 2005: 189)

How then might an alliance between Bible/Christianity and Marxism/
socialism make a contribution to re-engaging prophetically with the South
African government's macro-economic policy? Here too I follow Jobling,
who suggests that, "The greatest theoretical debt which Biblical Studies
owes to Marxism ... is the understanding of historical modes of production"
(Jobling 2005: 192). Given that the Bible is a significant and accessible silo
in South Africa, and given that African Christians, who are the vast majority
of South Africans across all sectors of South African society, readily look for
and construct analogies between the biblical world and their contexts, an
analysis of biblical modes of production may provide a way of talking about
modes of production in the South African context (and globally) within a
faith-based community which does not normally talk about economic
matters. Here biblical and Marxist analysis would join forces to offer both
a structural account of our current economic situation and additional
categories and concepts with which to do their own further analysis.

As Jobling illustrates from examples of his own praxis (Jobling 2005:
195, 198), and I could illustrate from examples of the work of the Ujamaa
Centre with which I work (West 2006a), there is both a tactical and
pedagogic value to such analogies. Tactically, they enable us to mobilize
support from Christian-based organizations (and perhaps even faith-based
organizations in general). And even when we, as socially engaged biblical
scholars, have to admit that though the Bible does offer paradigms of
resistance within the tributary and slave-based modes of production, it
does not, by definition, address resistance to capitalism, this very admission
has a positive side. First, it enables us to show the relationship between
successive modes of production, for, as Jobling says, capitalism, like any
mode of production, "continues to be 'inhabited' by all the MPs [modes
of production] that preceded it – not least because ancient texts like
the Bible continue to exert power within it". And second, admitting the

difference enables us "to present responsible 'translations'. In each case, we have to ask how words of power spoken within one pervasive mindset are capable of being heard within another" (Jobling 2005: 194).

Pedagogically, because of its engagement with Marxism, Biblical Studies is able to take up the task, among other disciplines, in this period after the collapse of the Soviet Union, "to *represent* Marxism in locations where it is weak or absent" or discredited (Jobling 2005: 198). And just as Jobling was able to provide the basics of Marxism to his students as part of his biblical studies teaching (Jobling 2005: 198–199), so too I regularly use a Marxist modes of production form of analysis with my students, and with the communities of unemployed youth with whom we in the Ujamaa Centre work (West 2006b), giving them an additional array of categories and concepts with which to do their own analysis of why they are unemployed (instead of lashing out at the "foreigners" who are simply struggling to survive in the same systemic economic conditions as they are). Such biblical analogies also provide a Marxist vocabulary with which to forge links with COSATU and the SACP, for whom African socialism is still firmly an economic option, and with which to engage government, who still deploy Marxist rhetoric in the public realm.

Norman Gottwald is right to caution those of us who would mobilize around the Bible for economic transformation of the limits of our analogies. "Given the reality that economic systems cannot be 'imported' from the Bible to meet our needs", Gottwald says, "the ethical force of the Bible on issues of economics will have to be perspectival and motivational rather than prescriptive and technical" (Gottwald 1993: 345). Yet this kind of force is considerable, particularly if we agree with Gottwald that, "The dominant voices in biblical economic ethics are emphatically communitarian, resolutely critiquing tributary power by seeking state reforms, urging resistance to oppressive power, upbraiding ruthless exploiters and speaking to the collective religious conscience of a nation with a communitarian premise at its base" (Gottwald 1993: 345). And, "When we interface communitarian biblical economic ethics with our own economic systems, the results are instructive", says Gottwald. "The biblical premise of the primacy of communal welfare over individual achievement is much closer to the premise of socialism than to those of capitalism" (Gottwald 1993: 346).

Notwithstanding the very real differences and the distance between the realities of biblical economic ethics and our own economic ethics, what connects the two "is a common thread of economic inequity and oppression and a common thread of struggle against needless economic suffering, a struggle fuelled by religious convictions and aspirations" (Gottwald 1993: 346). For the socially engaged biblical scholar "we must exegete the biblical world and our world separately while we also lay claim to their continuities" (Gottwald 1993: 346).

In the conclusion to his essay on the Bible as a resource for economic ethics, Gottwald wonders aloud, "is it possible to identify a perspective emerging from biblical economics that will orient our analysis and reflection on capitalist/socialist economic systems in our time?" (Gottwald 1993: 346) He thinks we can, and so do I.

> Biblical economic ethics, in their several strands, show an abiding concern for the welfare of persons in damaged but perfectible communities. People matter. People are social and communal creatures. In important ways community structures, especially economic production, distort, and destroy people. As creatures of God, it is both possible and obligatory to build better forms of economic community in which more people benefit more equitably in deciding economic priorities and in the production and consumption of goods, services, and ideas. What the God of the Bible "reveals", behind and within all the many voices of the biblical traditions, is that this building of a materially just society is an indispensable precondition for the spiritual welfare of humanity. (Gottwald 1993: 347)

Conclusion

The return of the Bible to the public realm in the Nelson Mandela Lecture is a sign that religion cannot be relegated to the periphery of South African political life. However, Mbeki's attempt to take up but restrict the Bible to matters of the soul and the ANC's attempt to place religion in its own separate policy document will not suffice. Neither will the recent attempts by the new ANC President, Jacob Zuma, who has invoked God to justify eternal ANC rule, claiming that the ANC "will rule until Jesus comes back" (Jasson da Costa 2008).

Mbeki is wrong. The Bible has as much to say about bread as it does about soul. So we progressive prophets will take up the challenge of the ANC's "The RDP of the Soul" policy document, by mobilizing the memory of African socialism, by forging alliances with the Congress of South African Trade Unions and the South African Communist Party, by working in solidarity with those who do not have "decent work" (Cochrane 2008) and those who are unemployed and unemployable, by recognizing and rallying around our religious resources (including the Bible), so that we can engage with the state for an RDP of the economy. There will be no RDP of the soul in South Africa until there is an RDP of the economy.

Notes

1. Here there is perhaps an echo of Takatso Mofokeng (see below).
2. I have inserted verse numbers for reference sake; Mbeki's version is from the King James Version (which clearly appeals to his "classical" ear), but does not include the chapter and verse references.
3. Mbeki returns here to the "almost biblical" character of the Reconstruction and Development Programme, citing some of its tenets. A sub-text of Mbeki's invocation of the RDP is, I think, his response to the critique levelled at the ANC by the South African Communist Party, as argued in the May 2006, Special Edition of *Bua Komanisi*: Information Bulletin of the Central Committee of the South African Communist Party (SACP 2006). This incisive analysis considers in depth the ANC's betrayal of the African socialist vision of the RDP in favour of its neo-capitalist replacement project, GEAR.
4. Mbeki seems acutely aware of his two audiences and of their rather different attitudes to the Bible.
5. Mbeki recognizes that his immediate educated audience would recognize his biblical allusions/quotations, even though (as he has implied earlier) they may not take the Bible seriously. Beyond this immediate audience is another larger less educated audience who would not only recognize but also "believe" the Bible.
6. In his speeches Mbeki regularly appropriates Marxist rhetoric. In his more recent appropriations, including this instance, the appropriation is ambivalent. Rhetorically, he shows he knows his Marx, but he also indicates that ideologically he is not fully persuaded.
7. As indicated above, it is at this point that Mbeki makes an aside, saying, "Do not worry, I am not about to become a priest" (Mbeki 2006b).

Bibliography

Achebe, Chinua. 1958. *Things Fall Apart*. London: Heinemann.

African National Congress. 2007. *Section 7: RDP of the Soul* 2007 [cited 7 June 2007]. Available from http://www.anc.org.za/ancdocs/policy/2007/discussion/rdp.html

Campbell, John. 1822. *Travels in South Africa, Undertaken at the Request of the London Missionary Society; Being a Narrative of a Second Journey in that Interior of that country*, 2 vols. London: Francis Westley.

Cochrane, James R. 2008. *Work, Decency, being human: justice still to come*. Available from www.Ujamaa.org.za

Comaroff, Jean, and John L. Comaroff. 1991. *Of Revelation and Revolution: Christianity, Colonialism and Consciousness in South Africa*, Vol. 1. Chicago, IL: University of Chicago Press.

_____ 1997. *Of Revelation and Revolution: The Dialectics of Modernity on a South African Frontier*, Vol. 2. Chicago, IL: University of Chicago Press.

de Kock, Leon. 1993. Postcolonial analysis and the question of critical disablement. *Current Writing* 5: 44–69.

Gottwald, Norman K. 1993. How does social scientific criticism shape our understanding of the Bible as a resource for economic ethics? In *The Hebrew Bible in Its Social World and in Ours*, ed. N. K. Gottwald: 341–347. Atlanta, GA: Scholars Press.

Gumede, William Mervin. 2007. *Thabo Mbeki and the Battle for the Soul of the ANC*. Cape Town: Zebra Press.

Jasson da Costa, Wendy. 2008. Religion versus politics ... *The Mercury*, 2.

Jobling, David. 2005. "Very limited ideological options": Marxism and biblical studies in postcolonial scenes. In *Postcolonial Biblical Criticism: Interdisciplinary Intersections*, eds S. D. Moore and F. F. Segovia: 184–201. London and New York: T&T Clark.

Legassik, Martin. 2007. *Towards Socialist Democracy*. Pietermaritzburg: University of KwaZulu-Natal Press.

Legum, Margaret. 2002. *It Doesn't Have to be Like This! A New Economy for South Africa and the World*. Kenilworth: Ampersand Press.

Mbeki, Thabo. 1995. *A national strategic vision for South Africa: address by Deputy President T. M. Mbeki, at the Development Planning Summit, hosted by the Intergovernmental Forum* [cited 06/12/2006. Available from http://www.anc.org.za/ancdocs/history/mbeki/1995/sp951127.html

_____ 2006a. *4th Annual Nelson Mandela Lecture by President Thabo Mbeki: University of Witwatersrand, 29 July 2006* [cited 06/12/2006]. Available from http://www.info.gov.za/speeches/2006/06073111151005.htm

_____ 2006b. *The Nelson Mandela annual lecture: transcript of President Thabo Mbeki's lecture, 29 July 2006*: Nelson Mandela Foundation. DVD.

Mofokeng, T. 1988. Black Christians, the Bible and liberation. *Journal of Black Theology* 2: 34–42.

Philip, John. 1828. *Researches in South Africa; Illustrating the Civil, Moral, and Religious Condition of the Native Tribes*, 2 vols. London: James Duncan.

SACP. 2006. Special edition. *Bua Komanisi!: Information Bulletin of the Central Committee of the South African Communist Party*: 31.

Saul, John S. 2005. *The Next Liberation Struggle: Capitalism, Socialism and Democracy in Southern Africa*. Pietermartizburg: University of KwaZulu-Natal Press.

Seekings, Jeremy, and Nicoli Nattrass. 2006. *Class, Race, and Inequality in South Africa*. Pietermaritzburg: University of KwaZulu-Natal Press.

Terreblanche, Sampie. 2002. *A History of Inequality in South Africa, 1652–2002*. Pietermaritzburg: University of Natal Press.

Theologians, Kairos. 1986. *The Kairos Document: Challenge to the Church*. Revised Second Edition. Braamfontein: Skotaville.

West, Gerald O. 2006a. Contextual Bible reading: a South African case study. *Analecta Bruxellensia* 11: 131–48.

_____ 2006b. Contextuality. In *The Blackwell Companion to the Bible and Culture*, ed. J. F. A. Sawyer: 399–413. Oxford: Blackwell.

_____ 2006c. The vocation of an African biblical scholar on the margins of biblical scholarship. In *Voyages in Uncharted Waters: Essays on the Theory and Practice of Biblical Interpretation in Honor of David Jobling*, eds W. J. Bergen and A. Siedlecki: 142–71. Sheffield: Sheffield Phoenix Press.

_____ 2004.Early encounters with the Bible among the BaTlhaping: historical and hermeneutical signs. *Biblical Interpretation* 12: 251–281.

_____ (forthcoming). Thabo Mbeki's Bible: the Role of Religion in the South African Public Realm After Liberation. In *Religion and Spirituality in Postcolonial South Africa*, ed. D. Brown. Pietermaritzburg: University of KwaZulu-Natal Press.

Part III

PROSPECTS FOR APPLICATIONS OF BIBLE AND JUSTICE

The Old Testament and the Environment

J. W. Rogerson[a]

There is no such thing as "the environment". "Environment" is a word which describes the external factors or circumstances in which a system can function; and since the natural and the human worlds can be described in terms of many systems, so there are many environments in which these systems operate (Luhmann 1988: 36–7). Luhmann (2005: 326–6) notes that the German word *Umwelt* was coined around 1800 and that the English "environment" was coined in the nineteenth century. While many systems are identified on the basis of scientific analyses, there are also aesthetic and moral considerations that come into play. For example, the siting of wind turbines can provoke very strong disagreements. On the one hand there are those who may argue that placing wind turbines in a particular spot will ruin the surrounding landscape. Against them will be those who argue for the necessity for energy to be produced from renewable sources such as wind farms if the harmful effects of burning oil and coal are to be combated. These disagreements can be seen as a conflict between two views of systems and their environments. The anti-wind-farm-in-a-particular-spot view is understanding environment in terms of the immediate surroundings of the wind farm. The opposite viewpoint is defining environment in more global terms. The basis of the disagreement is aesthetic, not scientific, and those opposing wind farms in a particular spot may be just as committed to the need for renewable sources of energy as their opponents in this particular case.

[a] J. W. Rogerson is Emeritus Professor of Biblical Studies, Sheffield University, and an active Anglican priest. He has published widely in the fields of the social and historical backgrounds to the Old Testament, the history of biblical interpretation, and the use of the Bible in ethics.

The fact that decisions, including aesthetic and moral considerations, have to be made about how to define systems and their environments is important for the present chapter for the following reason. The Old Testament writers and their presumed readers/hearers knew nothing about the ecological crises that are faced by today's world, or about the scientific causes according to which they are currently understood. The question could therefore be fairly raised about the value of examining what the Old Testament contains on the subject of the environment. Given, however, that aesthetic and moral considerations are involved in defining systems and environments and differing attitudes to them, a space is made for the possibility that the Old Testament might contain something from which we could learn. To this can be added the point made by Jürgen Habermas (2003: 256–57), that religious traditions can constitute a kind of archive on which modern thought can draw for inspiration and guidance.

The biggest difference between the Old Testament writers and ourselves, and one that they shared with the human race until the eighteenth or nineteenth centuries, is that for us, there is almost no part of planet earth that is unexplored, except for parts of the oceans. For earlier generations parts of the earth were as yet undiscovered. This fact affected how the systems that maintain the life of the planet were analysed, and how their environments were defined. For Old Testament writers the undiscovered or unknown world was something that impinged upon their lives, not in the sense of an environment that was vital to support their life systems, but as a sphere of chaos and disorder that was a threat to their life systems. One of the most striking instances of their interaction with this sphere was in the ritual of the Day of Atonement (Leviticus 16) when a goat for Azazel was led from the camp (the sphere of ordered relationships) to the wilderness. This goat symbolically bore the iniquities of the people from the sphere of order to that of the disorder and chaos that lay beyond the camp. The prevailing scholarly view is that Azazel was some kind of demon, and that the "elimination rite" of transferring iniquities from the ordered to the disordered sphere was a pre-Israelite ritual that was taken over into the Priestly traditions (Janowski 1982: 268–70). Some commentators have wondered how such belief could have found a place in the supposedly strongly monotheistic religion of the Priestly traditions. The answer is surely to be found in the fact that ancient Israelites, whatever the nature of their monotheism, were very conscious of the unknown and potentially dangerous world that surrounded them, and which they could well believe was populated by malign powers as well as dangerous wild animals. What is interesting is that the Priestly tradition saw the Day of Atonement ritual not as a way of propitiating the powers that inhabited the dangerous outside world, but as a convenient dumping process for the people's iniquities. Here, if you like, was a case of environmental pollution; but the more important point was that for the Priestly traditions, the establishment of justice *within* the sphere of ordered relationships was the means of ensuring that the ordered sphere would be protected from the potential dangers that surrounded it. It was not the powers that ruled in the disordered sphere that needed to be appeased; it was the God who was ruler of the world, and whose main requirement was justice.

This method of self-critical acknowledgement of iniquities and their symbolic removal to a sphere of disorder can be contrasted with what happens in many societies, including our own. Instead of self-critical acknowledgement of failure and wickedness, there is self-justifying blaming of others for failures and wickedness. If there is a symbolic transfer of perceived wrongness in today's world, it is not to a disordered and impersonal sphere, but to minority groups such as immigrants, who can be made to carry the blame. In this scenario, groups such as immigrants also symbolize disorder, and are perceived as a threat to an ordered society. It has to be acknowledged that the Old Testament itself was not free from the practice of scapegoating other human groups. The Deuteronomic traditions saw in those they called Canaanites a constant threat to the ordered life of the people (Deut. 7:1–5), although it was also acknowledged that fault lay with Israelites for being willing to be led astray by Canaanite beliefs and practices.

All this may seem to be a long way from environmental issues; but it is not. There is a connection between how groups within societies view other human groups, and how they view the so-called natural world. There is a connection between how societies divide humanity into them and us, and how they treat the world of nature. An environmentalist has remarked that if, in a particular country, the number of people killed on the roads each day was attacked and killed by packs of wolves, action would quickly be taken to eliminate this threat to human life (Kinzelbach 1995: 144). That being so, why is nothing apparently done to eliminate the threat to human life posed by motor transport? The answer is that motor transport has become such an essential part of our economic and social systems that its curtailment or abolition would be unthinkable. Wolves, on the other hand, are considered to be external to human systems. If they became extinct (as is the case in Britain) this would in no way affect human life. As such, therefore, they are seen as a threat, which would have to be eliminated if it became serious.

To return to the Old Testament, one of its notable emphases is that there is a link between the moral order and the created order. Indeed, in the Old Testament the created order includes the moral order, so that if the moral order is violated, this has an effect on the world of nature. In the story of Cain and Abel in Genesis 4, after Cain has murdered his brother Abel, he is told by God that Abel's blood is crying out from the ground, and that when Cain tills the ground, it will no longer yield its strength (Gen. 4:10–12). Although, from a modern point of view, it is impossible to accept the theory of causality implicit in the particular judgement spoken by God against Cain, there is no doubt that, as a general rule, human injustice can and does have a detrimental effect on the natural world in relation to the human race.

I want now to look at environmental issues, and then to comment on them from the perspective of the Old Testament. For the sake of convenience I shall refer to the German environmental scientist Ragnor Kinzelbach. In his *Ökologie, Naturschutz, Umweltschutz* (Kinzelbach 1995) he outlines two main approaches to thinking about, and seeking to deal with, the current environmental crisis. What is common to both these approaches is their analysis of the causes of the crisis, namely, over-population and over-production, and the consequent divergence of the human economic system from the eco-systems of the natural world so that the eco-systems are under threat from the economic system. The first strategy for dealing with the problem he describes as *die ökologische Versöhnungsstrategie*, the strategy of reconciling the economic system with the eco-systems. This involves the following goals, and means to their attainment. First, there is the protection of nature and its environments, including the protection of land, air and water and the animal and plant worlds, against the harmful effects of human use of these things (Kinzelbach 1995: 111). Second, there must be a restriction on or reduction of population growth and a reversal of the cycles of economic over-production. Needless to say, this latter goal has consequences for the life-styles especially of those who live in the affluent parts of the world (Kinzelbach 1995: 139–43). Third, a drastic recasting of financial systems is required so that it becomes clear who, and what practices, are responsible for environmental degradation, so that those responsible can be penalized financially. In this connection, it would not be possible to exempt those who manufacture, sell and use motor vehicles.

These points are familiar, as are most of the observations made about them by Kinzelbach. On the matter of protecting the natural world he points out that this amounts to an intervention on the part of the human race. During the history of the world many species have become extinct either because of regional or global changes of temperature, etc., or because they have been unable to protect themselves against other species. The modern protection of species implies a recreation of the natural world in the image of those doing the protecting; and it can be added that if, say, aboriginal peoples were doing the recreating of nature in their image the results might be different from those produced by western environmentalists. Put another way, protection of nature is essentially protection of the human race (Kinzelbach 1995: 116). This does not invalidate it, but raises the question, to which I shall return, of the kind of human race that is protecting itself via the protection of nature.

The acknowledgement of the subjective element in nature preservation leads to observations about two assumptions, which may (but not must) be part of the reconciliation-with-nature strategy. The first is that nature has intrinsic value; the second is that it maintains a kind of equilibrium that human economic activity has disturbed, and which human action must try to restore. Both assumptions are questionable, according to Kinzelbach. The first is based upon a sentimental view of nature which ignores its violent manifestations such as earthquakes, floods and outbreaks of deadly diseases. The second view, that concerning equilibrium, is too simplistic and needs to be replaced by a dynamic model in which systems are constantly changing by means of diversification and adaptation, something that has been going on for the entire history of the world. Kinzelbach makes a nice German distinction between *Da-Sein* and *So-Sein*, between what is actually in existence (*Da-Sein*) and what people would ideally like to be or to remain in existence (*So-Sein*) (Kinzelbach 1995: 136–37). The strategy of reconciliation with nature will be flawed if nature is seen as a benign system in harmony with itself. It must be seen rather as an ongoing process, not a condition.

These observations lead to the second strategy outlined by Kinzelbach, and the one he prefers, *die ökologische Entwicklingsstrategie*, (the ecological development strategy). What this boils down to is that the human race can only save itself and the world that it inhabits, first, by emancipating itself from nature, and second, by steering nature in a direction determined by human values. This, however, raises the question of the nature of humanity and its values and calls, in the view of Kinzelbach, for a new conception of the nature of humanity and the structure of its society in the world of the future (Kinzelbach 1995: 166: "zur Behebung der ökologischen Krise bedarf es eines neuen Entwurfes vom Bild des Menschen und von der Struktur der Weltgesellschaft der Zukunft").

According to the Hebrew lexicon of Brown, Driver and Briggs, the word *rà'àv* meaning famine, or hunger, occurs 101 times in the Old Testament (Brown *et al.* 1907: 944). It does not always refer to famines, of course, but even a superficial knowledge of the content of the Bible will indicate that famines play a part in the story of Abram (he goes down to Egypt to escape it in Genesis 12), the story of Joseph in Genesis 41 (the seven fat and seven lean years) and the story of Ruth in the book of Ruth (Naomi and her family leave Bethlehem for Moab because of famine). The world of nature was not, therefore, a benign environment in which Israelites lived out their lives, and the foundation myth of Genesis 3 describes the circumstances in which Israelites were to win food from the soil:

> cursed is the ground because of you;
> in toil you shall eat of it all the days of your life;
> thorns and thistles it shall bring forth to you ...
> In the sweat of your face you shall eat bread. (Gen. 3:17–18)

Strategies to cope with famine had to be devised such as migration from Canaan to Egypt (where the Nile inundation usually guaranteed the fertility of the crops) or migration from Bethlehem to Moab, where the high Moabite plateau was cold enough to produce early-morning dews that moistened the ground. The stratagem of Joseph in storing up grain in the good years as an insurance against bad years was another way of coping with an uncertain climate and natural conditions (Skinner 1910: 472 has a note on Egyptian responses to famines). If, as I think, the poem in Eccl. 3:1–9, expresses the unrelenting routine imposed upon the human race in its attempts to produce food by the world of nature, it is another piece of evidence that Israelites had no cause to think of the natural world sentimentally (Rose 1999: 195–200). There were, of course, those in the ancient world who sought to imitate the fertility rhythms of nature, the bull being one of the symbols of this outlook. But such outlooks also transferred into human society the observation that, in the natural world, bigger, stronger creatures preyed upon smaller, weaker ones. The result was the kind of injustice that is illustrated by the story of Naboth's vineyard in 1 Kings 21, in which Queen Jezebel used false evidence in order to get Naboth executed for blasphemy, so that King Ahab could take possession of his vineyard.

At its best, the Old Testament did not try to imitate nature, although its writers did draw lessons from the behaviour of animals and birds in order to show that they had a better sense of loyalty or understanding than their human counterparts. Isa. 1:3 declares that

Even the ox knows its owner,
and the ass its master's crib;
Israel has no such knowledge,
my people does not understand.

In Jer. 8:7 it is observed that

Even the stork in the heavens knows when to migrate,
the dove, the swift and the crane when to return.
But my people know not the ordinances of the Lord.

But drawing lessons from nature was as far as Old Testament tradition went. When it came to dealing with the natural world and its non-human inhabitants, the biblical writer did so in terms of a story – a story grounded in cultural memory and shaped by celebration and retelling – the story of the exodus. From our holier-than-thou perspective, of course, the perspective of a world in which the destruction of human life has been brought technologically to a fine art, a perspective which eminently qualifies us to pass moral judgements on earlier ages, the story of the exodus is problematic. But let us forget our moral superiority for a moment and consider what the Old Testament writers did in applying the exodus story to the treatment of the natural world. The *locus classicus* is Exod. 23:9–12 which reads as follows in my translation:

A stranger you shall not treat harshly. You know what it is like to be a stranger, for you were strangers in the land of Egypt. Six years you may sow your land and harvest its produce, but in the seventh you shall let it lie fallow and leave it unattended. The poor of your people shall eat from it, and what remains may be eaten by the wild animals. You shall do the same to your vineyard and to your olive orchard. For six days you may do your work, but on the seventh day you shall desist, so that your ox and your ass may have rest and your slave and the stranger residing with you may refresh themselves.

The passage begins with a command that the Israelites must deal graciously with strangers, that is Israelites or non-Israelites who are estranged from their families and taking refuge with those who are not their kin (Bultmann 1992 discusses the relevant Hebrew terms). The command is grounded in the fact that the Israelites were themselves estranged in Egypt. Also implied is the fact of their having been freed from Egyptian enslavement by the gracious act of God. Both their sympathy born of suffering and their gratitude for deliverance must be translated into generosity towards others. But not just towards others. This generosity must also be extended to the natural order.

The origins of the sabbatical year for agriculture have been sought in ancient tabu practices that set a boundary against the extent to which humans could use nature for their own purposes (Albertz 1998: 394). The addition of vineyards and olive yards, and the injunction to allow the poor and wild beasts to eat the produce from the sabbatical year would therefore be later developments, as would the linking of these practices with the exodus story. But the end result is a theologizing which is impressive and which calls for attention.

Because of the lack of fertilizers in ancient Israel, fields were fallowed every other year (Hopkins 1985: 200–03), which means that the sabbatical year was not an agricultural necessity made into a theological virtue. No doubt it helped fields to recover their growing potential, but this was not the primary purpose. The primary purpose was to establish and preserve a triple relationship between God, the users of the land and the land itself, where the limits set upon the use of the land also contributed to human self-understanding, by setting limits to human ambition. This is indicated by the later addition of vineyards and olive orchards to the text, things that do not need to be fallowed every seven years to assist their growing potential. These items are most likely to have been added to the text in the post-exilic period when land use in Judah seems to have switched from the growing of barley (its main cereal crop) to the production of oil and wine (Kippenberg 1982: 44–7). The continuation of the passage to embrace the weekly sabbath moves in the same direction, that of imposing upon the use of domesticated animals a practice derived from compassion and graciousness. The first stated beneficiaries or the sabbath rule in Exod. 23:12 are the ox and the ass.

There are, of course, other well-known passages in which compassion for aspects of the natural order are enjoined. Deut. 20:19–20 forbids the felling of fruit trees that belong to a city that is besieged in warfare. Trees which do not yield fruit may be used to build siegeworks, but trees are not otherwise to be felled. As the most recent research indicates, this injunction was not simply an expression of solidarity with the world of nature; it was a way of expressing outrage at the military practices of the neo-Assyrian empire, which showed no mercy either to human foes or the world of nature. Eckhart Otto in his recent *Krieg und Frieden in der Hebräischen Bibel* (Otto 1999: 99–100) not only quotes from Assyrian texts which boast about the wholesale destruction of fruit trees, and indeed of anything that produced food for human consumption, he also reproduces a scene from an Assyrian relief which shows Assyrian soldiers felling the fruit trees outside a besieged city. However, the Hebrew legislation is not simply an outraged human reaction against brutal practices; it is driven by the divine command for compassion rooted in God's act of compassion in freeing his people from slavery; and the same motive is behind the injunction in Deuteronomy 22 which commands compassionate treatment for straying and lost animals, animals that have fallen down in some way, mother birds with their young, and asses that must not be made to plough with the much stronger oxen.

Thinking about these passages in the light of Kinzelbach's observations on the current ecological crisis and its possible solutions has driven me to reconsider some famous, and crucial, verses in Genesis 1. In the translation of the RSV they command the human race to fill the earth and subdue it, and to have dominion over all living creatures (Gen. 1:28). As is well known, these verses became especially sensitive because of an article by Lynn White Jr., in the 1967 number of *Science* (White 1967: 1203–07), which blamed Christian arrogance towards nature for the present ecological crisis. Obviously, this view is based upon a very inadequate understanding of the history of biblical interpretation and the history of science, but it has thrown a spotlight upon Gen. 1:28. The potentially awkward fact is that the two Hebrew verbs, *kàvash* and *ràdàh*, rendered as "subdue" and "have dominion" by the RSV, are far from benign in their usage in the Hebrew Bible. The Sheffield *Dictionary of Classical Hebrew* gives as meaning equivalents for *kàvash* "subdue, make subservient" and in one case (Esth. 7:8) "to rape" (a woman) (Clines 1998: 361). For *ràdàh*, the dictionary of Brown *et al.* gives the meaning equivalents of 'have dominion, rule, dominate' (Brown *et al.* 1907: 921–22).

These far-from-reassuring meanings have been examined, for example, by Norbert Lohfink, who has argued that *kàvash* means to place the foot upon something in order to take possession of it, and that *ràdàh* means basically "to wander around" (*umherziehen*). In the context of Genesis 1, therefore, verse 28 means that having multiplied, the human race is to take possession of the earth, and to wander around it in company with other life forms (Lohfink 1977: 165–68). However, no standard translation of the Bible has attempted to ameliorate the force of the traditional renderings of *kàvash* and *ràdàh*, and even the recent and radical *Bibel in gerechter Sprache* warns in an endnote against any attempt to weaken their meaning (Bail 2006: 2280 note 2; see also Neumann-Gorsolke 2004).

One way out of the impasse may be to interpret the verse in the light of Kinzelbach's alternative strategy: that the solution to the ecological crisis is for the human race to save itself from the world by emancipating itself from nature and by steering it in a direction determined by human nature. This would do justice to the element of coercion implied by the Hebrew verbs. Of course, this way out of the impasse would be disastrous if the human values that determined the process were those of a humanity driven by greed and exploitation, a humanity that continues to fell rain forests, pollute the atmosphere, and be indifferent to thousands of deaths each day in road accidents. This, however, is not what is intended. As Kinzelbach says at the end of his book the overcoming of the ecological crisis requires "a new conception of the nature of humanity and of the structure of the world community of the future" (Kinzelbach 1995: 166). This is what the Old Testament is about, looked at as an over-arching narrative. It is about God's project to create a humanity that will be capable of living in a world that is the kind of world that God intends.

That ideal world is pictured briefly in Genesis 1 by way of vegetarianism (Rogerson 1991: 20–22; Barr 1992: 76; a contrary view is argued by Neumann-Gorsolke 2004: 233–36), a world at harmony with itself, but the harmony is soon broken as Cain murders his brother Abel, Lamech kills a man for striking him, and the whole creation has to be destroyed on account of the wickedness of the human race. The compromise world that emerges after the flood – the world of our experience – is one designed to accommodate its most violent and aggressive creature, the human race. The story of the chosen people is the story of God working through one people in order to bring blessing to the whole human race and the world that it inhabits. This is why the scriptures of the chosen people contain many inspiring visions of a new humanity and a new world. "A new heart I will give you, and a new spirit I will put within you; and I will take out of your flesh the heart of stone and give you a heart of flesh" says Ezek. 36:26. Isa. 65:17–25 envisages new heavens and a new earth free from sorrow, pain, violence and injustice, in which the vegetarian notion of a creation at harmony with itself returns. In the Psalms of the kingship of God the sea, the cultivable land and the trees of the wood rejoice at the prospect of God coming to judge the world and its people with righteousness and truth (Ps. 96.12–13). Isaiah and Micah contain the vision of swords being beaten into ploughshares and spears into pruning hooks (Isa. 2:4; Mic. 4:3) and of war being no more.

The Old Testament cannot tell us what to do in the face of the environmental crisis that threatens us, and we may be divided about our attitude to the alternatives outlined by Kinzelbach, or feel that both contain important insights that might claim our allegiance. Where the Old Testament comes into its own is in its insistence that the world cannot be as it is intended to be without a radical alteration in our understanding and practice of what it means to be human. This no doubt entails moral and historical discussion and reflection. It also entails drawing on the strength that God supplies, through prayer, worship and the study of the scriptures. I began rather tentatively when it came to the contribution of the Old Testament to the debate about "the environment". I hope that I have ended rather more positively!

Bibliography

Albertz, R. 1998. "Sabbatjahr." In *Neues Bibel-Lexikon,* vol 3, 394–95. Zürich and Düsseldorf: Benzinger Verlag.

Bail, U. (ed.). 2006. *Bibel in gerechter Sprache,* Gütersloh: Gütersloher Verlagshaus.

Barr, J. 1992. *The Garden of Eden and the Hope of Immortality.* London: SCM Press.

Brown, F., S. R. Driver and C. A. Briggs. 1907. *A Hebrew and English Lexicon of the Old Testament,* Oxford: Clarendon Press.

Bultmann, C. 1992. *Der Fremde im antiken Juda. Eine Untersuchung zum sozialen Typenbegriff ‚ger‘ und seinem Bedeutungswandel in der alttestamentlichen Gesetzgebung* (FRLANT 153). Göttingen: Vandenhoeck & Ruprecht.

Clines, D. J. A. 1998. *Dictionary of Classical Hebrew,* vol. IV. Sheffield: Sheffield Academic Press.

Habermas, J. 2003. "Glauben und Wissen. Friedenspreisrede 2001." In *Zwölf Essays 1980–2001,* 249–62. Frankfurt am Main: Suhrkamp Verlag.

Hopkins, D. C. 1985. *The Highlands of Canaan. Agricultural Life in the Early Iron Age* (SWBA 3). Sheffield: Almond Press.

Janowski, B. 1982. *Sühne als Heilsgeschehen. Studien zur Sühnetheologie der Priesterschrift und zur Wurzel KPR im Alten Orient und im Alten Testament* (WMANT 55). Neukirchen-Vluyn: Neukirchener Verlag.

Kinzelbach, R. K. 1995. *Ökologie, Naturschutz, Umweltschutz.* Darmstadt: Wissenschaftliche Buchgesellschaft.

Kippenberg, H. G. 1982. *Religion und Klassenbildung im antiken Judäa. Eine religionssoziologische Studie zum Verhältnis von Tradition und gesellschaftlicher Entwicklung,* (StUNT 14) (2nd edn). Göttingen: Vandenhoeck & Ruprecht.

Lohfink, N. 1977. "Wachstum. Die Priesterschrift und die Grenzen des Wachstums." In *Unsere Großen Wörter. Das Alte Testament zu Themen dieser Jahre,* ed. N. Lohfink, 156–171. Freiburg: Herder Verlag.

Luhmann, N. 1988. *Soziale Systeme. Grundriß einer allgemeinen Theorie,* 2nd edn. Frankfurt am Main: Suhrkamp Verlag.

_____ 2005 *Einführung in die Theorie der Gesellschaft.* Darmstadt: Wissenschaftliche Buchgesellschaft.

Neumann-Gorsolke, U. 2004. *Herrschen in den Grenzen der Schöpfung. Ein Beitrag zur alttestamentlichen Anthropologie am Beispiel von Psalm 8, Genesis 1 und verwandten Texten,* (WMANT 101). Neukirchen-Vluyn: Neukirchener Verlag.

Rose, M. 1999. *Rien de nouveau. Nouvelles approches du livre de Qohéleth,* (OBO 168). Fribourg: Editions Universitaires; Göttingen: Vandenhoeck & Ruprecht.

Otto, E. 1999. *Krieg und Frieden in der Hebräischen Bibel und in Alten Orient. Aspekte für eine Friedensordnung in der Moderne (*Theologie und Frieden 18). Stuttgart: Kohlhammer Verlag.

Rogerson, J. 1991. *Genesis 1–11* (OTG). Sheffield: Sheffield Academic Press.

Skinner, J. 1910. *Genesis* (ICC). Edinburgh: T. and T. Clark.

White, L., Jr. 1967. "The Historical Roots of our Ecologic Crisis." *Science* 155: 1203–07.

Ecojustice in the Bible? Pauline Contributions to an Ecological Theology[*]

David G. Horrell[a]

Introduction

The question about whether, and in what way, the Bible supports the ecojustice agenda has been provoked both by the general rise in awareness of the extent of the environmental challenges facing us and by the specific criticism of the Christian tradition articulated by Lynn White Jr and others. In broad terms, as with other ethical issues which stimulate investigations of the biblical material – issues concerning poverty, war, sex, and so on – it is the contemporary context which puts environmental questions onto the agenda of biblical studies. In recent years, environmental issues have moved from the fringes of political and ethical debate to the very centre, rapidly and widely becoming acknowledged as among the most crucial and pressing issues faced by the whole global community at the beginning of the third millennium. More specifically, Christian theologians and biblical scholars have been forced to consider the ecological implications of the biblical tradition by the now famous Lynn White thesis (White 1967). White argued that the (Western) Christian worldview, rooted in the creation stories and the notion of humanity made in God's image, had

[a]   David Horrell is Professor of New Testament Studies and Director of the Centre for Biblical Studies at the University of Exeter, UK. From 2006–2009 he directed a research project on "Uses of the Bible in Environmental Ethics" and is the author of *The Bible and the Environment* (Equinox, 2010), co-author of *Greening Paul: Rereading the Apostle in an Age of Ecological Crisis* (Baylor, 2010), and co-editor of *Ecological Hermeneutics* (T. and T. Clark, 2010). He has also published widely on Paul, 1 Peter, New Testament ethics and social-scientific approaches to the New Testament.

swept aside other worldviews, with their sacred views of nature and cyclical notions of time, introducing instead a dualism between humanity and nature, and the notion that it was God's will that humanity exploit nature to serve human interests. Thus Christianity, according to White, bears "a huge burden of guilt" for introducing the anthropocentric Western worldview that has permitted and promoted the active and aggressive conquest of nature to serve human ends (White 1967: 1206). White does not explicitly cite biblical texts, giving only an overview of the biblical creation story, and his arguments concentrate much more on the historic development of Christian thought and early science during his own period of specialism, the medieval era. Nonetheless, his forceful critique of the impact of the biblical tradition, especially the creation story of Genesis 1, has raised a serious question about the Bible's green credentials, to which there has been a variety of responses.

Responses to the Lynn White Thesis: the Bible as an Eco-Friendly Book?

One kind of Christian response has essentially taken the form of an affirmation of the kind of perspective White offers, albeit from an utterly contrary standpoint: Christianity's anthropocentric focus on personal salvation is accepted and affirmed. While White proposes that we need a religion that can reorientate our relationship to nature and help us out of our ecologic crisis (White 1967: 1205–06), this approach, represented primarily by some American fundamentalists, sees the call to save the planet and discipline human activity in accord with this aim as a form of neo-pagan "New Age" pantheism, or as a distraction from the business of saving human souls through evangelism – as if a surgeon were to abandon an operation to go and unblock a toilet, as Todd Strandberg somewhat tastelessly puts it.[1] From this perspective, humanity, made in the image of God, is indeed supreme over non-human creation, which does indeed exist to serve human needs (cf. Beisner 1997: 48–49, 53, 117–23). Furthermore, the construal of biblical eschatology among some such fundamentalist groups – with their expectation of an imminent parousia, or a rapture of Christians from the earth – adds further weight to a theology in which sustaining the earth is a pointless, even dangerous preoccupation.

Yet many evangelical (and other) responses to White's thesis specifically, or to the environmental crisis generally, have taken quite the opposite stance, arguing, *contra* White, that the Bible does not support aggressive human dominion over the earth in the interests of serving human needs and desires. Instead, it is argued, the Bible affirms the value of the whole created order and calls humanity to responsible stewardship of the earth (see, e.g., Granberg-Michaelson 1987; Wilkinson 1980: 203–38; Hall 1990 [1982]). Indeed, a focus on stewardship as a biblical image of humanity's role in the world is central to the realignment of major evangelical leaders and bodies behind a more environmentally-conscious vision of Christian responsibility, as expressed, e.g., in An Evangelical Declaration on the Care of Creation (1994; in Berry 2000: 17–22) and the Evangelical Climate Initiative (2006).[2] In many works of ecotheology, whether evangelical or not, the (often implicit) claim is that the Bible, rightly and constructively read, offers a positive vision of creation's value and a clear mandate for environmental concern.

In clear contrast to such an approach is the stance adopted by the Earth Bible Team, as presented in their five-volume Earth Bible series. Norman Habel, main editor of the series, is evidently concerned to confront and to challenge the naïve assumption "that the Bible is environmentally friendly" (Habel 2000: 30). The Earth Bible Team approach the biblical texts with a prior commitment to a clear and explicit set of "ecojustice principles", set out at the beginning of each volume in the series. These are as follows (from Habel 2000: 24):

1. *The principle of intrinsic worth*: The universe, Earth and all its components have intrinsic worth/value.
2. *The principle of interconnectedness*: Earth is a community of interconnected living things that are mutually dependent on each other for life and survival.
3. *The principle of voice*: Earth is a subject capable of raising its voice in celebration and against injustice.
4. *The principle of purpose*: The universe, Earth and all its components, are part of a dynamic cosmic design within which each piece has a place in the overall goal of that design.
5. *The principle of mutual custodianship*: Earth is a balanced and diverse domain where responsible custodians can function as partners, rather than rulers, to sustain a balanced and diverse Earth community.
6. *The principle of resistance*: Earth and its components not only suffer from injustices at the hands of humans, but actively resist them in the struggle for justice.

In effect, these principles form an ethical standard, an ecojustice canon, against which the biblical texts are measured: the key task is to discern whether "the text is consistent, or in conflict, with whichever of the six ecojustice principles may be considered relevant" in any particular case (Earth Bible Team 2002: 2). Where the texts cohere with the principles, they may be fruitfully and positively read; where they do not, exposing and resisting may be more appropriate interpretative strategies.

Critical Evaluation: Towards an Ecological Hermeneutic

Each of these approaches may be subjected to critical evaluation, in the interests of developing a more adequate basis for an ecojustice hermeneutic which is at the same time a form of Christian theological engagement with the Bible.[3] Fundamentalist and evangelical readings can often be criticized for obscuring the extent to which what they present as "biblical teaching" is not simply a repetition of "what the Bible says", despite claims to the contrary, but a particular construal of certain biblical texts, prioritized over other biblical texts, and read in the light of a particular understanding of the reader's contemporary context. The claim that stewardship, for example, constitutes the biblical view of humanity's responsibility towards creation, fails to acknowledge the extent to which this is a doctrinal construction, prioritizing a certain reading of humanity's role in the creation stories (e.g. Gen. 2:15), construing "dominion" to mean stewardly responsibility (Gen. 1:26–28), and generally applying a model of divine and kingly oversight to the human-nature relationship. Furthermore, just as the model of divine/ kingly dominion may be suspected of having its less benevolent side, so the model of stewardship may be more problematic for environmental theology than its proponents appreciate (see Palmer 1992; Bauckham 2000; Southgate 2006). Of course, a particular (and high) view of biblical authority, when combined with a commitment to the need for environmental concern, *requires* a positive construal of the Bible's ecological message: without a cogent case that the Bible supports the environmental commitment, one or other of the convictions must give (cf. Horrell *et al.* 2008: 231–32).

By contrast, the Earth Bible Team's approach is ready both to recover and (crucially) to resist the range of biblical perspectives, depending on their coherence with the ecojustice principles. These principles, we are informed, were worked out "in dialogue with ecologists" and are deliberately not formulated using biblical or theological terms, so as "to facilitate dialogue with biologists, ecologists, other religious traditions … and scientists" (Earth Bible Team 2000: 38). In other words, the Bible is granted no explicit authoritative status in this project – authority effectively lies with the ecojustice principles – nor are the ecojustice principles presented as emerging from the biblical or Christian tradition. The problem here is to see why, in the project as it is presented, what the biblical texts say should matter.[4] It may be interesting to see how some biblical texts, read in a certain way, seem to support some of the ecojustice principles, while other biblical texts do not. But it is the ecojustice principles that set out a set of ethical norms to inspire and instruct human belief and action. Those for whom such ecojustice principles are a compelling vision may find the principles useful, but it is unclear why they should be concerned about whether and where the biblical texts support or contradict the principles, unless they are Christians or Jews with some commitment to the value and status of these texts. On the other hand, for those for whom these texts do carry some authoritative force, it is unclear why the ecojustice principles should acquire the kind of status to stand as the arbiter of scripture. In other words, the Earth Bible Team's approach, which effectively makes a set of contemporary values the court of appeal, the canon, against which biblical texts are tested, fails to show how these contemporary values might emerge (or indeed have emerged) from a (particular) reading of the tradition, and thus, crucially, severely limits its ability to be *persuasive* for those within that tradition. To be potentially persuasive as an attempt to reshape Christian ethics, an ecological reading of the Bible would need to demonstrate that it offers an authentic appropriation of the Christian tradition.

In sum, we might criticize both evangelical environmentalism and the Earth Bible Team – without, let it be stressed, meaning to deny the immensely valuable work that has been produced – with two corresponding points. The former, with its strong commitment to a particular understanding of the Bible's authority, tends to deny or veil the extent to which the work of interpretation is a constructive act, with doctrine and ethics made in the encounter between the (ancient) text and the (modern) reader, whose constructions are shaped by the contemporary reading context. The latter, with its strong and explicit commitment to the ecojustice principles, denies the Bible any explicit role in the construction of doctrine and ethics, and effectively measures the biblical texts against its adopted set of values.

What is needed, at least as a model for engaging the Bible in contemporary Christian theology and ethics, is an approach that falls somewhere between these two alternatives. Just such an approach has been helpfully outlined, specifically in the context of an attempt to develop an ecological hermeneutic, by Ernst Conradie.[5] For Conradie, it is important to appreciate how appropriation of the Bible in Christian theology is shaped by heuristic or doctrinal keys – "justification by faith" in the Lutheran tradition, "liberation" in liberation theology, "stewardship" in some recent ecotheology, and so on (Conradie 2006: 306–09). The crucial point is that these doctrinal constructs "are not directly derived from either the Biblical texts or the contemporary world but are precisely the product of previous attempts to construct a relationship between text, tradition and context". They are *made* in the ongoing encounter between reader and text, and in the attempt to fuse the distant horizons of both. As such, doctrinal keys have a "double function ... They provide a key to unlock the meaning of *both* the contemporary context *and* the Biblical texts and simultaneously enable the interpreter to establish a *link* between text and contemporary context' (Conradie 2006: 306, original emphasis). Just as any key offers a positive new way to construct relevant meaning from the Bible, so also, Conradie insists, it will inevitably "distort" both text and context, perhaps ideologically – that is, in legitimating and concealing the interests of dominant social groups. Doctrinal keys should thus be subject to a hermeneutic of suspicion (Conradie 2006: 308). But precisely by identifying them as doctrinal or hermeneutical keys (or, perhaps better, lenses)[6] – rather than as simply what the text "says" – this critical suspicion is invited.

Such an approach invites an engagement with the biblical texts that is exegetically serious – otherwise it ceases to be a genuine attempt at reading – but which also acknowledges such an engagement to be, inevitably, a constructive and creative act, shaped by the perceived priorities of the contemporary context. To function as a form of constructive Christian theological engagement does not imply that such a reading must avoid any criticism of biblical texts. But it does mean that there will be some positive construction of (a) doctrinal lens(es), formed in the encounter between reader and text, which in turn may serve as a criterion for critical appropriation. Just as Luther found in Paul a message of justification by faith, through grace alone, which then became the hermeneutical and theological heart of the Lutheran tradition, shaping a whole tradition of (critical) biblical interpretation and theological doctrine, so our own context, with its ecological crises and environmental pressures, may inspire new kinds of engagement with the Bible, new readings with new doctrinal lenses at their heart.

In the remainder of this essay, I want to attempt to illustrate one way in which such work might possibly proceed, through an engagement with Pauline theology and ethics, focused on 2 Cor. 5:14–21. Needless to say, the Pauline texts are only one among many possible sites for such interpretative endeavour; but they are important ones, given their central place in the Christian (especially Protestant) theological tradition. This will then lead, finally, to some broader conclusions, outlined in brief, concerning the ways in which a reconfigured Pauline theology might contribute to the development of an ecotheological ethic.

On Becoming the (Eco)Justice of God? A Reading of 2 Cor. 5:14–21

A glance at the abundant ecotheological literature will quickly reveal two favourite Pauline texts: Rom. 8:19–23 and Col. 1:15–20.[7] There is good reason for this selection: in their different ways, these texts provide a basis for the conviction that the whole of creation is bound up in God's redeeming and reconciling purposes; or, to express the point in terms of ecojustice principles (see above), that the whole cosmos has intrinsic worth and purpose. This is an important foundation for an ecotheology, which must confront and reorientate a tradition that has largely focused on the salvation of human beings. These texts provide an important starting point, an initial orientation to certain potential doctrinal lenses. But an ecological hermeneutic must go beyond the citation of favourite proof texts and begin to generate fruitful (re)readings of the wider Pauline (and biblical) tradition.

At this point, we turn to 2 Cor. 5:14–21, a passage which can reasonably be regarded as a rich statement of central themes in Pauline theology: the vicarious death and resurrection of Christ and the participation of believers in these saving events; new life in Christ; reconciliation and righteousness. (Such a claim, of course, already makes clear how lenses quickly come into play: placing this text as central inevitably displaces others from such a role, prioritizing certain Pauline motifs over others. Nonetheless, there are good grounds, both exegetically and theologically, for some such prioritizations, though they should always be subject to critical scrutiny.)

After describing himself and his co-missionaries as controlled (*sunechei*) by the love of Christ, Paul reiterates a central early Christian creed. But instead of repeating the usual formula, that Christ died "for us", or "for our sins" (cf. Rom. 5:8; 1 Cor. 15:3; 1 Thess. 5:10), Paul here chooses to make the point that Christ died "for all" (*hyper pantōn*), and that therefore "all have died". Christ's death is not only, or even primarily, a sacrificial or representative death, but somehow a death in which all have participated (cf. Rom. 6:3–8; 1 Cor. 15:22). It is beyond question that Paul has humanity primarily in view here, and specifically the Corinthians to whom he is writing; his is an inescapably anthropocentric theology, though only in certain senses, as we shall see. Paul has little reason to pursue the question about the extent to which non-human creation might be affected by, or bound up in, the dying and rising of Christ. But there is scope enough in the Pauline texts (Rom. 8:19–23; 1 Cor. 8:6) to encourage the development of his thought in this direction, as is already evident in the cosmic Christology of Colossians.

The implication Paul proceeds to draw from Christ's death *hyper pantōn* is that those who live should live for Christ. In other words, while Paul's theology, his message of justification and reconciliation, is in a sense anthropocentric, focused on human beings, it is more profoundly christocentric or theocentric (cf. e.g., 1 Cor. 3:22–23; 1 Cor. 15:28). Since all have died, any life they now live can only be life in Christ, orientated to Christ and not to the self (cf. Gal. 2:20). The fundamental reorientation entailed in the death of the self is to Christ and, in Christ, to God. But this being in Christ – and conforming to the pattern of Christ's self-giving death (cf. Rom. 15:1–3; 1 Cor. 11:1; Phil. 2:4–8) – also means a fundamental reorientation to the other, and to the needs and interests of the other above the self (cf. Horrell 2005: 204–45). Once again it is beyond question that Paul's other-regarding ethic is focused on human relationships, and specifically relationships *en ekklēsia* – within the Christian community. And some might argue that the primary motivation for environmental action remains properly and inevitably anthropocentric, a matter, first and foremost, of *social* justice: to alleviate the impact of climate change on the most vulnerable poor, and so on (cf. Clifford 2007). But if our ethics are more radically shaped by the (theologically-grounded) "ecojustice" principles of the intrinsic worth and ultimate purpose of all things,[8] then we may want to take the more constructive and creative step to broaden the scope of the community of others not only beyond the church community but also beyond the human community. If Christ's death encompasses "all things" in its reconciling, peace-making act, then the "living for others" which is the ethical implication of dying to self may certainly be argued, logically if not in Paul's own expressions of the notion, to include all things, *ta panta*.

The new perspective on others which is the result (*hōste*) of the reorientation of the self that is now dead-but-alive-in-Christ includes everyone (presumably, though, only humans are explicitly in Paul's purview here), even Christ himself, who is no longer to be known *kata sarka*, "according to the flesh" (v. 16). The corresponding, positive result (*hōste*, again) is new creation in Christ (v. 17). This is a famously elliptical phrase: *ei tis en christō, kainē ktisis*, "if anyone in Christ, new creation". The translator clearly needs to supply verbs, and the choices made often give the individual person the identity of "new creation": "if anyone is in Christ, he is a new creation" (ESV, NIV; cf. Thrall 1994: 427–28). But the ellipsis leaves room for a range of possible interpretations, discussed at length in the history of interpretation (on which see Mell 1989: 9–32; more briefly Hubbard 2002: 1–5). The only other occurrence of the phrase "new creation" (also in Paul) is similarly terse: *oute gar peritomē ti estin oute akrobustia alla kainē ktisis*, "for neither circumcision nor uncircumcision is anything, but new creation" (Gal. 6:15).

The phrase "new creation" occurs only twice in the entire Bible, both times in Paul's letters, though it is generally seen – as with the occurrences in intertestamental Jewish literature (e.g., *Jub* 4:26; *1 En* 72:1) – as originating as a motif in the eschatological hopes of the prophets, especially deutero-Isaiah (see esp. Isa. 43:18–19). This motif is developed in trito-Isaiah into a depiction of the eschatological renewal of creation and specifically the idea of a "new heaven and new earth" (e.g. Isa. 65:17–25; 66:22).

The contrasting interpretative proposals are well illustrated by the two most significant recent studies of this theme. In a wide-ranging study of both the developments in Jewish literature and its use by Paul, Ulrich Mell sees apocalyptic Judaism, notably in Jubilees and also Qumran (11Q Temple 29:9), as the tradition-historical precursors for Paul's use of the phrase *kainē ktisis*, "new creation" (Mell 1989: 172–73). He argues against reading 2 Cor. 5:17 (and Gal. 6:15) as anthropological "conversion" texts and for understanding them as referring to a cosmic eschatological transformation that the Christ-event has wrought.

By contrast, Moyer Hubbard's 2002 monograph argues for a thoroughly anthropological reading of the two texts in Paul, proposing that in each case the focus of Paul's thought is on the Spirit-wrought transformation of the individual believer, their transition from death to life. In identifying relevant Jewish background material, unlike Mell, Hubbard focuses not on the appearance of the precise phrase "new creation" but on the ways the broader idea and imagery is expressed. For Hubbard, the crucial material to compare with Paul is not in apocalyptic texts such as Jubilees – which he sees as a response to the specific dilemma faced by such writers (Hubbard 2002: 26–53) – but in *Joseph and Aseneth*, where new creation imagery (though not the phrase itself) is used to depict the outcome of conversion (2002: 54–76). Particularly important in Hubbard's argument is the attempt to set the two Pauline texts in their context in Paul's letters and thought. This, he maintains, "is the primary context for explicating Paul's new-creation motif" (p. 7). Thus, after examining the death-to-life imagery in Romans 6 and 7, and Paul's focus on the Spirit as the bringer of new life, Hubbard concludes that in 2 Cor. 5:17 "*kainh ktisij* is an anthropological motif relating to the new situation of the individual "in Christ" (2002: 183). A similar conclusion goes for Gal. 6:15.

A thorough comparison and critique of these works would require another lengthy work, and a few comments pertinent to the present task must suffice. It seems to me that Hubbard, with a method that looks at the broader exegetical and background material, makes some strong points in terms of seeing Paul's primary focus as anthropological, specifically on the experience of human beings like himself, who have found themselves taken from death to life. Yet there is a danger of misconstruing Paul when this focus is taken to imply the view that the transformation in view is that of the individual and that Paul's thought is anthropocentric. For a start, one must emphasize, as the "apocalyptic" readers of Paul since Käsemann have done, that the focus of Paul's thought is on the epoch-making action of God in Christ; it is more properly seen as theocentric or Christocentric than anthropocentric. As Mell rightly points out, what Paul sees as the achievement of the Christ-event is the inauguration of a new world, an eschatological transformation (*Umbruch*) (cf. Mell 1989: 365); the *apo tou nun*, "from now on", of 2 Cor. 5:16 is not "conversion terminology" but "eschatological terminology" (p. 366).

Moreover, while Paul's primary focus is undoubtedly on humanity, the background to the term "new creation" in the prophetic and apocalyptic depictions of the renewal of the whole creation strongly suggests that a notion of the Christ-event as having inaugurated a truly *cosmic* transformation may well be in view. Mell has shown this to be exegetically plausible in the two places where Paul uses this motif. It is notable that Paul does not say, in glossing what this new creation implies, that the old person has passed away, to be replaced by a new person. He does not speak here of the "outer person" (*ho exō anthrōpos*) and the "inner person" (2 Cor. 4:16), nor of the "new person" (*ho kainos anthrōpos*; cf. Eph. 4:24). Nor does he speak of the making of one new human, transcending the former division of humanity into Jew and Gentile (Eph. 2:15). Instead, Paul speaks of "the old things" (*ta archaia*) passing away, replaced by "new things" (*kaina*). And this is immediately followed by the assertion "and all things [come] from God" (*ta de panta ek tou theou*), a phrase which recalls similar formulations elsewhere in Paul, where the work of God in creation is in view (1 Cor. 8:6; 11:12). The Christ-event, in Paul's view, not only makes possible the transformation of individual believers but also, and more fundamentally, marks the decisive eschatological interruption which announces the end of the old age and the beginning of the new (cf. 1 Cor. 10:11: *ta telē tōn aiōnōn*).

In these new creation texts, then, Paul's thought is at least open to a construal focused less on the individual's new identity – a focus which may owe more to Western individualism than to Paul, as Krister Stendahl long ago argued (Stendahl 1963) – and more on the sense that what God has achieved in Christ (or is in the process of bringing about) is a cosmic "new creation": anyone who is in Christ belongs to, participates in, this new creation, in which the former distinctions (between Jew and Gentile, etc.) no longer count for anything (cf. Martin 1981: 104; Adams 2000: 227, 235). The Church is the locus where this new creation is (in Paul's view) acknowledged and made visible, but the whole cosmos is equally bound up in the Christ-event, and strains towards its eschatological consummation (Rom. 8:19–23).

To be sure, Paul immediately stresses the implications of this divine creative activity for "us" (*hēmas*), whom God "reconciled to himself through Christ", and to whom God "gave the ministry of reconciliation" (v. 18). This is immediately expanded once again in the parallel reformulation in v. 19 (cf. Thrall 1994: 431) to indicate that it was indeed the whole *kosmos* that God was in Christ "reconciling to himself".[9] Yet once again, it is hard to deny that Paul's primary focus is anthropological – that the primary referent of *kosmos* is, in Reimund Bieringer's words, *die Menschenwelt*, the world of human beings (Bieringer 1987: 318) – given that this reconciliation of the *kosmos* is immediately glossed with the phrase "not counting their trespasses against them" (cf. Adams 2000: 235). There is some scope for developing a broader construal of the extent of sin and thus of God's gracious forgiveness of it, given the depiction in Genesis 6–8 of the spread of corruption to "all flesh" (*kol-basar*), clearly referring to living creatures beyond only the human (Gen. 6:12, 13, 17; 7:21 – note esp. 7:21). Indeed, the covenant made after the flood is emphatically with the whole earth, and every living thing upon it (Gen. 9:9–17). But there would be little indeed to indicate that Paul saw any such wider picture here, though it might find some support in, or at least plausibly cohere with, Rom. 8:20–21, where Paul refers to creation's bondage to decay and subjection to futility (see Hunt *et al.* 2008). The positive insistence that the whole creation is bound up in God's redeeming purposes would then have its correlate in a negative depiction of a corruption that afflicts not only humanity but *ta panta*, "all things" – even if it is hard to make theological sense of this in a scientifically cogent way.[10]

However, the key point in this text is to consider how we might construe the sense of reconciliation (*katallagē/katallassō*), one of the few key expressions of this distinctively Pauline theme.[11] As Howard Marshall notes, there is a two-part structure to the act of reconciliation: the prior act of God in Christ and the appeal for a human response which it is the task of God's ambassadors to announce (Marshall 1978: 122). Typically for Paul, there is a tension here between the indicative of divine achievement and the imperative of human responsibility, just as there is, in the announcement of "new creation", an eschatological tension between the "already" and the "not yet".

Reconciliation-language in the ancient world and the biblical tradition generally concerned the restoration of relationships and the ending of enmity and anger (so, e.g., Marshall 1978: 118–21; Porter 1994: 13; Breytenbach 1989: 82) and is here depicted as specifically concerned with the relationship of people to God. What is most striking and unique in Paul, as both Marshall and Stanley Porter have stressed, is that the picture of reconciliation is one in which the offended party (here God) actively "reconciles" the offender to himself (Marshall 1978: 127–28; Porter 1994: 16, 143). Again, Paul's perspective is theocentric more than anthropocentric. This does not mean, however, that this reconciliation has no other dimensions than the human-divine one. The most obvious of these, though unstated by Paul, ever the astute politician, is that underlying Paul's appeal is a desire to effect and cement the fragile reconciliation between himself and the Corinthian church, previously riven by hostility and suspicion. Being reconciled to God means, at the same time, being reconciled to Paul and his co-workers. While this may certainly be criticized as part of a strategic and concealed use of power on Paul's part (cf. Castelli 1991) it does at least indicate that reconciliation with God and with (certain) others is inseparable. But the ancient parallels also imply that reconciliation was only conceived as involving personal beings. In other words, there is no precedent for the idea that the reconciliation in view here includes the totality of the non-human creation. As elsewhere in our text, then, we have to acknowledge that Paul's primary focus is anthropological rather than cosmic, on *die Menschenwelt* rather than the whole creation. The question, though, is not only one concerning Paul's intentions or focus, but also one about the ways in which his text might plausibly and constructively be read.

It is clear enough that the overcoming of divisions and the creation of unity is, for Paul, one of the key achievements of what God has done in Christ; reconciliation is one important way to express the character of this achievement (cf. Gal. 3:26–28; 1 Cor. 12:12–27; Boyarin 1994; Horrell 2005: 99–132). The ways in which Paul conceives and expresses this vision of unity or oneness reflect the particular contexts and arguments in which he is engaged. A prominent focus in Galatians and Romans, picked up as a *Leitmotif* by the author of Ephesians, is the unity and equality of Jew and Gentile. In 1 Corinthians it is the factional divisions in the church that evoke Paul's appeal that they be united (1:10; cf. Mitchell 1991). For rather obvious reasons – he was hardly faced with the need to respond to a global ecological crisis caused by humanity's exploitation of the planet – Paul did not reflect on this unity as a potentially *cosmic* achievement. But the author of Colossians does, of course, go some way towards developing the motif of reconciliation in a cosmic direction, perhaps in response to a philosophically influenced popular anxiety about the stability and duration of the cosmos (Schweizer 1976: 217–20; cf. Liedke 1979: 158–61). While Paul's own notion of reconciliation is, then, focused on the relationships of humans with God and with one another, the Pauline trajectories already evident in the New Testament indicate the potential for constructive broader development, given new and pressing issues to address.

Finally we must consider v. 21, perhaps the most dense and disputed crux in our passage. Many issues regarding its interpretation must be left aside. Here we find another key Pauline theological phrase: *dikaiosunē theou*, "the righteousness of God". Much ink has been spilt on the topic of justification and righteousness in Paul, not least because of the central place this holds in Protestant theology. Paul's statements about the "justification" of the believer can reasonably be held to express an idea central to his gospel (especially in Romans and Galatians), though how central, and how the idea should be understood, is much more open to debate. The phrase *dikaiosunē theou* adds further complications, since in some places it seems to refer to the saving power of God (Rom. 1:17; 3:21) and elsewhere to the righteousness bestowed by God (note both of these senses together in Rom. 10:3). It is therefore unnecessary to assume or insist that it must always mean precisely the same thing, and here in 2 Cor. 5:21 it seems most likely to mean essentially the state of being justified, or made righteous, with the genitive thus a genitive of origin: "(righteousness) deriving from God", "bestowed by God" (so Thrall 1994: 442–43 with n. 1776; Porter 1994: 143). It remains striking, though, that Paul expresses the "interchange" of Christ and believers in such vivid terms, with Christ "becoming sin for us in order that we might become the righteousness of God in him" (cf. Hooker 1990; *pace* Wright 1993).

It also remains to be considered whether this "becoming the righteousness of God" might have more theological and ethical relevance than would seem to be conveyed in the rather bland interpretation of it as effectively a statement about being justified. We might first note the evident parallel with reconciliation in our passage: being reconciled to God is closely related to becoming the righteousness of God (cf. Marshall 1978: 124–25; Porter 1994: 142–43). That Paul sees the two terms as closely parallel ways to express the relationship established between the Christian community and God is equally apparent from the other important reconciliation text in Paul: Rom. 5:9–10. "Being justified/righteoused by his blood" (5:9) is equivalent to "being reconciled to God through the death of his son" (5:10), both phrases being immediately followed by statements about the promise of future salvation (*sōthēsometha*).[12]

Just as reconciliation implies more than the restoration of friendly relations with God, so too righteousness implies more than the removal of sin and guilt before God. It is also a moral category, describing both the character of God and the expected character of those who share God's righteousness/justice. As such, and typically for Paul, it constitutes both an *is* and an *ought*. Just as God's act of reconciliation – something somehow already achieved – undergirds an appeal to be reconciled, so being righteoused/justified carries with it the obligation to be righteous/just. Paul's ethics, and specifically the relationship between identity and action, have often been encapsulated in the catchphrase "be what you are", an attempt to express the intrinsic relationship between the indicative of God's achievement and the imperative of human responsibility (see further Furnish 1968; Horrell 2005: 10–15). So here, reconciliation and justice encapsulate both divine achievement and human calling.

It is clear enough, as I have stressed throughout, that Paul does not envisage cosmic or ecological dimensions to such moral imperatives, the "oughts" that follow from being reconciled and from becoming the righteousness of God. It would be anachronistic to expect them. Yet if we find sufficient grounds, in both the exegesis of Pauline texts and the demands of our contemporary context, for developing a truly cosmic understanding of the reconciliation and unity of *ta panta* in Christ, then the corresponding ethical imperatives become equally cosmic in their scope. In other words, if new creation in Christ is a cosmic and not merely personal or human transformation, then the responsibilities incumbent on those who respond to the vision are cosmic in scope and not merely interpersonal; they encompass, we might say, not merely social justice, but ecojustice too. Needless to say, Paul gives us little indication of what, in concrete terms, such responsibilities might entail. Indeed, Paul's ethics are generally "underdeveloped" in terms of specific exhortations and duties (cf. Lategan 1990: 320). The prophetic texts from which Paul's new creation language derives might fill out the vision a little further, with their depictions of an eschatological peace that brings an end to enmity among animals and people as well as social justice in the human realm (Isa. 11:1–10; 61:1–11; 65:25; cf. Bauckham 1994). Yet discerning what ethical responsibilities might follow from the conviction that the decisive inauguration of this eschatological vision has already taken place, and doing so in a way which is scientifically cogent, is a difficult task with few unambiguously clear answers. Suggestions as to appropriate actions range, for example, from a commitment to vegetarianism (e.g., Linzey 1994; Webb 2001), to attempts to end the extinction of species (Southgate 2008), perhaps by physically relocating them in view of the impact of climate change (Southgate *et al.* 2008). But the fact that one finds no explicit answers, no proof-texts to detail eco-ethical responsibilities, either in Paul or elsewhere in the Bible, does not make this topic any different from most other issues in contemporary Christian ethics, where the task is precisely to reflect on what commitments and actions, what form of Christian vocation, might appropriately reflect the narrative vision which the Christian is called to share.

Conclusion: Towards an Ecological Reconfiguration of Pauline Theology

It should be clear that in this essay I have not intended to offer a proposal as to "what Paul really said". I am not arguing – crudely put, but in more subtle ways reflecting a stance that underpins a good deal of biblical interpretation – that Paul wanted to work for the reconciliation of the whole of creation so we should too. Rather, I am attempting a constructive exercise in which a rereading of the Pauline tradition is explicitly shaped by the perceived priorities of the contemporary context, yet at the same time draws on and develops potential latent in the Pauline texts.

My main proposal is that God's act of cosmic reconciliation in Christ should stand as a doctrinal lens at the centre of an ecologically reconfigured Pauline theology. Various Pauline texts, especially Rom. 8:19–23 and Col. 1:15–20, provide an exegetical foundation for the conviction that non-human creation is not merely the stage on which the drama of human redemption takes place, but is fully bound up in the process of reconciliation and salvation. 2 Cor. 5:19a – "God was in Christ reconciling the cosmos to himself" – can stand as a concise expression of the heart of this theology. Making such a lens central to an engagement with Paul may help to move the tradition away from a focus on the justification and salvation of human beings and towards a focus on God's reconciliation of the entire created order and the associated human responsibilities to enact – in relation to the whole cosmos – the imperatives of reconciliation and justice.

Other Pauline themes may also be reconfigured around this central notion of cosmic reconciliation. While placing reconciliation centre stage inevitably displaces "justification" from that position, it does not imply that being righteoused is unimportant in an ecologically-orientated Pauline theology. On the contrary, it remains significant both as a depiction of the kind of reconciliation that is in view – the restoration of (covenant) relationship to God – and as an indication of the moral responsibilities entailed for the people of God – embodying the justice of God in the world.

To this extent an ecojustice ethic finds roots in Paul, but requires substantial and constructive development beyond, even against, Paul. Paul's explicit contribution to an ecojustice ethic is severely limited by his focus on relationships *en ekklēsia* and his generally anthropocentric sphere of concern. Nonetheless, if God's act of reconciliation in Christ is deemed to be cosmic in scope, then it seems reasonable to take the constructive step to develop the ethical motif of other-regard in relation not only to all people, but also to "all things". But what this might mean, in concrete ethical terms, in the context of current ecological issues and global climate change, remains unspecified and – crucially – requires contemporary theological and ethical work, in careful and attentive dialogue with science. In saying this I mean to reject the claim in some quarters that to have done exegesis is effectively to have done systematic theology and Christian ethics (cf., e.g., Grudem 1994: 21, 26, 127–35). Paul may help to resource our efforts to reconfigure our vision of the world around us, and to ground a revised theology which (re)integrates humanity into solidarity with the whole community of creation – crucial tasks indeed – but neither he nor any of the biblical writers can give us substantive answers to the question as to what, in concrete terms, we then should do.

Notes

* This essay is an output from a project on "Uses of the Bible in Environmental Ethics", funded by the Arts and Humanities Research Council (Grant No. AH D001188/1; see http://humanities.exeter.ac.uk/theology/research/projects/uses/). I would like to thank the AHRC for their support, the members of the project team for the ways in which our shared work has shaped my thinking as expressed here, and participants in the Sheffield conference for their comments and suggestions on the paper as presented there. I am especially grateful to Cherryl

Hunt and Christopher Southgate for our collaborative work, cited below, which significantly informs this essay.

1. See Strandberg (n.d.). Examples of this kind of response to environmentalism are found in Cumbey (1983, 1985) and Hunt (1983).
2. Cf. also http://www.cornwallalliance.org/articles/read/the-cornwall-declaration-on-environmental-stewardship/ (accessed 15 September 2008).
3. For a fuller survey and critical evaluation of different approaches to using the Bible in ecotheology and environmental ethics, see Horrell *et al.* (2008).
4. Francis Watson, interestingly, traces this type of modern approach back to Kant's attempt, in *Religion within the Limits of Reason Alone* (1793), to offer an account of how the truths embodied in biblical and Christian doctrine can be independently discerned by "reason". Watson comments: "Kant's work is the forerunner of all more recent attempts to interpret scripture on the basis of an ethical-political criterion that is already known independently of the texts. Scripture can only say what the criterion allows it to say [Or, we might add, is criticized and resisted where it does not say this], and what it is allowed to say is only what we can already say to ourselves even without scripture. The textual embodiment of the criterion is of only limited usefulness, for the particularity of biblical narrative is an imperfect and potentially misleading vehicle for the universal truths of reason or for the various contemporary projects of liberation" (Watson 2008: 18–19).
5. See Conradie (2004, 2006). This paragraph also draws on our more detailed articulation of this approach in Horrell *et al.* (2008: 233–38).
6. Cf. Horrell *et al.* (2008: 235). Lenses shape the encounter between reader and text, bringing certain themes into clear and central focus, blurring, distorting, or marginalizing others.
7. For a treatment of Rom. 8:19–23, see Hunt *et al.* (forthcoming). Colossians 1:15–20 will be treated in a forthcoming collaborative work.
8. These two principles can, for example, be grounded in the notion that all creation is called to praise God (Ps. 148, etc.), and finds its *telos* in fulfilment of this calling; see Horrell and Coad (forthcoming).
9. On the various possible construals of the crucial phrase in v. 19a, see Bieringer (1987).
10. In what way, for example, could one consider animals "fallen", not to mention inanimate things? Michael Lloyd's (1998) argument that evil in the natural world – which he takes to include the "evil" of predation – "is the result of the distortion of creation brought about by the angelic Fall" (1998: 160), illustrates the difficulties, since taking Darwin seriously (as Lloyd does, see p. 156) makes it impossible to accept that animals ever existed in some pre-Fall herbivorous paradise, even if a pre-human Fall can be conceptualized, albeit speculatively. On the wider issues involved here, see Southgate (2008).
11. Both noun and verb appear only in the Pauline letters in the NT, and are heavily concentrated here in 2 Corinthians 5: *katallagē* (Rom. 5:11; 11:15; 2 Cor. 5:18–19); *katallassō* (Rom. 5:10 (*bis*); 1 Cor. 7:11; 2 Cor. 5:18, 19, 20).
12. Breytenbach 1989 argues strongly, and importantly, that reconciliation language (*katallassein ktl.*) does not stand in a close relationship to atonement language (*hilakesthai ktl.*). The two are not related in Paul, who does not use the two terminological groups in the same contexts (pp. 99, 220, etc.). Nonetheless, Paul clearly does, Breytenbach stresses, connect reconciliation with the death of Christ:

*"Paulus interpretiert die Versöhnungsvorstellung so, daß Versöhnung durch
den stellvertretenden Sühnetod Christi ermöglicht wird"* (p. 221, italics original;
see further pp. 193–215, 222–24).

Bibliography

Adams, E. 2000. *Constructing the World: A Study in Paul's Cosmological Language.*
SNTW; Edinburgh: T. & T. Clark.

Bauckham, R. J. 1994. "Jesus and the Wild Animals (Mark 1:13): A Christological
Image for an Ecological Age." In *Jesus of Nazareth: Lord and Christ. Essays on the
Historical Jesus and New Testament Christology,* eds J. B. Green and M. Turner,
3–21. Grand Rapids, MI/Carlisle: Eerdmans/Paternoster.

_____ 2000. "Stewardship and Relationship." In *The Care of Creation,* ed. R. J. Berry,
99–106. Leicester: IVP.

Beisner, E. C. 1997. *Where Garden Meets Wilderness: Evangelical Entry into the
Environmental Debate.* Grand Rapids, MI: Acton Institute for the Study of Religion
and Liberty/Eerdmans.

Berry, R. J. (ed.). 2000. *The Care of Creation,* Leicester: IVP.

Bieringer, R. 1987. "2 Kor 5,19a und die Versöhnung der Welt." *Ephemerides Theologicae
Lovanienses* 63(4): 295–326.

Boyarin, D. 1994. *A Radical Jew: Paul and the Politics of Identity.* Berkeley. CA:
University of California Press.

Breytenbach, C. 1989. *Versöhnung: Eine Studie zur paulinischen Soteriologie.* WMANT
60; Neukirchen-Vluyn: Neukirchener.

Castelli, E. A. 1991. *Imitating Paul: A Discourse of Power.* Louisville, KY: Westminster
John Knox.

Clifford, P. 2007. *"All Creation Groaning": A Theological Approach to Climate Change
and Development.* London: Christian Aid.

Conradie, E. M. 2004. "Towards an Ecological Biblical Hermeneutics: A Review Essay
on the Earth Bible Project." *Scriptura* 85: 123–35.

_____ 2006. "The Road Towards an Ecological Biblical and Theological Hermeneutics."
Scriptura 93: 305–14.

Cumbey, C. E. 1983. *The Hidden Dangers of the Rainbow: The New Age Movement
and Our Coming Age of Barbarism.* Shreveport, LA: Huntington House.

_____ 1985. *A Planned Deception: The Staging of a New Age "Messiah".* East Detroit,
MI: Pointe Publishers.

Earth Bible Team. 2000. "Guiding Ecojustice Principles." In *Readings from the Perspective
of Earth,* ed. Norman C. Habel, 38–53. Sheffield: Sheffield Academic Press.

_____ 2002, "Ecojustice Hermeneutics: Reflections and Challenges." In *The Earth Story
in the New Testament,* eds Norman C. Habel and Vicky Balabanski, 1–14. Sheffield:
Sheffield Academic Press.

Evangelical Climate Initiative. 2006. http://christiansandclimate.org/learn/call-to-action/
(accessed 15 Sept 2008).

Furnish, V. P. 1968. *Theology and Ethics in Paul.* Nashville, TN: Abingdon.

Granberg-Michaelson, W. (ed.). 1987. *Tending the Garden.* Grand Rapids, MI:
Eerdmans.

Grudem, W. 1994. *Systematic Theology: An Introduction to Biblical Doctrine.* Leicester:
IVP.

Habel, N. C. 2000a. "Introducing the Earth Bible." In *Readings from the Perspective of Earth*, ed. Norman C. Habel, 25–37. Sheffield: Sheffield Academic Press.

_____ 2000b. *Readings from the Perspective of Earth*. The Earth Bible 1. Sheffield: Sheffield Academic Press.

Hall, D. J. 1990. *The Steward: A Biblical Symbol Come of Age*. Garden Rapids, MI/New York: Eerdmans/Friendship Press.

Hooker, M. D. 1990. *From Adam to Christ: Essays on Paul*. Cambridge: Cambridge University Press.

Horrell, D. G. 2005. *Solidarity and Difference: A Contemporary Reading of Paul's Ethics*. London and New York T & T Clark.

_____ Forthcoming. "'The Stones Would Cry Out' (Luke 19:40): A Lukan Contribution to a Hermeneutics of Creation's Praise." *Scottish Journal of Theology*.

Horrell, D. G., C. Hunt and C. Southgate. 2008. "Appeals to the Bible in Ecotheology and Environmental Ethics: A Typology of Hermeneutical Stances." *Studies in Christian Ethics* 21: 219–238.

Hubbard, M. V. 2002. *New Creation in Paul's Letters and Thought*. SNTSMS 119; Cambridge: Cambridge University Press.

Hunt, C., D. G. Horrell and C. Southgate. 2008. "An Environmental Mantra? Ecological Interest in Romans 8:19-23 and a Modest Proposal for its Narrative Interpretation." *Journal of Theological Studies* 59: 546–79.

Hunt, D. 1983. *Peace Prosperity and the Coming Holocaust: The New Age Movement in Prophecy*. Eugene, OR: Harvest House.

Lategan, B. C. 1990. "Is Paul Developing a Specifically Christian Ethic in Galatians?" In *Greeks, Romans, and Christians: Essays in Honor of Abraham J. Malherbe*, eds D. L. Balch, E. Fergusson and W. A. Meeks, 318–28. Minneapolis, MN: Fortress.

Liedke, G. 1979. *Im Bauch des Fisches: Ökologische Theologie*. Stuttgart and Berlin: Kreuz.

Linzey, A. 1994. *Animal Theology*. London: SCM.

Lloyd, M. 1998. "Are Animals Fallen?" In *Animals on the Agenda*, eds Andrew Linzey and Dorothy Yamamoto, 147–60. London: SCM.

Marshall, I. H. 1978. "The Meaning of 'Reconciliation.'" In *Unity and Diversity in New Testament Theology: Essays in Honor of George E. Ladd*, ed. Robert A. Guelich, 117–132. Grand Rapids, MI: Eerdmans.

Martin, R. P. 1981. *Reconciliation: A Study of Paul's Theology*. Atlanta, GA: John Knox Press.

Mell, Ulrich. 1989. *Neue Schöpfung: Eine traditionsgeschichtliche und exegetische Studie zu einem soteriologischen Grundsatz paulinischer Theologie*. BZNW 56; Berlin/New York: Walter de Gruyter.

Mitchell, M. M. 1991. *Paul and the Rhetoric of Reconciliation*. Louisville, KY: Westminster/John Knox.

Palmer, C. 1992. "Stewardship: A Case Study in Environmental Ethics." In *The Earth Beneath: A Critical Guide to Green Theology*, eds I. Ball, M. Goodall, C. Palmer and J. Reader, 67–86. London: SPCK.

Porter, S. E. 1994. *Καταλλάσσω in Ancient Greek Literature, with Reference to the Pauline Writings*. Cordoba: Ediciones El Almendro.

Schweizer, E.1976. *Der Brief an die Kolosser*. EKKNT; Zürich/Neukirchen-Vluyn: Benziger/Neukirchener.

Southgate, C. 2006. "Stewardship and its competitors: a spectrum of relationships between humans and the non-human creation." In *Environmental Stewardship: Critical Perspectives, Past and Present*, ed. R. J. Berry, 185–95. London/New York: T. & T. Clark.

_____ 2008. *The Groaning of Creation: God, Evolution, and the Problem of Evil.* Louisville, KY: Westminster John Knox.

Southgate C., C. Hunt and D. G. Horrell. 2008. "Ascesis and Assisted Migration: Responses to the Effects of Climate Change on Animal Species." *European Journal of Science and Theology* 4 (2): 99–111.

Stendahl, K. 1963. "The Apostle Paul and the Introspective Conscience of the West." *Harvard Theological Review* 56: 199–215 repr in *idem, Paul Among Jews and Gentiles*, 78–96 (London: SCM, 1977).

Strandberg, T. (n.d.). "Bible Prophecy and Environmentalism", http://www. raptureready.com/rr-environmental.html (accessed 15 September 2008).

Thrall, M. E. 1994. *A Critical and Exegetical Commentary on the Second Epistle to the Corinthians*, Vol. 1. ICC; Edinburgh: T. & T. Clark.

Watson, F. 2008. "Hermeneutics and the Doctrine of Scripture: Why They Need Each Other." Conference paper, forthcoming.

Webb, S. H. 2001. *Good Eating.* Grand Rapids, MI: Brazos/Baker.

White, L., Jr. 1967. "The Historical Roots of our Ecologic Crisis." *Science* 155: 1203–207.

Wilkinson, L. (ed.). 1980. *Earthkeeping: Christian Stewardship of Natural Resources.* Grand Rapids, MI: Eerdmans.

Wright, N. T. 1993. "On Becoming the Righteousness of God: 2 Corinthians 5:21." In *Pauline Theology. Volume II: 1 & 2 Corinthians*, ed. D. M. Hay, 200–08, Minneapolis, MN: Fortress.

CAN THE BOOK OF REVELATION BE A GOSPEL FOR THE ENVIRONMENT?

Simon P. Woodman[a]

Introduction: From Genesis to Revelation

This paper could be said to find its "G/genesis" in a process of reflection on the nature of the "dominion" over the earth which is granted to humanity in Gen. 1:26–28, coupled with my own personal engagement with the topic of global warming and its attendant environmental devastation; see (Woodman 2008: 209–12). For some time I found myself obsessed, even depressed, as I sought to understand the emotions I experienced whenever I contemplated this troubling reality. I asked why it should be that I was responding with such uncharacteristic intensity, and initially I wondered if it was as simple as being afraid of dying, but concluded that this was unlikely, as one who rides a sports motorbike can never be entirely risk-averse. Neither was it a fear about the end of the world, as growing up in the shadow of the cold war had adjusted me to that terror at an early age; for a fascinating analysis of this fear from a North American perspective see (Mojtabai 1997). Eventually I had a moment of what might be called "R/revelation". I realized that I had fallen in love with Babylon, and that I was standing alongside the merchants and seafarers of Rev. 18:9–19, weeping for the loss of my beloved empire.

For many readers, the "gospel", or *good news* of the book of Revelation involves inevitable environmental destruction. The apocalyptic message

[a] Simon Woodman is a Baptist Minister. He is Tutor in Biblical Studies at South Wales Baptist College, Cardiff, and a lecturer at Cardiff University. His SCM Core Text on The Book of Revelation was published in 2008, and he has recently co-edited a volume on Baptist Hermeneutics to be published by Mercer University Press in 2011.

of hope is perceived as a message of rescue, with the elect transported from a disintegrating creation into an eternity of bliss within a re-created and perfected environment. Those who take such views tend towards a pessimistic outlook on the earth's future, equating visions of destruction drawn from the Apocalypse with destructive events either already occurring within their own context, or imminently anticipated. For example, the former American president Ronald Reagan, speaking about the global-political events of the early 1980s, commented:

> You know, I turn back to your ancient prophecies ... and the signs foretelling Armageddon and I find myself wondering if we're the generation that is going to see that come about. I don't know if you've noted any of those prophecies lately, but, believe me, they certainly describe the times we're going through. (Mojtabai 1997: 152)

In a similar vein James G. Watt, US Secretary of the Interior 1981–83, commented "I do not know how many future generations we can count on before the Lord returns" (Boyer 1992: 141). For further analysis of this approach see the chapter "Apocalyptic Politics in the New Christian Right" (O'Leary 1994: 172–93). It is salutary to note that there have been those in almost every age who have sought to equate the imagery of Revelation with events in their own times; for example there were seventeenth-century British Baptists who identified the Cromwellian protectorate as the millennial reign (Woodman 2009).

The mid-twentieth-century fear of impending nuclear holocaust readily lent itself to such interpretative measures, with an anticipated World War III equated with the battle of Harmagedon (cf. Rev. 16:16) and the subsequent end of the world (Kovacs and Rowland 2004: 175). Hal Lindsey, in a book which reportedly sold over forty million copies in the three decades following its publication (Howard-Brook and Gwyther 2001: 3), makes this correlation with astonishing confidence:

> It is extremely important to note the accuracy of the Bible prophecy in relation to this last conflict ... Imagine, cities like London, Paris, Tokyo, New York, Los Angeles, Chicago – obliterated! John ... predicts that entire islands and mountains would be blown off the map. It seems to indicate an all-out attack of ballistic missiles upon the great metropolitan areas of the world. (Lindsey and Carlson 1970: 153, 155)

In support of this message of impending nuclear environmental destruction, Lindsey marshals the prophet Isaiah, interspersing biblical quotations with his own commentary:

> Isaiah predicts in chapter 24 concerning this time: "Behold, the Lord will lay
> waste the earth and make it desolate, and he will twist the surface and scatter
> its inhabitants." "The earth lies polluted under its inhabitants." (Perhaps this
> refers in part to water and air pollution.) "Therefore, a curse devours the
> earth, and its inhabitants suffer for their guilt; therefore the inhabitants of
> the earth are scorched [burned], and few men are left" (verses 1, 5, 6). In the
> same chapter Isaiah says: "The earth is utterly broken, the earth is rent
> asunder, the earth is violently shaken. The earth staggers like a drunken
> man, it sways like a hut ..." (verses 19, 20). All of these verses seem to indicate
> the unleashing of incredible weapons the world over. (Lindsey and Carlson
> 1970: 155)

Lindsey then concludes with a bleak prediction of environmental
catastrophe, mitigated only by the return of Christ. He challenges those
reading his book to prepare themselves spiritually to meet the messiah:

> As the battle of Armageddon reaches its awful climax and it appears that all
> life will be destroyed on earth – in this very moment Jesus Christ will return
> and save man from self-extinction. As history races toward this moment, are
> you afraid or looking with hope for deliverance? The answer should reveal to
> you your spiritual condition. One way or another, history continues in a
> certain acceleration toward the return of Christ. Are you ready? (Lindsey and
> Carlson 1970: 157)

Writing to those living under the shadow of nuclear holocaust, Lindsey
offered a message of hope. Instead of fearing the destruction of the earth, or
working to avoid it, his readers were encouraged to welcome such a
catastrophe as part of God's plan for the judgement of the wicked and the
salvation of the elect. As long as their spiritual status was such that they
were ready for Christ's return, they had nothing to fear if the world
disintegrated around them; they would be delivered from the disaster and
given a new earth on which to live out eternity. In this way the future of
humanity is seen as resting with the church, who function as a righteous
remnant, emerging from environmental catastrophe to re-establish
humanity in a purified creation.

Lindsey's approach has clear echoes of the story of Noah emerging from
the ark to repopulate a purified earth (cf. Gen. 8:15–22), and also of the
Old Testament theme of a "remnant" from Israel surviving the Assyrian
and Babylonian assaults to re-establish the people of God in the land (cf.
Isa. 6:13; 10:20–23; Jer. 23:3). This motif of destruction followed by a fresh
start becomes paradigmatic for Lindsey's concept of the annihilation of the
earth followed by the creation of a "new heaven and new earth" (Rev. 21:1)
as the eternal destination of the righteous.

The ending of the cold war and the consequent receding threat of global nuclear annihilation, coupled with the increasing public awareness of a likely impending ecological catastrophe, has meant that such "catastrophic" interpretations have readily transferred themselves over to the disaster scenarios associated with global warming. As Tina Pippin has observed:

> In fundamentalist interpretations of the Apocalypse in the United States believers are told not to worry about or be responsible for the possible human ending of the world through nuclear accident or environmental pollution. The Rapture will occur first and all the believers will be taken up into the clouds with Jesus and will not suffer the tribulation on earth. (Pippin 1999: 98)

Robert Thurman similarly comments:

> In America the very dominant Protestant (fundamentalist) interpretation ... promotes an overwhelmingly anti-natural message, in which the text of Revelation is used to justify the destruction of the environment, because it is seen as a book of judgment. (Thurman and McCleary 1997: 191). See also Guyatt (2007: 127–55) and Palmer (1992: 177–84).

The doctrine of the "rapture" to which Pippin refers lies at the heart of the popular view that the followers of Jesus will be spared the experience of earthly "tribulation" by being removed to heaven, leaving the rest of humanity behind to face judgement along with creation. Whilst this doctrine is primarily drawn from biblical passages beyond Revelation (cf. Mt. 24:40–42; Jn. 14:2–3; Phil. 3:20–21; 1 Cor. 15:49–55; 1 Thess. 4:15–17; 2 Thess. 2:1–7), it nonetheless informs the premillennial dispensationalist interpretation of Revelation found in the recent and bestselling series of fictional *Left Behind* novels by Tim LaHaye and Jerry Jenkins (pub. 1995–), in which faithful Christians are removed from the earth before the sequences of judgement from Revelation begin. For a critical analysis of these novels see (Hertzler 2000). The environmental quietism, or even fatalism, which this position attracts is an outworking of the belief that human sin has put creation on a downward spiral towards destruction, and that the answer to this problem lies in the maintenance of moral and spiritual purity on the part of the elect until the time arrives for departing the doomed earth and journeying with Christ to the new earth (cf. 2 Pet. 3:10–14). Harry Maier comments on the importance of engaging this theology from an environmental perspective:

> If premillennialism continues to fascinate and enthral the consumers of Western popular culture and their leaders, then it is a matter of great urgency to return that reading with a critical evaluation that seconds Earth's voices of

resistance to its inevitable destruction. This is all the more urgent if ... one place where that voice of resistance is loudest is in the Apocalypse itself ... The need to second Earth's voices of resistance becomes all the more pressing once it is recognized that premillennialist dispensationalism arises out of and expresses the economics and politics that makes the majority of the Earth's inhabitants slaves to greed and Earth-destroying ambition. (Maier 2002: 171–72)

Images of Environmental Judgement
The scenes of environmental destruction found in the Apocalypse form part of the broader picture of John's representation of divine judgement on evil. The various images of judgement which John utilizes serve a double purpose: on the one hand, they demonstrate that evil in all its forms will not be allowed to continue into eternity (cf. 19:20; 20:10, 14), while on the other hand they serve as warnings intended to provoke repentance on the part of the nations of the earth (cf. 9:20–21; 11:13; 16:9–11).

The images of final judgement on evil offer John's audience an assurance that, however powerful the forces currently opposing their faithful witness, these satanic systems will ultimately be called to account for their opposition to God's in-breaking kingdom. However, it is in the depictions of judgement as a warning intended to provoke repentance that John depicts the desolation of the created order along with humanity itself. Environmental damage and human suffering are presented as inseparable partners. In the sequences of seals, trumpets and bowls, John depicts scenes of environmental devastation with increasing intensity. The opening of the sixth seal triggers the shaking of the entire cosmos, with a great earthquake, the darkening of sun and moon, stars falling to the earth, the sky being rolled away, and every mountain and island being displaced (Rev. 6:12–14). The sounding of the trumpets leads to the burning away of a third of the earth, trees, and all green grass, the death of a third of all sea creatures, the poisoning of the earth's waters, and the darkening of a third of the sun, moon and stars (Rev. 8:7–12). The pouring out of the bowls triggers the death of every living thing in the sea, the poisoning of all waters, burning from an intensified sun, and a time of darkness (Rev. 16:2–12). Richard Woods suggests that "the Seven Bowls of Wrath comprise, in effect, a powerful ecological parable for the twenty-first century" (Woods 2008: 65), and evocatively suggests that the seven bowl plagues might more accurately be called "the Seven Wounds of Creation" (Woods 2008: 67). These visions of environmental destruction are interspersed with scenes of judgement on humanity, with the entire created order depicted as suffering the effects of humanity's rejection of God.

John's intent in constructing these images of warning judgement, encompassing the entire creation in their scope, was to provide his audience with an alternative perspective on their current earthly situation. From the perspective of those in the seven cities of Asia Minor to whom John was writing, the unbridled expansion of the Graeco-Roman cultural, economic and military empire could appear a noble and beneficent project. However, when viewed through John's visionary lens, the imperial machine is seen as a corrupting whore and a violent beast demeaning or destroying all who come into contact with it (Rev. 13, 17, 18) (Bauckham 1993: 17–18, 35–36). The series of judgements on the earth thus represent John's vision of the inevitable end-result of the human obsession with empire. Whether it be the death of a third of humankind through war (Rev. 9:15, 18), or environmental devastation on a global scale, these are to be seen as the direct consequences of human imperial aspiration.

In his subversive portrayal of empire as a violent and destructive system, John provides a powerful critique of all such systems that seek to centralize wealth and privilege at the expense of exploitation at the margins. The environmentally exploitative effects of empire were well attested in John's time, for example the Levitical perspective on the Babylonian exile was that it allowed the land its overdue "Sabbath" which had been denied it under the pre-exilic Jewish empire (Lev. 26:34–35, 42). Abimelech son of Gideon sowed the ground at Shechem with salt, making it useless for growing crops and so underlining the totality of his conquest over the people who lived there (Judg. 9:45). In John's own time, the Syrian Elephant was hunted to near-extinction to supply the trade in carved ivory (Bauckham 2005: 99), while the Roman system of *latifundia* farming pressurized land into non-productivity through intensive farming, as well as forcing peasant farmers to the brink of starvation (Howard-Brook and Gwyther 2001: 98, 248). This situation was so severe that Pliny the Elder (23–79 CE) commented on these large-scale farms: "[W]e must confess the truth, it is the wide-spread domains [*latifundia*] that have been the ruin of Italy, and soon will be that of the provinces as well. Six proprietors were in possession of one half of Africa, at the period when the Emperor Nero had them put to death" (*Natural History* 18.7.35; Bostock and Riley 1856: 14–15). In a contemporary parallel, consider the following by George Monbiot:

> It doesn't get madder than this. Swaziland is in the grip of a famine and receiving emergency food aid. Forty per cent of its people are facing acute food shortages. So what has the government decided to export? Biofuel made from one of its staple crops, cassava. The government has allocated several

thousand hectares of farmland to ethanol production in the county of Lavumisa, which happens to be the place worst hit by drought. It would surely be quicker and more humane to refine the Swazi people and put them in our [fuel] tanks. (Published in *The Guardian* newspaper on 6 November 2007 and retrieved from http://www.monbiot.com/archives/2007/11/06/an-agricultural-crime-against-humanity/. Accessed 22.1.10)

Pablo Richard, in his liberationist reading of Revelation, interprets John's plagues of judgement for his own time:

These [plagues] are not natural disasters [such as] (earthquakes, volcanic explosions, floods, droughts, cyclones, hurricanes, plagues), since such disasters fall not on the empire and its partisans but basically on the poor. Cosmic agonies of this kind ... [are] rather direct consequences of the structure of domination and oppression: the poor die in floods because they are pushed out of safe places and forced to live alongside rivers; in earthquakes and hurricanes the poor lose their flimsy houses because they are poor and cannot build better ones; plagues, such as cholera and tuberculosis, fall primarily on the poor who are malnourished, uneducated, and lacking in sanitation infrastructure. Hence the plagues of the trumpets and bowls in Revelation refer not to "natural" disasters, but to the agonies of history that the empire itself causes and suffers; they are the agonies of the beast caused by its very idolatry and lawlessness. Today the plagues of Revelation are rather the disastrous results of ecological destruction, the arms race, irrational consumerism, the idolatrous logic of the market, and the irrational use of technology and of natural resources. (Richard 1995: 86)

The Call to Repentance

Simply portraying the effects of empire through images of suffering and destruction is, however, not sufficient for John. He also offers a theological commentary on the globally catastrophic results of empire, lamenting that those who have experienced the judgements still "did not repent" (Rev. 9:20, 21; 16:9, 11). Within John's scheme, the judgements are not personally targeted punishments aimed at those who have denied the lordship of Christ, neither are they God punishing the earth for its opposition to the kingdom of Christ. Rather, they are presented as warnings to the nations of the effects of their ongoing investment in empire, in the hope that the nations of the earth will "repent" and turn from their exploitative and destructive practices. As Woods notes, the plagues of judgement

are primarily meant to move people to repentance, not to harm them or Creation ... [they] are profoundly and prophetically apt as a metaphorical catalogue of the disasters humankind brings upon itself and the planet through greed, oppression, cruelty, exploitation, and indifference to the suffering of the innocent. (Woods 2008: 68, 69)

The tragedy of John's presentation is that the nations remain unrepentant in the face of the warning judgements. He portrays the imperial aspirations of the nations as so all-pervasive that, even when faced with increasing levels of human and environmental catastrophe, still they remain committed to the exploitative practices of empire. In this way, kings, merchants and seafarers are heard mourning the destruction of Babylon, because they have so invested themselves in the economic systems of empire that they are unable to comprehend its ending as anything other than disaster (Rev. 18:9–19). This is in contrast to the response which John expects of those who have entered with him into his visionary world to gain heaven's perspective on empire. They are invited to, "Rejoice over her, O heaven, you saints and apostles and prophets! For God has given judgment for you against her" (Rev. 18:20).

If the nations fail to heed the warnings, John offers a bleak assessment of the future of the empire in which they are investing themselves. It is portrayed as an ultimately self-destructive system, which begets violence, suffering and environmental catastrophe. Against this background John offers his theological assertion that systems of oppression and destruction will themselves ultimately face judgement, something which he vividly depicts in the vision of the destruction of the great whore and the great city (Revelation 17–18). As Ian Boxall comments: "Evil and injustice bear within themselves the seeds of their own destruction, and ultimately the whole edifice will come tumbling down" (Boxall 2006: 249).

The Extent of Environmental Judgement

One could be forgiven for thinking at this point that, from an environmental perspective, all is lost. After all, if the nations remain unrepentant in the face of the increasingly severe and catastrophic results of their actions, surely the end result will be the breakdown of the entire created order. However, John does not leave his audience with a scenario of ecological despair. From John's perspective, God has not yet written creation off as irredeemably tainted by human sin and therefore destined for destruction.

The judgements against the environment which John describes are not total, and it is ultimately Babylon, the satanic empire, which is destroyed rather than the earth. As Barbara Rossing coments: "The strong sense of eschatology in Revelation promises that Rome will not last forever. The book is not so much about the end of the world as about the end of Rome" (Rossing 2002: 189). In this way, the results of imperial ecological devastation are seen to be limited rather than limitless: The four angels who have power to damage earth and sea are restrained from harming the sea and the trees (Rev. 7:3); at the sounding of the trumpets it is only a *third* of the earth which is destroyed (Rev. 8:7–12; 9:15–18); and the locusts from the bottomless pit are told not to damage the grass or any green growth or any tree (Rev. 9:4).

The warning judgements of environmental destruction which John describes are thus severe, but restricted. Rather than depicting a downward spiral resulting in the end of the world, John rather presents the effects of imperial ecological violence as warnings to be heard alongside his repeated call for "repentance" (cf. Rev. 2:5, 16, 21–22; 3:3, 19). John's scheme thus finds clear echoes in the contemporary prophetic call for imperial environmental "repentance", that "there is still time to avoid the worst impacts of climate change if we act now". Sir Nicholas Stern, author of the Stern Report into climate change.[1]

The End of Environmental Exploitation

The hope which John presents is not restricted to mere divine limitation of the extent of environmental damage. Rather, John points to divine judgement on those very systems that oppress and destroy creation. Following the seventh trumpet, the 24 elders sing that the time has come, "for destroying those who destroy the earth" (Rev. 11:18). The destruction of Babylon represents, for John, the final and fitting judgement on empire. As Boxall perceptively notes: "The apocalyptic imagery of destruction and cosmic collapse is shown ... as a challenge to all that would itself destroy the creation, all that keeps it out of kilter and removed from its divinely ordained destiny" (Boxall 2006: 171). Those systems which have placed themselves in opposition to the peace and stability of creation are, it seems, not eternal. Richard Bauckham underlines this point, commenting that "[t]he coming of God's rule on earth will not only liberate people from evil, but will liberate the earth from those who are destroying it" (Bauckham 2008: 63).

John also presents a positive role for creation. As a counterpart to his negative vision of the destruction of the ecologically destructive empire, John evokes the Noahic covenant, recalling God's promise to remain faithful to creation in his description of the rainbow around the divine throne (Rev. 4:3; cf. Ezek. 1:28; Gen. 9:13–16) (cf. Boxall 2006: 84). The earth itself is seen playing an active part in the rescue of humanity from the attack of the satanic beast, swallowing the river sent from the mouth of the dragon (Rev. 12:15; cf. Bredin 2008: 78), while the whole of creation participates in the offering of worship to the one seated on the divine throne (Rev. 5:13; cf. Phil. 2:10). Due to the telescopic nature of Revelation, Rev. 5:13 is actually a proleptic vision of the worship offered in the new Jerusalem (cf. Page 2006: 99; Woodman 2008: 43, 46). In her discussion on the "heroic action" of the earth in Revelation 12 Rossing suggests that:

> In the lament of Rev. 12:12 God gives voice to the Earth ... lamenting Rome's unjust domination over the whole Earth as a manifestation of Satan's presence ... Earth's heroic swallowing of the dragon's river in Rev. 12:16 is an action that models ... the principle of resistance. (Rossing 2002: 181)

The swallowing of the river by the earth is thus interpreted as an act of "resistance against Roman conquest" (Rossing 2002: 190).

The four living creatures before the heavenly throne (Rev. 4:6ff) depict the created order offering a united song of worship before the throne. It is significant that only one of the four living creatures has a human face (Rev. 4:7), indicating that the worship offered by those on the earth is merely one facet of the totality of worship offered to God by the whole of creation. As Bauckham comments:

> If creation needs priests, here they are in heaven, the central worshippers in creation, worshipping continuously in the immediate presence of God and doing so representatively, offering all creation's worship until the time when all creation will perfectly and fully follow them in their worship. (Bauckham 2005: 101–02).

Given the anthropocentric propensity of many biblical environmental readings, reinforced by the divine injunction for humans to have "dominion" in Gen. 1:26, the image of the four living creatures provides a useful corrective. As Bauckham further notes:

> The vision in chapters 4–5 is ... thoroughly theocentric, centred on the throne of God who made all things and for whose glory all things exist ... This theocentric and non-anthropocentric view of creation is even more apparent in the living creatures considered as the representatives of the animate creation ... As creatures engaged in the worship of God, humans find themselves not set over but alongside other creatures, caught up with them in the common worship of their common creator. (Bauckham 2008: 62)

Through these images, creation is seen as having a hopeful future. Rather than facing eventual destruction at the hands of human imperial exploitation, it rather has a role in drawing all things towards unity with the creator. The violence which the environment endures at the hands of humanity points the way to a new future beyond slavery to the forces of empire. Once released from the tyranny of the satanic powers that oppress and destroy, creation is freed to fulfil its function as the context for a renewed relationship between humanity and God.

A New Heaven and a New Earth

John's image of a new heaven and a new earth (Rev. 21:1–5; cf. Isa. 65: 17–25) represents his vision of what it means for humanity to finally "repent" of their obsession with empire, learning to live in a new relationship with both creation and creator. It is no coincidence that John evokes the language of Eden in his description of the new earth; he envisages a context where the effects of the fall are reversed, where human idolatrous pretensions no longer wreak destruction on the face of the planet, and where God is present and at ease with humanity (Rev. 21:22–23; cf. Gen. 3:8). As Howard Peskett and Vinoth Ramachandra comment: "What is 'new' about this creation? The creation is now filled with the immediate presence of God … No longer present in hiddenness and contradiction, the throne of God moves from heaven to the earth" (Peskett and Ramachandra 2003: 264). See also Bouma-Prediger (2001: 115).

John uses the image of the new Jerusalem to represent the church, the bride of Christ (Rev. 21:2, 9–10), at the heart of the renewed creation. In true Edenic fashion, the new Jerusalem has a tree at its centre, but whereas the tree in Eden was implicated in the fall of humanity, the tree in the new Jerusalem has the opposite effect. The leaves of this tree are said to be, "for the healing of the nations" (Rev. 22:2; cf. Gen. 3:2–7; Ezek. 47:12), an image which presents creation and church collaborating in the drawing of humanity away from the destructive seductions of empire, to a new place where true healing can occur (cf. Rev. 21:4). Accordingly, the nations walk by the "light" of the new Jerusalem, and the kings of the earth are seen bringing their "glory" into it (Rev. 21:24).

The transition to the new heaven and new earth is not one which involves the total destruction of the existing created order before re-creation can occur. Rather, the new creation is brought into being as the oppressive powers of the satanic empire are destroyed. Larry Rasmussen thus rightly describes the new creation as, "a radical transformation *of* the created order and not its utter obliteration in favor of realms literally out of this world" (Rasmussen 1996: 256). Ernest Lucas agrees, commenting that the divine statement, "See, I am making all things new" (Rev. 21:5) indicates, "a renewing of the old by a radical transformation, not the abolishing of it to start again *de novo*" (Lucas 2005: 83). See further Adams (2007: 238); Bauckham (1993: 49); Deane-Drummond (1996: 24–25); and Russell (1996: 6). The picture that John draws of the new earth is therefore one which encompasses redeemed aspects of the present earth, as Lucas comments:

> It may be significant that this picture of the culmination of God's purpose is not a simple return to the Garden of Eden, but a City of Eden. In Genesis 4 the city is a human artefact, with the first one being built by Cain. This might imply that in the New Jerusalem that has come from heaven to earth God has incorporated the best of human endeavours in the working out of his purposes. (Lucas 2005: 83)

Bruce Reichenbach and V. Elving Anderson make a related point, commenting, "the garden has become the city, but the city is reminiscent of the garden" (Reichenbach and Anderson 2006: 124).

It is significant that the new Jerusalem is seen by John descending from heaven, with this image carrying a rhetorical function which is not usually noted. Having initially drawn his audience through the open door into the heavenly realm (Rev. 4:1), John has shown them heaven's perspective on their earthly situation. Here at the end of his visionary work, he returns them back to the earth as the new Jerusalem, transformed through their participation in his symbolic scheme (Woodman 2008: 235–36). Having experienced John's representations of the divine judgements on the satanic empire, and having seen both the effects of empire and its ultimate fate, John's audience finds that when they return from the heavenly vision to the earth, everything is different. No longer do they look at the empire which surrounds them and see strength, beauty and righteousness; rather, they see weakness, corruption and judgement. Those who witness the vision of the burning of Babylon become those who are already living the proleptic reality of the new creation, because they have been freed from their ideological slavery to Babylon. John's vision of the new heaven and earth therefore has a timeless aspect to it, with the one seated on the throne declaring in the present tense "see, I am making all things new" (21:5; cf. Isa. 43:19). George Caird similarly comments:

> The pastoral relevance of the new Jerusalem to the needs of the seven churches becomes still clearer ... [T]his voice from the ultimate future has something urgent to say about the critical present: "I am making all things new". This is not an activity of God within the new creation, after the old has been cast as rubbish into the void; it is the process of re-creation by which the old is transformed into the new. In Smyrna and Thyatira, in Sardis and

Laodicea, in all places of his dominion, God is for ever making all things new, and on this depends the hope of the world. (Caird 1984: 265–266)

Peskett and Ramachandra also note that "God promises not to make 'all new things' but, rather, *all things new*" (Peskett and Ramachandra 2003: 270) while Maier compares the economic systems of new Jerusalem with the "Giveaway" of the North American indigenous population, whereby "wealth or objects of value are ritually given away in order to acknowledge dependence on others for success". He observes: "Earth's voices in Revelation tell us there is indeed a new world coming whenever and wherever there are those courageous enough to live and express the Giveaway of the tree and water of life" (Maier 2002: 179).

This vision of the new heaven and the new earth, with the new Jerusalem at their centre, is therefore primarily a vision for the here-and-now of John's audience. It presents them with a challenge that they are to be those who give testimony to the in-breaking kingdom of God, those who live as citizens of new Jerusalem rather than as citizens of Babylon. The renewal of the created order is therefore not solely something to be anticipated at some decisive point in the future, as the divine answer to the environmental destructions wrought by empire. Rather, it is to be found in the present as the idolatrous claims of the satanic empire are exposed, opposed and rejected, and as humanity responds to the prophetic witness to the existence of an alternative to slavish devotion to the beast of empire. As Ron Elsdon comments: "The promise of the renewal of creation still lies in the future, but what the New Testament adds to the Old is the way that the kingdom of God has already broken into the present world order through the Incarnation, death and Resurrection of Jesus Christ" (Elsdon 1992: 161).

The Prophetic Call

By this reading of the book of Revelation, the hope for creation-under-empire lies in John's prophetic challenge to the destructive ideology of empire. It is only once the idolatrous claims of Babylon are rejected that a new relationship between humanity and creation becomes possible. The first thing confronting John's audience, as they journey with him through the open door into heaven, is a startling and dramatic vision of God on the heavenly throne (Rev. 4:1–11). This image poses a direct and overt challenge to the imperial claims made by the one on the throne at the heart of the empire. Within John's first-century context, the challenge to the dominion and authority of the emperor of Rome is clear. However, John's use of the image "Babylon" to depict Rome indicates that there is a timeless applicability to his message. Through this presentation of God as the lord of the cosmos, John enables those experiencing his work in any age to become a prophetic people, challenging the world to step away from the destructive ideology of empire.

Within John's scheme, it is when God is named as lord of creation that the idolatrous powers of empire are challenged (Rev. 3:14; 10:6; 11:4; 14:7). In this way, the many worship scenes of Revelation acquire distinctly political overtones, as they challenge the dominant oppressive and destructive powers in the world. Worship in Revelation is therefore not about making God feel good about himself, it is about reversing the effects of the fall. As God is named lord of creation, the idolatrous imperial aspirations of humanity are challenged, and the way is cleared for humanity, God and creation to recover that which was lost at Eden. The new song which only the 144,000 can sing (Rev. 14:3) therefore becomes a song of prophetic challenge, with those who recognize the lordship of the one on the throne in heaven challenging the nations of the earth to join them in resisting the seductive yet destructive call of the satanic empire. It is to this end that Michael Northcott notes:

> [T]he writer of the Book of Revelation [speaks] of a time when the whole cosmos will be brought into a relationship with the supreme justice of the Lord who is God in Christ. Christians have often proclaimed this justice to people of their own race and gender and class. They have more rarely proclaimed it amongst people different from themselves. Far more rarely has it been proclaimed to those orders of life which are not human flesh and blood. But the connections between human justice, and the good of the land and its non-human inhabitants, remain as clear today in environmental disasters which destroy the land of greedy land-owners who have burnt the tree and leaf, as they did in the time of Isaiah and Amos. (Northcott 1996: 326)

Can the Book of Revelation Be a Gospel for the Environment?
The only occurrence of the term "a gospel" in the Johannine writings is found in the description of an angel flying in midheaven (although the verb form is used in Rev. 10:7). The angel is described as having, "an eternal gospel to proclaim to those who live on the earth – to every nation and tribe and language and people" (Rev. 14:6). It becomes clear that this "eternal gospel", this *good news* to all the peoples of the earth, is the certain arrival of the hour of the judgement of God (Rev. 14:7 cf. 15:5–16:21) (Smalley 2005: 361). The gospel, or *good news*, of Revelation is therefore seen to revolve around God's justice: Justice against evil, justice for the righteous, and justice for creation.

The sequences of warning judgements, calling the nations to repentance of their imperial idolatry, pave the way for the ultimate judgement on those satanic systems which oppress and destroy. Creation is finally and fully freed from satanic oppression as the forces of empire are destroyed at the great battle of Harmagedon. The armies of the kings of the earth are defeated by the sword that comes from the mouth of the rider on the white horse, with the word of God from the mouth of the messiah victorious over the satanic deceptions of the beast (Rev. 19:21). The imperial forces which destroy the created order, oppress humanity, and violently suppress opposition are ironically seen to be themselves destroyed by nothing other than the "gospel" itself.

Though John's own antidote to imperial idolatry involves an acknowledgement of the lordship of the divine figure on the heavenly throne as a precursor to the redemption of creation, his work also makes a powerful environmental critique of empire available to a wider humanity. Although John was writing to those within the Christian congregations of first century Asia Minor, nonetheless his prophetic call to the church, to enact a faithful witness to a non-exploitative view of humanity and the earth, retains a clear challenge to the contemporary world. John's call to "come out" of Babylon (Rev. 18:4), coupled with his presentation of empire as a destructive, and ultimately self-destructive, system present a persistent challenge to those who want to combine life-under-empire with environmental justice. Harnessing the strengths of empire in the search for solutions to pressing environmental concerns may or may not solve imminent problems; but in the long-term, those who dance with empire still end up embracing Babylon. John's core question thus remains as pertinent as ever: If you do not serve the Emperor, just whom do you serve?

Note

1. (http://www.timesonline.co.uk/tol/news/uk/article619828.ece. Accessed 21.1.10).

Bibliography

Adams, E. 2007. *The Stars Will Fall From Heaven: Cosmic Catastrophe in the New Testament and its World*. London: T&T Clark.

Bauckham, R. 1993. *The Theology Of The Book Of Revelation*. Cambridge: Cambridge University Press.

_____ 2005. "The New Testament Teaching on the Environment: A Response." In *A Christian Approach to the Environment* eds R. C. J. Carling and M. A. Carling. London: The John Ray Initiative.

_____ 2008. "Creation's praise of God in the Book of Revelation." *Biblical Theology Bulletin*, 38 (2): 55–63.

Bostock, J. and H. T. Riley. 1856. *The Natural History of Pliny*. London: Henry G. Bohn.

Bouma-Prediger, S. 2001. *For the Beauty of the Earth: A Christian Vision for Creation Care.* Grand Rapids, MI: Baker Academic.

Boxall, I. 2006. *The Revelation of St John.* London: Continuum.

Boyer, P. 1992. *When Time Shall Be No More: Prophecy Belief in Modern American Culture.* Cambridge, MA: Harvard University Press.

Bredin, M. 2008. "God the Carer: Revelation and the environment." *Biblical Theology Bulletin*, 38 (2): 76–87.

Caird, G. B. 1984. *The Revelation Of St John The Divine.* London: A & C Black.

Deane-Drummond, C. 1996. *A Handbook in Theology and Ecology.* London: SCM Press Ltd.

Elsdon, R. 1992. *GreenHouse Theology,* Tunbridge Wells: Monarch.

Guyatt, N. 2007. *Have A Nice Doomsday: Why Millions of Americans are Looking Forward to the End of the World.* Chatham: Ebury Press.

Hertzler, D. 2000. "Assessing the 'Left Behind' Phenomenon." In *Apocalypticism and Millennnialism,* ed. L. L. Johns. Kitchener, ON: Pandora Press.

Howard-Brook, W. and A. Gwyther. 2001. *Unveiling Empire: Reading Revelation Then and Now.* New York: Orbis Books.

Kovacs, J. L. and C. Rowland, C. 2004. *Revelation.* Oxford: Blackwell.

Lindsey, H. and C. C. Carlson. 1970. *The Late, Great Planet Earth.* Grand Rapids, MI: Zondervan.

Lucas, E. 2005. "The New Testament Teaching on the Environment." In *A Christian Approach to the Environment,* eds R. C. J. Carling and M. A. Carling. London: The John Ray Initiative.

Maier, H. O. 2002. "There's a New World Coming! Reading the Apocalypse in the Shadow of the Canadian Rockies." In *The Earth Story in the New Testament,* eds N. C. Habel and V. Balabanski. London: Sheffield Academic Press.

Mojtabai. 1997. *Blesséd Assurance: At Home with the Bomb in Amarillo, Texas.* Syracuse, NY: Syracuse University Press.

Northcott, M. S. 1996. *The Environment & Christian Ethics.* Cambridge: Cambridge University Press.

O'Leary, S. 1994. *Arguing the Apocalypse: A Theory of Millennial Rhetoric.* Oxford: Oxford University Press.

Page, R. 2006. "The Fellowship of All Creation." In *Environmental Stewardship: Critical Perspectives – Past and Present,* ed. R. J. Berry. London: T.& T.Clark International.

Palmer, M. 1992. *Dancing to Armageddon.* London: Aquarian Press.

Peskett, H. and V. Ramachandra. 2003. *The Message of Mission – The Glory of Christ in All Time and Space.* Leicester: Inter-Varsity Press.

Pippin, T. 1999. *Apocalyptic Bodies: The Biblical End of the World in Text and Image.* London: Routledge.

Rasmussen, L. L. 1996. *Earth Community, Earth Ethics.* Geneva: WCC Publications.

Reichenbach, B. R. and V. E. Anderson. 2006. Tensions in a Stewardship Paradigm. In *Environmental Stewardship: Critical Perspectives – Past and Present,* ed. R. J. Berry. London: T.&T. Clark International.

Richard, P. 1995. *Apocalypse: A People's Commentary on the Book of Revelation.* New York: Orbis Books.

Rossing, B. R. 2002. "Alas for Earth! Lament and Resistance in Revelation 12." In *The Earth Story in the New Testament*, N. C. Habel and V. Balabanski. London: Sheffield Academic Press.

Russell, D. M. 1996. *The "New Heavens and New Earth": Hope for the Creation in Jewish Apocalyptic and the New Testament*. Philadelphia, PA: Visionary Press.

Smalley, S. S. 2005. *The Revelation to John: A Commentary on the Greek Text of the Apocalypse*. London: SPCK.

Thurman, R. and J. McCleary, J. 1997. "Facing the Future with Hope: A Discussion from an American Perspective." In *Revelation and the Environment AD 95–1995*, eds S. Hobson and J. Lubchenco. Singapore: World Scientific Publishing Co. Pte. Ltd.

Woodman, S. 2008. *The Book of Revelation*. London: SCM Press Ltd.

_____ 2009. "The Plain and Literal Meaning of the Text: A 17th Century Particular Baptist Perspective on Revelation 20:1–7." In *The Way the World Ends? The Apocalypse of John in Culture and Ideology*, eds W. J. Lyons and J. Økland. Sheffield: Sheffield Phoenix Press.

Woods, R. 2008. "Seven Bowls of Wrath: the Ecological Relevance of Revelation." *Biblical Theology Bulletin*, 38 (2): 64–75.

THE KINDNESS OF STRANGERS: BIBLICAL HOSPITALITY AND THE POLITICS OF INTERVENTION

Diana Lipton[a]

In this paper I shall bring to bear Hebrew Bible texts from Amos and Genesis on the endlessly difficult question of what makes someone else's business our business?[1] When should we intervene in the affairs of an external entity – household, institution, or nation (my focus here) – because some of its members are suffering, whether at the hands of hostile outsiders or other members? When would intervention bring a positive outcome, and what factors can help us to determine that? Although I shall not discuss specific cases, I have in mind the Twentieth Century's most consequential failure of timely intervention (Nazi Germany), and what I see as the Twenty-first Century's most consequential example of untimely intervention (the allied invasion of Iraq).

As well as asking when we should intervene, I shall ask the corollary question: when should we not intervene? In particular, when should we avoid intervention because it would not merely be counter-productive, but positively immoral? And what justifies intervention on behalf of members of one oppressed group and not another? My starting point is that intervention on behalf of a group with whom the intervening party

[a] Diana Lipton's career includes an English degree at Oxford, investment banking, full-time motherhood, and a Cambridge Ph.D on dreams in Genesis. In 2007, she left a Fellowship at Newnham College, Cambridge for a Lectureship in Hebrew Bible and Jewish Studies at King's College London. Diana loves teaching and happily agrees with Rabbi Hanina: I have learned much from my teachers, more from my colleagues, and from my students most of all. Her most recent book is *Longing for Egypt and Other Unexpected Biblical Tales* (2008), and her new project is on the Bible and Talmudic narrative.

has a particular connection, such as fellow-members of a family or social or national entity, requires no explanation. The common bond explains, if not always justifies, the special interest. My concern is rather with cases where there is no obvious reason to be activist on behalf of one group rather than another. In these cases, nations that could have benefited from intervention are overlooked because intervening parties focus instead on countries they cannot help, and countries that are targeted for intervention are harmed by well-wishers with only the slightest understanding of the issues involved and no hope of bringing benefit. Although I shall not discuss it explicitly, I have in mind what I take to be an inordinate and inexplicable desire to intervene in the affairs of Israel/Palestine by groups with no personal connection to either people who consistently overlook similar or worse conflicts in other regions of the world.[2]

I am addressing my questions not from the perspective of a *beneficiary* of third party intervention, but from the perspective of a party that is *contemplating intervention*. In theory, the conclusions should be the same, but they will not be, and the decision-making process will certainly be different. I shall not look at biblical texts concerning Assyrian or Babylon invasions of Israel, partly because they were arguably motivated by straightforward expansionist desires, which, as I will explain, are not my interest, but mainly because we will inevitably view them from the wrong point of view – the perspective of the invader rather than that of the invaded.

My biblical discussion texts are Amos 1–2, the so-called "oracles against the nations", and Genesis 18–19, the account of Sodom and Gomorrah. Amos is often characterized as the first prophetic universalist, partly on account of his concern for social justice, but mostly because God in Amos seems interested in the nations in their own right, and, according to many commentators, judges them as he judges Israel.[3] The Sodom and Gomorrah narrative is less obviously universalist, since the a-historical context makes it less clear how those cities should be classified, but I have presented an argument for understanding them as "foreign" cities in my recent book, *Longing for Egypt* (2008: 108–140). At any rate, Abraham's sole connection with them was with Lot and his family, which is all that matters for my present purposes.

Noting the preoccupation in Amos's oracles against the nations with the getting and keeping of territory, Michael Walzer characterizes the oracles as "Geneva Conventions".[4] They are demands of the kind that can legitimately be made of other nations and societies – not domestic policy (particularist), where the absence of shared values makes it difficult or impossible for outsiders to intervene effectively, even if intervention is morally justifiable, but foreign affairs (universal), the interaction that occurs at borders where agreed – though not necessarily shared – values are essential. I want to build on Walzer's analysis to offer a provisional profile of what justified and effective intervention might look like.

Intervention Following Country's A's Invasion Country B

Here I have in mind the situation in which country A has invaded country B in order to expand its own territory, gain access to natural resources, enhance its national security, or similar. This primary invasion is not, however, my concern. Without wishing to justify or defend invasions of this kind, I take it that they are the standard fare of international politics, and that, in any case, neither the morality of the decision to invade, nor the welfare of the invaded country, are generally at issue for the invader and it is of little practical use to discuss them. What interests me rather is what might occur when country A has invaded country B, and country C is considering whether or not to intervene on behalf of country B. Here, the morality of the decision to intervene is certainly at issue, and so is the welfare of country B. To be sure, there are circumstances in which country C's intervention might be motivated by self-interest – its own destabilized borders, for example, if countries B and C are adjoining – but even then the justifications offered usually involve an altruistic component without which intervention would not take place. This altruistic component is my focus and what follows is set of terms and conditions which should be met if altruistically motivated intervention is to be successful. These terms and conditions are not my own; I have derived them exegetically, as I shall go on to show, from the opening chapters of Amos.

Conditions That Should be Met When Country C Is Considering Intervention on Behalf of Country B Following an Invasion of Country B by Country A

1. Intervention within the borders of country B, the invaded nation, should in the first instance be avoided. Retaliation should be focused on country A, the invader. Reasons for this include inevitable collateral damage to the citizens and resources of any invaded country, even when the invasion (in this case, country C's intervention on behalf of country B) is motivated by a desire to protect its citizens and their resources. While the innocent civilians of country A may not

themselves deserve to be victims of collateral damage, military action within their borders is more justifiable than action within the borders of country B. They are, unfortunately, citizens of an aggressor nation and must expect to pay a price.

2. Country A's ordinary expansionist activities would not in themselves justify intervention by country C, as noted above. The balance in favour of intervention would be tipped by cruel and unusual behaviour on the part of country A. Determining what is cruel and unusual in times of war is no easy feat, as we have seen in recent times, but I have in mind above all gratuitous violence against civilians that is sanctioned by the government or even a component of its military strategy.

3. The citizens of country B need not necessarily merit intervention in this situation – their status as victims of aggressive invasion by country A is sufficient to justify the intervention of country C.

Intervention Within the Borders of Country B When Retaliation in Country A Was Not Effective; or When Country B is at Civil War or Otherwise Internally Divided

My concern here is with intervention within the borders of a non-aggressor nation, where punishment is not justified or intended. While it is true that even an aggressor nation will have citizens who were in no sense involved in the aggression and do not deserve retaliation, it is also true that damage in their cases can only be limited, not avoided, once the decision to invade has taken place. If the nation in question is democratic, and its citizens should therefore take a measure of responsibility for the actions of their elected government, or if it can reasonably be claimed that the citizens created in some other way a culture that encouraged or allowed aggressive actions by their government, it could even be argued (though I would not go so far) that no citizen of an aggressive invader can escape pay-back. By contrast, when intervention is planned not as part of a process of retaliation, but within a country that has already been invaded or is suffering from significant civil or political unrest, the cost/benefit calculations are entirely different. Intervention could not be justified if the country's citizens were worse off after it than before, whereas in the case of an aggressor nation, intervention could perhaps be justified regardless of the welfare of its citizens.

Conditions That Should Be Met When Country C Is Considering Intervention Within the Borders of Country B, Whether Following Invasion by Country A or During Civil Unrest

1. When intervention occurs within the borders of country B, the invaded nation, the distinction between countries A and B, the invader and invaded, must be clear to country C before intervention occurs. In many cases, this is likely to be self-evident, especially if country C's intervention occurs soon after country A's invasion. Unfortunately, however, it is easy to imagine situations in which the distinction is not obvious. For example, a country considering intervention following the invasion of one African or central European country by another may find itself unable to draw clear lines, especially if both countries were recently created and have mixed populations. In these cases, a country considering intervention could not readily draw distinctions based on ethnic origins of the population, religion, language and so forth, or on the political origins of the country. All the above applies all the more in cases of civil war or other kinds of internal division, when there are significant difficulties in drawing distinctions between the parties involved.

2. The beneficiaries of intervention must actively merit it. It is not sufficient that they be innocent victims of military aggression; they must be "righteous". This is not a matter of raising a barrier or presenting an obstacle to external aid. It is rather the case that external support will be ineffective at best and counter-productive and even dangerous at worst if abused by its beneficiaries.

3. The beneficiaries of intervention must not just merit but welcome it. It is unlikely that intervention will be effective and productive if its beneficiaries are hostile to it. An all too familiar dichotomy of perspective comes to mind. Those intervening can see themselves as liberators; their beneficiaries see them as colonizers. These differences must usually be resolved in advance of intervention, difficult though that may be.

4. The beneficiaries of intervention must be willing to accept an intermediate, liminal state in advance of a return to the status quo or, more likely, to a new post-intervention state. Beneficiaries can harbour unrealistic expectations about what intervention can achieve, and, more to the point, what its executors want to achieve. Even if an intervening party has no interest in promoting its own values (democracy, equality of the sexes, e.g.), its presence will almost

inevitably have a short-term effect, and possibly long-term influence, on the "host" society.

I shall now attempt to show how these principles can be derived from Amos 1–2 and Genesis 18–19. For present purposes, I read Amos's oracles collectively and cumulatively, not individually. I am not concerned with the details of the historical context that Amos describes, or with the book's history of composition. A brief analysis of Amos 1–2 yields the following points concerning the terms and conditions set out above.

Retaliation Within the Borders of an Invading Country Following Acts of Unusual Cruelty

[3]Thus said the LORD: For three transgressions of Damascus, For four, I will not revoke it: Because they threshed Gilead With threshing boards of iron. [4]I will send down fire upon the palace of Hazael, And it shall devour the fortresses of Benhadad. [5]I will break the gate bars of Damascus, And wipe out the inhabitants from the Vale of Aven And the sceptered ruler of Beth-eden; And the people of Aram shall be exiled to Kir—said the LORD. [6]Thus said the LORD: For three transgressions of Gaza, For four, I will not revoke it: Because they exiled an entire, *shlemah*, population, Which they delivered to Edom. [7]I will send down fire upon the wall of Gaza, And it shall devour its fortresses; [8]And I will wipe out the inhabitants of Ashdod And the sceptered ruler of Ashkelon; And I will turn My hand against Ekron, And the Philistines shall perish to the last man—said the Lord God (Amos 1:3–8).[5]

These oracles present retaliation as measure for measure retribution for unacceptable behaviour, not as self-defence. It is this emphasis that makes Amos relevant to the issues at hand. The retaliation clearly occurs within the borders of the invading country, not within the invaded country; God promises to destroy palaces, fortresses and walls within Damascus and Gaza (v.5). It is clear too that the original military activity cannot be classified as ordinary imperialism, though it may have begun as such. The "threshing boards of iron" (v.3) hint at war crimes,[6] and the exiling of an *entire* population (v.6) suggests disproportion. It is to this disproportion and excess that God responds: "Because they exiled an entire ... population ... I will send down fire" (vv. 6,7).

War Crimes and Unacceptable Means to Acceptable Ends

[9]Thus said the LORD: For three transgressions of Tyre, For four, I will not revoke it: Because they handed over An entire population to Edom, Ignoring

the covenant of brotherhood. [10]I will send down fire upon the wall of Tyre, And it shall devour its fortresses. [11]Thus said the LORD: For three transgressions of Edom, For four, I will not revoke it: Because he pursued his brother with the sword And repressed all pity, Because his anger raged unceasing And his fury stormed unchecked. [12]I will send down fire upon Teman, And it shall devour the fortresses of Bozrah. [13]Thus said the LORD: For three transgressions of the Ammonites, For four, I will not revoke it: Because they ripped open the pregnant women of Gilead In order to enlarge their own territory. [14]I will set fire to the wall of Rabbah, And it shall devour its fortresses, Amid shouting on a day of battle, On a day of violent tempest. [15]Their king and his officers shall go Into exile together – said the LORD. (Amos 1:9–15)

Here, God attacks Edom for repressing compassion, and for fighting with raging anger and unchecked fury. Even if the invasion was based originally upon a defensible military strategy, those involved lost sight of its strategic motivations and were either indifferent to the harm they inflicted upon their enemies, or, worse still, bent on inflicting harm. This is presented most starkly in relation to Ammon's attack on pregnant women. In fact, none of this is best understood as condemning the actions of individual soldiers during the course of battle, unacceptable as they might be. Rather, Amos seems to focus on considered military strategy, intended perhaps to deal with future population growth, or to demoralize the population. This is indicated by the highly causative thrust of verse 13; they ripped open pregnant women *in order* to expand their own territory.[7] This was not a case of invading and then losing control, but an example of unacceptable military practice – an officially sanctioned means that cannot be justified by the ends. Rightly or wrongly, imperialists do not necessarily provoke divine wrath, but these imperialists bring it upon themselves by behaviour that was considered morally repugnant (in their own time as well as ours). The distinction between the unplanned immorality of individual soldiers (regrettably inevitable during conflict) and the planned strategy of military leaders is crucial. We can infer from Amos that retaliation based on the unsanctioned and uncondoned criminal misbehaviour of individual soldiers is not justifiable, or at least unlikely to be effective, whereas the same behaviour licensed by the aggressor nation as part of its government-sponsored campaign does justify intervention.

Thus far Amos's oracles against the nations support my claims above concerning third party intervention when retaliation takes place in the invader's own territory. Amos emphasizes that the invaders committed war crimes, and makes no reference to the *righteousness* of the citizens of the invaded country, though he does spell out that they are weak, defenceless and innocent (pregnant women and their unborn babies). Questions about intervention within the borders of the invaded country motivated by a desire to help a third party do not arise. But can we glean information from these oracles about what rules might then apply? To be sure, it was not the intention of Amos's nations to benefit the countries they invaded, but the charges levelled against them may nevertheless signal behaviour that might be found particularly reprehensible in the contexts that interest us. Tyre's indifference to the "covenant of brotherhood" (1:9), and Edom's pursuit of his brother with the sword (1:11), suggest a failure on the part of the invaders to make proper distinctions between the inhabitants of the invaded countries. That homogenization of potential beneficiaries of intervention is problematic may also explain why Gaza's exiling "an entire nation" (1:6) is specifically mentioned. The oracles against Ammon and Moab, by contrast, show evidence that God, unlike Tyre and Gaza, was making distinctions. God exiled only the king of Ammon and his officers (1:15), not the entire population, and in Moab he removed the ruler and killed his officials (see 2:3 below). This selectivity may reflect an interest in social engineering – not an arbitrary punishment of innocent civilians, but an effort to remove those who were responsible (the government) and thus to transform the country.

> Thus said the LORD: For three transgressions of Moab, For four, I will not revoke it: Because he burned the bones Of the king of Edom to lime. [2]I will send down a fire upon Moab, And it shall devour the fortresses of Kerioth. And Moab shall die in tumult, Amid shouting and the blare of horns; [3]I will wipe out the ruler from within her And slay all her officials along with him – said the LORD. (Amos 2:1-3)

Yet this possible glimpse of social engineering in Amos raises problems that have not been addressed by any of the oracles cited thus far. As we can infer from Walzer's discussion in "Amos as Social Critic", not to mention from recent international events, intervention into the internal affairs of another nation is potentially dangerous and destructive, and very unlikely to succeed. The intervening party fails to understand the beneficiary's social, legal, and political infrastructure, and the absence of shared values and a common code of behaviour makes it difficult or impossible to correct social ills. This negative situation may be exacerbated by an absence of support for the intervening party among the intended beneficiaries. Does Amos indicate how an intervening party might determine whether or not there exists among intended beneficiaries sufficient commonality and support to merit intervention? I shall attempt to show that the internal, domestic focus of the oracle against Israel may be a source of valuable advice on precisely these problems.

Altruistically Motivated Intervention

[6] Thus said the LORD: For three transgressions of Israel, For four, I will not revoke it: Because they have sold for silver Those whose cause was just, *tsaddiq,* And the needy for a pair of sandals. [7][Ah,] you who trample the heads of the poor Into the dust of the ground, And make the humble walk a twisted course! Father and son go to the same girl, And thereby profane My holy name. [8] They recline by every altar On garments taken in pledge, And drink in the House of their God Wine bought with fines they imposed. [9] Yet I destroyed the Amorite before them, Whose stature was like the cedar's And who was stout as the oak, destroying his boughs above And his trunk below! [10] And I brought you up from the land of Egypt And led you through the wilderness forty years, To possess the land of the Amorite! (Amos 2:6–10)

According to Walzer, Amos's oracle against Israel confirms that his expectations of Israel are qualitatively different than his expectations of the nations. This corresponds to Walzer's important emphasis on the prophet as social critic. Amos can make these specific, detailed, *domestic* demands of Israel because it is his own country, he understands it, and its citizens share his values and are indeed aware of them. When it comes to other nations, Walzer argues, Amos can do little more than appeal to an ancient equivalent of the Geneva Conventions based on behaviour is considered appropriate "at the borders". Walzer does not consider altruistically motivated third party intervention, but I suggest that we can extrapolate from the mutual understanding and shared values that enabled Amos to perform as Israel's social critic to identify a level of incomplete understanding and partly shared values that justifies intervention into the affairs of a country with whom the intervening country has no special relationship or prior connection.

Making Distinctions and Demonstrating Merit

In Amos's oracle against Israel, there are no invaders or invaded parties, but two distinct groups within a single society – the oppressors and the oppressed. The oppressed are clearly identifiable. This is not a case of an inevitably doomed attempt to distinguish between two groups with political or ethnic differences imperceptible to the outside viewer. Rather, the oppressed are an instantly recognizable subset of all societies, equivalent to Deuteronomy's poor, widows, orphans. Moreover, they are clearly identified by the laws just alluded to. There is, then, no difficulty in distinguishing between the two groups involved, the oppressors and the oppressed, and intervention is justified by the requirement to protect the vulnerable.[8] But would intervention be effective in this case, even if justified? This question is answered by a crucial move in Amos's oracle against Israel. The oppressed group is explicitly identified as, *tsaddiq*, "just" according to NJPS as above, but I shall render it henceforth as "righteous". I see this designation as confirmation not merely that the beneficiaries of intervention merit it, but that they would in fact benefit from it. I shall attempt now to explain why.

Amos's designation of the victims of oppression as righteous, *tsaddiq*, raises a question that lies at the heart of the politics of intervention. How do we decide who is righteous? In the case of Israel, it is clear that the benchmark is Torah law. With respect to the general population this would presumably be a matter of observance; some degree of adherence to, or at least respect for, Torah law would signify righteousness. In the case of the poor, widows and orphans, observance of Torah law is not required and nor are they expected to demonstrate righteousness in other ways. Regardless of their individual characters and attributes, this collective group is identified as deserving external support and protection, and their special status is designated by reference to their righteousness. They are righteous not because they are necessarily good (though they might be), but because they are categorized as such within the Hebrew Bible's legal system. This works because all parties involved are operating within this single system, and share its values. But how would we identify the righteous in a society whose values were different from our own, or in whose legal system we did not participate? Would poverty, a disadvantaged social status, or some form of victimhood, be sufficient indicators in all cases? Amos does not, I think, answer these questions, but holding on to his notion of righteousness, and working on the additional assumption that victimhood alone is not sufficient, we can make some progress by turning now to Genesis 18–19.

Intervention and Righteousness at Sodom and Gomorrah

The account of Abraham's encounter with God over the fate of Sodom and Gomorrah is a parade example of the politics of intervention. The episode begins with God's internal debate over whether to tell Abraham that he plans to destroy the cities:

[16]The men set out from there and looked down toward Sodom, Abraham walking with them to see them off. [17]Now the LORD had said, "Shall I hide

from Abraham what I am about to do, [18]since Abraham is to become a great and populous nation and all the nations of the earth are to bless themselves by him? [19]For I have singled him out, that he may instruct his children and his posterity to keep the way of the LORD by doing what is just and right, in order that the LORD may bring about for Abraham what He has promised him." [20]Then the LORD said, "The outrage of Sodom and Gomorrah is so great, and their sin so grave! [21]I will go down to see whether they have acted altogether according to the outcry that has reached Me; if not, I will take note" (Gen. 18:16–21)

God's monologue sets the stage for Abraham's dramatic response. Without hesitation, Abraham begins to bargain with God over the fate of two cities the vast majority of whose inhabitants are in every sense strangers to him. The exceptions are Lot and his family, and on one reading, Abraham's negotiations with God were no more than an elaborate case of plea-bargaining designed to save his own family members.[9] Intriguing as this is, however, I do not think it does justice to the text, or to Abraham. As I read this episode, Abraham's family members are saved in the first instance (though ultimately not without further action on their parts) because they are the group on whose behalf his intervention was automatically justified. The narrative focus is rather the residents of Sodom and Gomorrah with whom Abraham has no relationship, and Genesis 18–19 explores the merits of Abraham's intervention on their behalf, and why it ultimately failed.

Before Abraham utters a word in the defence of the citizens of Sodom and Gomorrah, God is moved to act more compassionately (justly) in relation to them than was suggested by his opening position. Just as he was on the brink of destroying both cities in total, God stopped to contemplate Abraham, the mere thought of whom seems to have convinced him that he should ascertain that *all* the citizens of Sodom and Gomorrah are guilty of the crimes attributed to them (18:21). God's willingness to make distinctions represents a crucial stage in the process of third party intervention, and it is upon precisely this impulse to distinguish that Abraham builds in his subsequent dialogue. Abraham sees his task as convincing God that he must, if possible, differentiate between the citizens of the cities, and to this end he sets out a distinction between the guilty and the others, *tsaddiqim*:

[22]The men went on from there to Sodom, while Abraham remained standing before the Lord. [23]Abraham came forward and said, "Will You sweep away the innocent along with the guilty? [24]What if there should be fifty innocent, *tsaddiq*, within the city; will You then wipe out the place and not forgive it for the sake of the innocent fifty who are in it? [25]Far be it from You to do such a thing, to bring death upon the innocent as well as the guilty, so that

innocent and guilty fare alike. Far be it from You! Shall not the Judge of all the
earth justly?"

But how does Abraham think that he (or God) can determine who deserves
to be wiped out and who does not? The NJPS translation of *tsaddiqim* as
"innocent" appears at first glance to solve this problem. God has already
alluded to unacceptable behaviour that seems to him to justify the
destruction of the cities (18:20). His task now is merely to discover whether
or not all (v. 21) the inhabitants of the city engaged in this behaviour. If
they did, he can destroy them all with impunity. If some did not, they will
be saved and, indeed, save others along with them. Unfortunately, it is not
so simple, not least because the precise nature of their crime is not identified,
but merely called a great sin (outrage in NJPS). If, however, we retain the
component of righteousness that I identified with *tsaddiq* in Amos, as I
think is in any case desirable in this text, we can begin to move towards a
solution. We are looking now not for avoidance of a particular crime, but of
evidence of particular behaviour or attributes that might constitute or
signal righteousness. What form will they take? The answer comes in the
ensuing narrative. In the meantime, it is sufficient to note that social
disadvantage or some sort of victimhood cannot have been an adequate
measure, as we speculated above was the case with Amos. There were surely
poor, widows, and orphans living in Sodom and Gomorrah, newborn infants
who could not possibly have sinned, and surely some citizens oppressed
others, creating a class of victims. Yet none of these count towards the ten
who might have saved the city.

Righteousness and Hospitality

By the time the angels approach Sodom, it is clear that there are no righteous
people in the cities. As the story unfolds, we are given evidence that this is
indeed the case, as well as a picture of the precise areas in which the citizens
failed to be righteous. Countless analyses have been written of the sin of
Sodom, and it would add little to this paper to reproduce them. My sole
focus at present is hospitality, a theme highlighted by Abraham's interaction
with the angelic figures who announce the birth of Isaac, and developed in
Lot's encounter with the two of the three "angels" who come to Sodom.

> The two angels arrived in Sodom in the evening, as Lot was sitting in the gate
> of Sodom. When Lot saw them, he rose to greet them and, bowing low with
> his face to the ground, [2]he said, "Please, my lords, turn aside to your
> servant's house to spend the night, and bathe your feet; then you may be on
> your way early." But they said, "No, we will spend the night in the square."

[3]But he urged them strongly, so they turned his way and entered his house. He prepared a feast for them and baked unleavened bread, and they ate. (19:1–3)

Commentators ancient and modern have contrasted Lot unfavourably with Abraham, citing for example his failure to rush to greet the angels, as Abraham did. This does not seem to me to be the pertinent contrast. Rather, I think, the similarly hospitable behaviour of Abraham and Lot towards their respective angelic visitors is contrasted with the complete lack of hospitality shown to them by the citizens of Sodom:

[4]They had not yet lain down, when the townspeople, the men of Sodom, young and old – all the people to the last man – gathered about the house. [5]And they shouted to Lot and said to him, "Where are the men who came to you tonight? Bring them out to us, that we may be intimate with them." [6]So Lot went out to them to the entrance, shut the door behind him, [7]and said, "I beg you, my friends, do not commit such a wrong. [8]Look, I have two daughters who have not known a man. Let me bring them out to you, and you may do to them as you please; but do not do anything to these men, since they have come under the shelter of my roof." (19:4–8)

The entire episode can be read as a meditation on hospitality, with the Sodomites' patent lack of it as the evidence that there were no righteous inhabitants there. Lot, in contrast to Abraham (18:4–8), is dealing not just with basic welcoming rituals and food, but with the more complex subject of sleeping arrangements. He convinces his visitors to stay not in the town square as they intended, but within the secure limits of his four walls (v. 2). Yet his walls turn out to be less secure than he must have hoped. The men of Sodom, so lacking in the most basic notion of hospitality, demand to have sex with these perfect strangers, thus violating Lot's private space and, crucially here, his capacity to share it with others. Lot's sense of hospitality leads him to try to protect his visitors and preserve his capacity to make them secure. He explains his obligation towards the angels by telling the townspeople "they have come under the shelter of my roof" (v. 8), and is willing to sacrifice even his own daughters to the cause. Finally, the theme of hospitality is underlined by the text's focus on entrances, gates, and doors (19:1, 6 [x2], 9, 10, 11[x2].[10] This emphasizes the centrality of notions of space in this narrative by highlighting the guests' movement from one side of the doorway to the other – who is inside and who is outside. More importantly for this discussion, it highlights the spatial transformation occurs when visitors cross a threshold.

No Direction Home?

Asked to construe hospitality spatially, we might envisage a motion directed outwards from the giver of hospitality towards its beneficiary. Yet hospitality is arguably better conceived as a motion directed inwards, drawing the beneficiary towards the giver. To be sure, the giver of hospitality might offer food and other amenities, outward motions in themselves, but hospitality's most significant consequence is not giving but the acceptance of an outsider into a designated space, and the subsequent transformation of the space that is entailed. This transformation may be effected actively and intentionally by the giver of hospitality, say by not smoking or cooking meat for guests with health concerns or dietary restrictions, or by modest dressing in the presence of visitors. Or it may be achieved passively by the mere presence of visitors and the altered spatial dynamics they create. If to offer hospitality is ultimately to be receptive and accommodating, it is thus an ideal indicator of a party's suitability to be a beneficiary of intervention. That is, the attribute of hospitality demonstrates that the potential beneficiary is capable of accepting both the intervention itself and the subsequent transformation of the beneficiary's space that will inevitably come in the wake of intervention.

The willingness of the beneficiary of intervention to accept transformation is crucial to the success of the endeavour. As noted above, beneficiaries who envisage an immediate return to the status quo are usually disappointed. The intervening party will bring its own goals and values, and, in the short or even long-term, a new entity will have been created by the amalgam of the intervening party and the beneficiary of intervention. Thinking about intervention from this perspective is helpful in several ways. It highlights the importance of envisaging realistically the nature and quality of the shared space following intervention, and it shows that accepting intervention is not a passive state of the kind associated with helpless victims, but a positive action, akin to offering hospitality. Using hospitality as a measure of whether intervention is justified and likely to be effective thus maximizes the chance that parties contemplating intervention will ask whether it is welcome, and that they will avoid the trap of viewing their intended beneficiaries as passive victims with no desire to play a determinative role in their own future (the downside of the troubling "liberation" model).

The notion of a liminal space created by hospitality (a temporarily vegetarian home, for example, where residents dress modestly out of respect for their company) helps to make sense of Walzer's allusion to the Geneva conventions in connection with Amos's oracles against the nations. It is clear from Walzer's analogy that new, shared rules (the Geneva Conventions) apply, accommodating both parties for a limited time. But precisely when and where do these rules apply? It is tempting to give a response that mentions borders, but borders that are (literally) construed more broadly than usual. The Conventions take effect not at the border between two countries, but after a border between two countries has been crossed. Once this has occurred, the country that has been entered becomes for the duration a virtual border, where both parties must agree during their interaction to the basic code of conduct entailed by the Conventions to which they have both agreed to adhere. As we can extrapolate from Abraham's experience at Sodom and Gomorrah, the onus is on the parties contemplating intervention to ensure that they can assess their potential beneficiaries and make relevant distinctions between them; and that they can determine in advance that their beneficiaries are equipped psychologically and practically to receive intervention, shape actively and live constructively with its consequences, and derive from it future, if not immediate, benefit.

International Relations as Domestic Hospitality

But is my equation of international relations and domestic hospitality justified in relation to ancient Israel and the Hebrew Bible, let alone as a practical guide to modern policy? I cannot help commenting that it is attractive to me in part because it avoids the unattractive orientalist tenor of discourse on this theme (Abraham rushed to be hospitable because excessive hospitality is what they do so well in the East). More to the point, and slightly unbelievably I must confess, it is *precisely* the equation made by the Deuteronomic authors when attempting to explain the exclusion of certain people from the congregation of the LORD. According to Deuteronomy 23, Ammon and Moab, both mentioned by Amos in his oracles, and, moreover, the very nations that are in some respects the biological and spiritual heirs of Sodom and Gomorrah (Gen. 19:36–38), are excluded for unjust treatment of refugees at the border characterized as lack of domestic hospitality to strangers: "No Ammonite or Moabite shall be admitted into the congregation of the LORD ... because they did not meet you with food and water on your journey after you left Egypt" (Deut. 23:4). Speaking biblically, then, it is hard to argue that this way of thinking through the politics of intervention is not justified or relevant. As to its practical application in one of the contemporary crises that made me want to write this paper, that remains to be tried and tested.

Notes

* The title of this paper alludes to one of the two most transformative articles I have read on the Hebrew Bible, Michael Walzer's "The Prophet as Social Critic", in *Interpretation and Social Criticism* (1987: 69–94). Walzer argues that the prophet's role as social critic entails intimate knowledge of the society being addressed and a body of shared values, both of which are incompatible with universalism. The oracles against the nations, then, do not reflect a universalist outlook, but represent ancient Israel's equivalent of the Geneva Conventions, namely, a code of behaviour that nations are entitled to expect of one another at times of war. Not every aspect of Walzer's paper will concern me here, but I am delighted to be engaging finally in print with a work that has inspired me and, I believe, several generations of my students, over more than ten years.

1. I want to convey my immense gratitude to Matthew Coomber for including a preliminary, oral version of this paper in his highly successful and stimulating conference on the Bible and Social Justice, Sheffield, May 2008, and for his great patience since then while I struggled to find time to write it up.

2. While it is not surprising that the Church of England is more interested in what happens in Israel/Palestine than in human rights abuses in other middle eastern countries or in the Far East, it is surprising (to me) that unions of university teachers and students should be similarly preoccupied.

3. See K. J. Dell, "The misuse of forms in Amos" (1995: 45–61) for an example of the "shock-value" reading of Amos's oracles (the oracles are a prelude to God's turning the tables on Israel).

4. Without knowing (I assume) Walzer's work on the same theme, Matthew Schlimm presented an interesting paper to the SBL Forum on using Amos 1–3 to engage students on war crimes and human rights. See Schlimm (2006: Online: http://sbl-site.org/Article.aspx?ArticleID=478).

5. All biblical translations based on *NJPS Tanakh*, JPS, Philadephia and New York, 1999.

6. See M. Schlimm, 'Teaching the Hebrew Bible amid the Current Human Rights Crisis', on threshing and war crimes.

7. I am grateful to participants of the Cambridge University's Jewish Students Egalitarian Minyan for helping me to see this important distinction during a discussion of an earlier version of my paper. To spell it out, on this account, we would differentiate Abu Ghraib from Guantanamo Bay.

8. This focus on the poor and vulnerable raises an issue I shall not pursue here, though it is highly relevant in our contemporary situation. Intervention costs money, as does its aftermath. Depending on the severity of the situation, it may be wrong to intervene in the absence of sufficient capital to build and sustain an economic infrastructure following intervention.

9. B. Visotsky, *The Genesis of Ethics*, New York (Crown Publishing: 1997).

10. For a different emphasis on the same theme, see B. Doyle, "'Knock, Knock, Knockin' on Sodom's Door': The function of *xtptld* in Genesis 18–19" (2004: 431–48).

Bibliography

Dell, K. J. 1995. "The misuse of forms in Amos." *Vetus Testamentum XLV/1*: 45–61.

Doyle, B. 2004. "'Knock, Knock, Knockin' on Sodom's Door': The function of *xtptld* in Genesis 18-19", *JSOT* 28: 431–48.

Lipton, Diana. 2008. *Longing for Egypt and Other Unexpected Biblical Tales.* Sheffield Phoenix Press, Sheffield.

NJPS. 1999. *NJPS Tanakh*, Philadelphia, PA: Jewish Publication Society.

Schlimm, Matthew R. 2006. "Teaching the Hebrew Bible amid the Current Human Rights Crisis: The Opportunities Presented by Amos 1:3–2:3." *SBL Forum*, n.p. [cited January 2006]. Online: http://sbl-site.org/publications/ article.aspx?articleId=478.

Visotsky, B. 1997. *The Genesis of Ethics*, New York: Crown Publishing.

Walzer, Michael. 1987. "The Prophet as Social Critic. In *Interpretation and Social Criticism*, 69-94. Cambridge, MA: Harvard University Press.

Prophets to Profits: Ancient Judah and Corporate Globalization

Matthew J.M. Coomber[a]

Introduction

For many Christian and Jewish social activists, the Hebrew prophets have become synonymous with a timeless struggle for a just world. From Martin Luther King Jr's use of Amos 5:24 in his call to "let justice roll down like waters and righteousness like a mighty stream" (King 1991: 297) in reference to eradicating segregation from the United States to Jewish activists' invocation of Mic. 6:8[1] in promoting the rights of Palestinians in the occupied areas (Serotta and Walt 2004), prophetic complaints against injustice have been employed by those who seek to use biblical texts to combat injustice.

While King's invocation of Amos 5:24 served as a powerful rallying cry for those who fought institutionalized racism during the Civil Rights movement, a deeper understanding and use of the contexts behind such prophetic texts may prove beneficial. Were it possible to move beyond a sound-bite usage of prophetic complaints against injustice by exploring the socio-economic contexts in which they were written, faith-based

[a] Matthew Coomber received his Ph.D in biblical studies from the University of Sheffield in 2010, where he developed a cultural-evolutionary approach to understanding the hidden contexts behind prophetic complaints against injustice. His primary interests include the effects of political and economic structures on textual interpretation in ancient and modern societies and the reciprocal ways in which biblical texts affect and are affected by the cultures and societies into which they are absorbed. Coomber has published *Re-Reading the Prophets Through Corporate Globalization* (Gorgias, 2010) and edited *Political Theology* 11 (3), which contains papers from the 2008 Conference on Bible and Justice.

activists and organizations might discover that the justice concerns that are addressed in texts like Isaiah and Micah share a more direct connection with modern social ills than had been previously realized.[2] Recent research on the contexts behind prophetic complaints attributed to eighth-century Judah suggests that some passages may be able to address a key target of many modern justice concerns with considerable authority: the negative effects of the neoliberal policies of corporate globalization.

Ever since the autumn of 1999, when globalization was brought to the forefront of the public consciousness in the West during the World Trade Organization protests in Seattle, Washington, the word "globalization" has become an umbrella term for a wide range of injustices. From the environmental destruction caused by clear cutting of rain forests in Latin America (Wallach and Woodall 2004: 44–45) and the exploitation of sweatshop workers in Vietnam (Hapke 2004) to the structural adjustment programmes (SAPs) that have undermined the sovereignty of developing nations and severely reduced their poorest citizens' standards of living (Thurow 1996; Woods 2000),[3] the exploitative practices of multi-national corporations and the international financial institutions (IFIs) that facilitate their activities have come under heightened scrutiny. While the Jubilee Campaign for debt relief is one way in which the Bible has been used to address the negative consequences of the world's most powerful nations' economic practices, another avenue has been largely overlooked: prophetic complaints against economic abuse in the eighth-century BCE. Despite the vast differences between modern-day global economics and the economic practices of Iron Age Palestine, prophetic complaints against landownership abuse in Judah, with all necessary caveats, may be uniquely placed to address the exploitative land reforms that have upset rural communities and cultures around the globe since the mid-twentieth century CE. Before connections between the ancient and modern contexts can be approached, a difficulty within the prophetic texts has to be addressed.

A Contextual Problem

While prophetic complaints against landownership abuse attributed to eighth-century Judah provide a damning verdict against those who would take the land of their neighbours, they also present a rather cumbersome obstacle for those who might want to gain deeper insights into their meanings: they fail to offer any real indication as to the socio-economic contexts in which they were written. Take Isa. 5:8, for example: "Woe to you who connect house to house, who attach field to field until there is room for no one but you, and you are left to live alone in the midst of the land".[4] While this verse offers a rebuke against the abuse of landownership rights, all that can be distilled of the verse's socio-economic context is that one generic group of perpetrators displaced another generic group of victims by joining houses and fields together. While the curses in verse 5:10 do indicate that those who were responsible had profited directly from Judah's agrarian industry, such information is of little use in reconstructing a socio-economic context, since *everybody* in an agrarian society profits directly from the agrarian industry. The key contextual variables, such as the motivations behind these land seizures, the identities of the perpetrators and victims who were involved, and the overall effects that these offences would have had on Judean society may have been apparent to the authors' intended audience, but they remain hidden from the modern reader. Such gaping holes in our contextual understanding of this passage makes any attempts to relate Isa. 5:8 to modern forms of exploitation very difficult.

There are other prophetic texts attributed to the eighth century that provide a few contextual clues, but these too are of limited value in revealing a clear socio-economic context. The land seizures referred to in Mic. 2:1 appear to have been carefully planned and facilitated by existing power structures. Without providing the modern reader with a motivation behind the act, the text simply informs us that land was taken because it was within the perpetrators' power.[5] Hosea 5.10 offers an additional clue by possibly pointing to the involvement of a ruling class, claiming that the princes of Judah were acting like those who remove landmarks.[6] The verse does not specifically claim that Judean princes were directly involved in the removal of landmarks, but the accusation that they engaged in such exploitative practices is inferred. Although, if the princes in question had engaged in land seizures, the claim that they acted *like those* who removed landmarks suggests that they were not the only ones engaging in this activity. However, even with such pieces of evidence, the greater socio-economic context to which these Hebrew Prophets referred remains vague, at best. Were they somehow available, answers as to the identities of those involved in these land seizures, the motivations behind their acts, and the effects that they had on Judean society might allow passages such as Isa. 5:8–10 to better address instances of landownership abuse in the modern world.[7]

Another approach that might be able to shed some light on the hidden contexts behind prophetic complaints against landownership abuse would be a more thorough understanding of landownership systems in the late eighth-century BCE. Unfortunately, while scholars such as C. J. de Geus, John Dearman and Joel Weinberg have worked to understand how land tenure was managed in ancient Palestine, they have run into the same problem that this chapter attempts to address: they have been forced to work with a very limited range of resources. As Baruch Levine notes, "biblical literature does not preserve any actual documents of land conveyance or deeds establishing [the] ownership of land in Israel. Nor do we possess court records, official correspondence or royal edicts from the kingdoms of northern Israel or Judah" (1996: 224). Such a limited range of materials not only frustrates a greater understanding as to how land tenure was managed, but also the ways in which land acquisitions would have affected Judean farmers. Despite the wide-range of possibilities that such a lack of contextual information presents, however, a general consensus on the nature of Judean landownership abuse has developed within biblical commentary.

Traditional Interpretations of Judean Landownership Abuse
Several twentieth-century commentators have interpreted Judean landownership abuse as a struggle that pit wealthy "merchants" or "businessmen" against poor farmers. James Mays' and Ralph Smith's commentaries on Mic. 2:1–2 each claim that businessmen had oppressed Judean *peasants* by taking their land. Mays argues that the land seizures referred to in Micah were the result of an "economic development which, supported by the policies of the royal court, had reached its climax in the eighth century" (1976: 64). As affluence increased, Mays concludes, government officials grew more susceptible to corruption and allowed these ancient businessmen to expand their wealth through seizing the lands of farmers. Such a scenario pits the wealthy against the impoverished.

Mays' interpretation of Mic. 2:1–2 is echoed in Ralph Smith's commentary, which also claims that the chief offenders mentioned in the passage were "a relatively small group of greedy, powerful businessmen who spent their nights devising schemes to take control over the lands of the small farmers" (1984: 24). As in Mays' account, Smith interprets eighth-century landownership abuse as a struggle between the wealthy and the poor, thus requiring the existence of a long-established Judean policy towards land tenure for corruptible judges and hypothetical businessmen to pervert. The theory that a few unscrupulous businessmen ruined the lives of vulnerable farmers is worth considering and, perhaps, is even justifiable, but these authors do not offer a justification for their hypotheses. Although they had been forced to work with the same limited resources that have faced so many who have tried to deconstruct the contextual foundation of passages such as Mic. 2:1–2 and Isa. 5:8–10, Mays and Smith offer a hypothesis that has been presented to their readers as fact.

Mays and Smith are not alone in their assessment of Judean land seizures. The motif of wealthy businessmen seizing the lands of the poor is also common in commentaries on Isa. 5:8–10. Edward Kissane, Otto Kaiser and A. S. Herbert each argue that Isa. 5:8 reflects the oppression of the poor by wealthy individuals who worked to bypass their land rights to accrue wealth. Kissane's heading for his commentary on Isa. 5:8–10, "The Rapacity of the Rich, and Jahweh's Threat of Requital", suggests such a socio-economic context (1941: 57). Published in the first half of the twentieth century, Kissane's commentary concludes that wealthy Judeans had been the culprits behind various schemes to displace poor farmers in an effort to build up large estates for themselves (1941: lx). As a result of their efforts, Kissane writes, "the poor were reduced to the position of slaves and hirelings" (1941: 57). Like Mays and Smith, Kissane contends that Judean landownership abuse was the result of greedy individuals who were able to corrupt an otherwise just and fair system of laws, without offering any justification for his conclusions. Despite the facts that Kissane's work was published in 1941 and that the limited information given in Isa. 5:8–10 offers a wealth of interpretive possibilities, very few subsequent commentaries and writings on this passage have deviated very far from his lead.

Kaiser puts forth the possibility that increased wealth among businessmen and Judah's growing "monetary economy" had "led to a crisis among small house owners and land owners ... who became totally dependent upon the large capitalists" (1972: 65),[8] while Herbert envisioned greedy merchants who "sought to buy up houses in the city and peasant holdings in the country" (1973: 51). In the tradition of Kissane, Kaiser and Herbert, John Bright understood the complaints against landownership abuse in Isaiah and Micah to address "the powerful and unscrupulous nobles and the venal judges who had conspired to rob the helpless of their rights" (1981: 278, 290). In each of these interpretations, the commentators present a few greedy businessmen or nobles who conspired to subvert what they saw as a just and sacred system of land tenure that had been practised throughout Judah. Why wouldn't they be drawn to make such assumptions? From a twentieth-century capitalist perspective, it is often the businessmen and banks, through court systems, who foreclose on poor and struggling farmers. However, when these prophetic texts are considered through recurring patterns of exploitation, new interpretive possibilities emerge.

While the above interpretations of prophetic texts speak to the problem of wealthy individuals who abuse the rights of the poor, Marvin Chaney and D. N. Premnath's use of cultural-evolutionary theory provides a more complex account that has breathed new life into a conversation that had become somewhat stagnant. Through using the recurring patterns of abuse that tend to accompany periods of rapid economic development in agrarian societies new understandings of Isa. 5:8–10 and Mic. 2:1–2 emerge. More pertinent to the topic addressed in this chapter and volume, as a whole, the presence of the catalysts for these patterns in both the late eighth-century BCE and modern-day agrarian societies could give certain prophetic texts a previously unrecognized relevance in addressing the negative effects of corporate globalization on agrarian communities. Before the potential value of integrating a modern case study with Chaney's and Premnath's interpretations can be assessed, an understanding of cultural evolution is needed.

The Theory of Cultural Evolution

Sociologists and economic anthropologists such as Gerhard Lenski, Stuart Plattner, Allen Johnson and Timothy Earle have found that agrarian societies tend to experience similar recurring patterns of development as they evolve from their reliance on subsistence strategies to more complex economic strategies that can better manage population growth and/or new trade opportunities, regardless of the culture or time in which they exist (Lenski 1966: 220–22; Johnson and Earle 2001: 256–57; Plattner 2002: 180–81). As the resource demands of population growth create a strain on a subsistence-based culture's carrying capacity, a higher level of administrative control is required to ensure the survival of the community. Whereas some societies succumb to disease and famine until numbers are reduced to levels that can be sustained by family-centred subsistence strategies (Cowgill 1975), others undergo an evolutionary process in which productive control is removed from the family or clan unit and given to a centralized administrative class that can orchestrate the cultivation, storage, protection, and redistribution of goods for the greater community (Johnson and Earle 2001: 24–27).

Similar to the patterns that emerge in order to maintain sudden increases in population growth, subsistence-based cultures that decide to take advantage of new trade opportunities require a greater level of centralized organization in order to orchestrate sufficient levels of food production while reallocating land for the cultivation and production of tradable goods.

While such strategic changes in productive management enable communities to increase in population, acquire new technologies, and introduce new goods, they do so at significant economic and social cost.

As subsistence farmers lose control over production and become increasingly dependent on redistribution mechanisms and the people who run them, a society's economic goals begin to shift from subsistence to profit. Anthropologist Stephen Sanderson explains that as a society's economy undergoes centralization, "at some point, some people get themselves into a position by means of which they can compel other people to work for them and produce substantial quantities of storable food" (2001: 300–01). By developing previously unknown levels of surplus, a society's ability to engage in interregional trade increases, whether for food, technological information, military hardware, or luxury items. As administrators find themselves in a position to take advantage of this situation, Johnson and Earle have found that they tend to use their influence to consolidate power and ensure that the wealth that is generated by the new economic landscape remains within their own class (2001: 26–27). They explain that in chiefdoms and states alike, "elites carefully manage the economy in order to maximize surplus production that may be translated into power and political survival", and that the "elite ownership of resources and technology is typically formalized in a system of legal property", to yet further this consolidation of power (Johnson and Earle 2001: 35). Evidence of this common pattern, which tends to occur in cycles that wax and wane with ever-changing levels of access to trade opportunities, can be found as early as Bronze Age Palestine and as recently as modern-day Vietnam and Peru (Richard 1987; Chossudovsky 2003: 180–83, 221–22).

The societal transformation that subsistence communities experience during the waxing of these cycles takes place through a set of recurring patterns. While these patterns will manifest themselves in different ways depending on cultural and meteorological environments in which the society exists, the rising class of elites will tend to exploit their region's resources by:

1. coercing farmers into abandoning traditional subsistence strategies and the socio-religious norms that support them;
2. consolidating land into large estates (or latifundia) in order to enable the mass production of export goods, a process known as *latifundialization*; and

3. hoarding the benefits of these developments amongst themselves and their supporters through various systems of patronage and exclusion.[9]

In the end, the productive efforts that had once been focused on the wellbeing of the community's producers become refocused on the wellbeing of the markets, leading to a loss of self-sufficiency and increased hardship for small-scale farmers (Johnson and Earle 1987: 273). Biblical scholars like Marvin Chaney and D. N. Premnath have recognized the interpretive value of these evolutionary patterns in their approaches to the contextually ambiguous prophetic texts attributed to eighth-century Judah, when the area experienced a series of rapid societal developments that are not entirely dissimilar to those taking place in agrarian societies today.

Cultural Evolutionary Theory and Eighth-Century Judah

Rather than reiterating the undefended contextual assumptions of previous biblical commentaries, Chaney's and Premnath's interpretive approach offers a new way of understanding prophetic complaints against landownership abuses that are attributed to eighth-century Judah. Breaking free from the commonly held view that the prophets addressed a few immoral merchants who had taken land from poor farmers, Chaney and Premnath suggest that a pan-Judean shift in economic strategy took place in the late eighth-century that reshaped the region's entire approach to agrarian production and land management. By reading Isa. 5:8 and Mic. 2:1–2 through the vibrant socio-economic context of Judah's absorption into the Assyrian trade nexus, Chaney and Premnath propose a more widespread problem than many previous commentators have offered. Chaney writes that while

> many modern readers of the prophetic books assume that these texts excoriate a few venal individuals who deviated from norms otherwise observed in what was a healthy and just economic system ... little could be farther from the realities of ancient Israel and Judah. As a careful reading of the oracles concerning economic dynamics makes clear, the prophets critique certain changes in the political economy as an integrated whole. (1989: 16)

Through taking into account evidence of a heightened demand for olive oil from Mesopotamia to Southern Europe, increased access to trade opportunities as a result of Judah's absorption into the expanding Neo-Assyrian Empire's world system, and levels of population growth that would have demanded a greater centralization of agrarian production,

Chaney and Premnath claim that the prophetic complaints were composed in response to the negative effects that accompanied a period of rapid cultural evolution, not the actions of a few greedy individuals (Chaney 2005: 146–49; Premnath 2003: 43–109).

Through considering the transformative changes that took place in late eighth-century Judah in light of cultural-evolutionary patterns, Chaney and Premnath both conclude that Judah was likely to have experienced a period of latifundialization that was facilitated by debt exploitation (Chaney 2005: 148; Premnath 1997). They each propose that Judean administrators led the farmers who had become dependent upon them to abandon their traditional risk-reducing subsistence strategies in favour of the risky, yet lucrative, specialized cultivation of olives and grapes. Such a practice would have made the Judean farmers more susceptible to Judah's unpredictable weather conditions and, in the end, crop failure and dependence on survival loans would have led to land foreclosures (Premnath 1997). Without the aid of risk-reducing subsistence strategies, which are used as a safety net against periods of drought and famine, farmers would have been especially vulnerable to this process. Chaney claims that the reduction:

> of risk-spreading measures rendered peasants ever more vulnerable to the vicissitudes of an erratic climate. When natural disaster struck, they were left no alternative to survival loans at *de facto* interest rates usurious by any standards. Foreclosure on family land and/or the indentured labor of family members pledged as collateral was often at the discretion of the wealthy urban creditors. (2005: 148)

For those who may have been reluctant to switch to specialized farming, Chaney offers the suggestion that rulers could simply have levied "a heavy tax upon grain produced 'inefficiently' by the subsistence farmers of the hill country" (1999: 107), to pave yet another way to survival loans and foreclosure. In the end, according to Chaney's argument, Judah's political elite would have profited from trade and expanded their landed estates as subsistence farmers lost their inheritance and traditional ways of life, thus angering the prophetic authors.

Material Evidence For Chaney's and Premnath's Theory

Chaney's and Premnath's theory that latifundialization occurred as a result of Judean societal transformation is supported by the archaeological record, which indicates that Judah experienced massive demographic changes accompanied by the development of a powerful political economy in the late eighth-century. In the last half of the eighth century alone, Jerusalem expanded from an area of about 6 hectares to cover 46 hectares (Shiloh 1984: 3) while its population is estimated to have grown by 10 to 15% in a single generation.[10] Rural areas also experienced unprecedented levels of growth at this time. Israel Finkelstein and Neil Silberman write that "settlements in the hill country to the south of Jerusalem swelled from perhaps thirty-four in Iron IIA to 122 in the late eighth century" (2006: 265). In addition to growth in and around the city of Jerusalem, the construction of urban waterway projects, massive defensive walls and fortresses in the Negev, irrigation systems and dams in previously unpopulated and uncultivated regions, new trade emporiums, and the introduction of standardized weights all attest to the development of a more powerful and centralized administration.[11] These economic and structural advances, none of which had been apparent before the late eighth century (Finkelstein and Silberman 2006: 277), indicate that a strong political economy and an increase in trade-based revenue streams had come to outweigh the simple and relatively low-maintenance subsistence strategies of previous generations.[12] It is in this way that the Judean response to population growth and increased trade opportunities dovetail with the recurring patterns that are associated with cultural-evolutionary patterns of abuse. Beyond internal motivations to centralize the management of production and redistribution in order to secure greater food surpluses and cope with such demographic upheaval, it is likely that Judah's Assyrian rulers, who sought raw materials for both trade and domestic consumption, would have also encouraged the economic advances that occurred in the eighth century (Sherratt and Sherratt 1993: 366–71).

Although latifundialization typically follows the sorts of changes that took place in this transformative period of Judah's history, population growth and the construction of various public works projects cannot prove that such land acquisitions took place; societal patterns can only be used as guides through which to interpret the evidence that we possess, not as historical evidence, in and of itself. However, there is another indicator that dovetails with prophetic complaints against landownership abuses during a time in which Judah appears to have experienced demographic upheaval: the development of a centrally orchestrated olive oil industry. Finkelstein and Na'aman find that a previously unseen large-scale olive oil industry arose in eighth-century Judah, with urban areas housing up to thirty oil-processing instillations (Finkelstein and Na'aman 2004: 73–74). Finkelstein and Na'aman write that "in the late 8th-century, the economy of Judah in general and the Shephelah in particular was well-planned and state-organized, with Tell Beit Mirsim and Beth Shemesh specializing in oil production. It also seems logical to assume that the land around these sites was given over to olive orchards" (2004: 74). A process of latifundialization, which allows those in either economic or political power to take greater control of the productive capability of a region's arable land, would have been an effective way to ensure an efficient and continued cultivation of olives for processing and trade or tribute.

Considering the meteorological environment with which Judean farmers had to contend, Chaney's and Premnath's assertions that crop failure and debt would have been used to take land from Judean farmers is plausible. Due to Judah's geographical position between subtropical and temperate atmospheric patterns, the highlands experience two distinct seasons in which farmers must calculate their annual planting strategies: a winter rainy season and a summer dry season (Ashbel 1971: 185; Borowski 2002: 47). In an environment that offers the prospect of complete crop failure as a result of unfavourable precipitation levels every three out of ten years, farmers who fail to spread risk are likely to find themselves in trouble before long, making survival loans a necessity (Hopkins 1985: 87–89, 215; Ashbel 1971: 185). These sorts of environmental conditions would have served those who had an interest in consolidating land into large estates by driving farmers into debt. It was against such a socio-economic context that Chaney and Premnath believe that the authors of Isa. 5:8–10 and Mic. 2:1–2 protested (Chaney 1989: 24–26; Chaney 1999: 107–09; Premnath 2003: 100–07).

The central question that remains is how can sociological patterns and archaeological findings from ancient Judah be of use to those who seek to address similar injustices in the modern world? Considering the recurring nature of cultural-evolutionary patterns, the events that took place in the late eighth-century are not unique, but are the manifestation of a system that has played itself out on both regional and inter-regional levels for millennia. This cycle's most recent manifestation is found in the neoliberal policies of corporate globalization.

World-Systems Evolution

The vast differences between corporate globalization and the world system that had such profound effects on Judean society in the eighth century BCE are both great and numerous. Farmers and merchants in eighth-century Judah had no concept of telecommunications or overnight trans-global shipping, nor did they have international financial institutions to regulate trade, let alone a functioning monetary system (Ronen 1996: 122).

While such important differences need to be considered when making comparisons between ancient and modern economic systems, world-systems theorists will argue that important connections do exist between the world systems of today and those of the ancient world. Corporate globalization is not an isolated economic phenomenon of the twentieth and twenty-first centuries[13] but, as Joachim Rennstich and George Modelski and William Thompson suggest, the culmination of up to five thousand years of world-systems evolution (Rennstich 2006: 204-08; Modelski and Thompson 1996).

The world system of the eighth and seventh centuries BCE and that of modern-day corporate globalization are connected by both a lineage and a key component: the motivations that drive them. Despite immense technological differences and the methods used to dominate the peripheral regions of a system's core, they share a common drive for power, wealth and growth. Rennstich explains that although technological contexts between successive world systems change alongside advances in agriculture techniques, the scope and efficiency of trade, and systems of management and control, "the driving logic (human agency) of this process remains the same [as] its context changes, constituting a 'social learning algorithm' of evolutionary change that is at work at all levels of the world system process (from the individual to the change of the world system itself)" (2006: 205). Although corporate globalization has developed into a far more efficient and expansive system than its Iron Age II ancestor, the motivating factors of profit and control – and the evolutionary transformations that they provoke in agrarian communities – remain common. It is this connection between the world systems of the Neo-Assyrian Empire and today's corporate globalization that allows prophetic texts attributed to the eighth century, including Isa. 5:8–10 and Mic. 2:1–2, to address a variety of modern economic injustices with a considerable level of relevance.

A very important Caveat
Naturally, the experience of Judean farmers cannot and should not be thought of as identical to those of modern farmers, but parallels may be found that could be useful to those who campaign for economic justice. For the purposes of this paper, I have examined the North African country of Tunisia, and the cultural evolution that it experienced as it entered into the current system of corporate globalization in 1956, after gaining independence from the French. The technological and economic differences between the agrarian societies of mid-twentieth-century Tunisia and eighth-century-BCE Judah are immense, but their experiences appear to be

connected by the recurring patterns of cultural evolution that arise as a result of being absorbed into a world economic system, and two important parallels: common agrarian challenges and religious-based systems of land management.

The Tunisian Example

The Tunisian experience is an excellent illustration of what tends to occur when agrarian societies undergo rapid economic growth. Since Tunisia gained its independence in 1956, a series of developments have changed the face of Tunisian land management, uprooted traditional economic and social norms, and changed the ways in which Tunisians interact with one another. Struggling to benefit from international capitalism, Tunisia surrendered several aspects of its cultural and religious identity to the will of its rulers and foreign financial interests. As a result, those whose families had depended upon semi-subsistence strategies for generations suffered greatly while a rising elite minority profited handsomely.

Soon after gaining independence, Tunisia underwent a period of rapid economic transformation in order to adhere to a common mid-twentieth-century paradigm, which blamed stunted economic development on a "dysfunctional attachment" to traditional production strategies (Shils 1960: 256–57). In order to facilitate a hurried process of modernization, the Tunisian government forced many of the country's rural communities to abandon their semi-subsistence practices so that the country could become a more competitive economic force and take advantage of the increased opportunities for trade of the post-war era (Duwaji 1968: 129; Shils 1960: 256–57). In line with the recurring patterns of cultural evolution, President Habib Bourguiba understood that in order to achieve the levels of agricultural efficiency required to compete in the global markets, his government would need to take control of Tunisian farmlands. To accomplish this, there would not only be a change in the way that land was managed in Tunisia, but the government would need to undermine the religious norms that supported the previous system. Bourguiba was able to accomplish both of these tasks through a series of latifundialist reforms that seized the lands from subsistence farmers and their religious patrons, abandoned traditional economic strategies to facilitate the cultivation of export goods (such as wine and olive oil), and redirected the benefits of the Tunisian agrarian economy from the religious establishment to the new ruling elite (King 2003; Anderson 1986: 242; Parsons 1965: 304; Radwan *et al.* 1991: 75). These ambitious goals were met through the closure of the *habous* land endowments.

The Closure of the Habous

The *habous* system of land management, which dates back to the beginnings of Islam in the first century AH (622–719 CE), was introduced to Tunisia by the Ottoman Empire in the sixteenth-century CE and covered one-fifth of Tunisia's arable land at the time of independence (Anderson 1986: 235).[14] Formed in part to give peasants communal access to farmland, the *habous* were designed to provide for both the material and spiritual wellbeing of rural communities (Powers 1989: 536). David Powers explains that when a *habous* was formed,

> a (*waqif*) [founder] would assign the usufruct of a revenue-producing property to either a person or an institution in a way considered "pleasing to God", while sequestering the property itself in such a manner that it became inalienable in perpetuity and could not be sold, given away as a gift, or inherited. (1989: 536)

Two types of these Muslim land endowments were maintained in Tunisia: the public *habous* and the private *habous*. While the private *habous* perpetuated the wealth and status of the old upper class families in Tunis, the public *habous* were a cornerstone of Tunisian agrarian culture. The public *habous* not only provided Tunisian farm communities with arable land for mixed-subsistence farming, they also funded schools, hospitals, and other charitable programmes (Powers 1989: 536; Duwaji 1968: 129). Despite the vital roles that these *habous* played in their communities, Bourguiba had them closed within the first six weeks of his presidency (Zaibet and Dunn 1998: 834).

The consequences of these *habous* closures for Tunisia's mixed-subsistence farmers were quick and dire. As control of the land from these endowments was transferred to the newly emerging state, the charitable services that were connected to them instantly disappeared. Aside from losing schools, hospitals and other benefits that rural Tunisians had enjoyed for generations, farming families were forced to purchase the same goods that they had once grown communally. This radical transformation of Tunisian culture caused outrage among small-scale farmers and religious leaders alike.

Many members of Tunisia's religious elite did not sit idly as the government dismantled their religious-based cooperatives. The country's more pious clerics protested the regime's callousness towards the needs of

rural Tunisians, and Bourguiba's disregard for the religious, social, and
financial significance of the *habous* (Tozy 1993: 105). Bourguiba's response
to these protests was well calculated. Rather than attempting to directly
marginalize Islam, which has been a key component of Tunisian society for
centuries, President Bourguiba demanded a reinterpretation of Muslim
teachings that would complement his government's economic and
developmental goals (Tozy 1993: 109–10).[15] Addressing a crowd in
Kairouan, Bourguiba entreated Tunisia's Muslim clerics to support his
reforms, stating,

> At a time [when] we are struggling against poverty, setting up programs and
> drawing plans to escape from underdevelopment, demanding an accounting
> from those who do not produce enough and who limit freedom of enterprise,
> at the time when our life and death are at stake, at a time when the recovery
> of this Muslim nation depends on our tenacious work, I enjoin you to take
> advantage of a dispensation clearly defined by a healthy conception of the
> religious laws. (Debbasch 1962: 148)

When the nation's more pious imams refused to comply, the government
forced them to resign and seized control of their educational institutions:
perhaps most importantly, the Zeitouna Mosque University (Tozy 1993:
105, 110). It had become very clear from the start that in the new Tunisia,
the influence of the markets would outweigh the authority of religious
tradition and the needs of the rural poor.

The disregard that the Tunisian government displayed towards religious
tradition is not surprising, from a cultural-evolutionary perspective, since
the overturn of religious ideals often goes hand-in-hand with socio-
economic transformation. Such tensions were experienced across the
world in the fifteenth century CE as trade opened up across the world and
religious norms pertaining to religious dietary habits were abandoned to
facilitate increased trade opportunities (Nussbaum 1933; Pomeranz 2000:
119–20; Bayly 2002: 52–53). Bernard Knapp explains that due to the often
inseparable connection that develops between agrarian economic
practices and religious tradition, as seen in agricultural festivals and land-
management strategies, "ritual activities serve as the interface between
religion and techno-economic or socio-political activities in agrarian
societies" (1988: 157). As a result of this intertwining of religion and
economy, Roy Rappaport observes, a society's economic concepts eventually
come to be perceived to be as infallible as the religious beliefs to which they
are connected (1971: 32–37). A greater understanding of this common
tension between religious and political leadership during periods of rapid
economic development may offer new perspectives on the motivations

behind prophetic complaints against economic injustice in eighth-century Judah. It is interesting to note that in 1960, economist Raymond Crist concluded his study of these transformations in Tunisian agriculture by quoting Isa. 5:8 (1960: 322). Apparently this economist saw a connection between the negative effects of land seizure on ancient and modern farmers.

Further Efforts to Consolidate Tunisian Farmland

In the 1970s the Tunisian government allowed wealthy individuals to confiscate even more communally held land, causing great hardship for small-scale farmers. Samir Radwan, Vali Jamal, and Ajit Ghose note that from 1961–62 to 1979–80 a marked decline in average numbers of people owning land was apparent as an affluent minority increased took control over the country's farmlands (1991: 37).[16] Addressing the presence of this common aspect of cultural evolution in agrarian societies, Douglas Ashford writes,

> As so often happens with abrupt shifts of policy over unpopular decisions, a good many of the aggrieved took matters into their own hands. A number of recently organised agricultural production co-ops were forcefully dissolved by the members and the managers simply driven off the land. Fall planting in some areas was seriously disrupted, while in the cities several long established co-ops for marketing and commerce were returned to private hands. (1973: 36)

With reduced access to local markets, small-scale landowners were coerced into producing exportable goods for a global economy rather than for their own communities and wellbeing. The additional financial demands of growing unreliable cash crops, such as refrigeration and fertilization, drove many of these farmers into unsustainable levels of debt. Forced to take out survival loans to compensate for added expenses, many lost their land to foreclosure (Ashford 1973: 36). Although Tunisia's GDP grew at an impressive annual rate of 9% between 1970 and 1976, the unemployment rate doubled, leading to civil unrest (Ashford 1973: 36). In 1978, when a general strike was called and demonstrations took place, the government responded by killing and imprisoning hundreds of Tunisian protesters (Disney 1978: 12).

Conditions for Tunisia's rural poor continued to decline throughout the 1980s, as the World Bank funded structural adjustment programmes that gave further legitimacy to the government's elite-centred policies (Payne 1993: 144). Similar to the methods used by Neo-Assyrian rulers, Tunisia's ruling elite further consolidated their economic control by gifting state-backed corporations to loyal supporters (Postgate 1969: 9–16; Payne 1993: 144). As is often the result of cultural-evolutionary shifts like the one that Tunisia experienced, by the end of the 1980s the wealthiest 3% of Tunisians controlled one-third of the country's farmlands while the poorest 46% held only 8%, and to devastating effect (Zaibet and Dunn 1998: 835–36). In 1989, citing increased food costs, decreased family wages, and a serious lack of access to medical facilities, UNICEF filed a complaint against the Tunisian government and the World Bank, blaming their developmental policies for the nation's rising infant mortality rate (United Nations Children's Fund 1989). As has often occurred during the waxing of previous world systems, the land consolidation and wealth-hoarding policies of this modern-day agrarian society's ruling elite had devastating effects on the country's rural producers.

The fact that Tunisia's experience in the latter half of the twentieth century CE was unique to its own time and cultural setting must be respected. The events that unfolded after Tunisia achieved independence from France were, in many ways, the product of the post-war era and the decline of European colonialism.[17] Aside from a massive loss of human life, the incredible economic and structural devastation that had been caused by the Second World War led many national leaders and policymakers to a realization that rapid reconstruction and lasting economic development throughout the world would be an essential element in ensuring lasting peace and stability (Smithies 1944: 785–86; MacGibbon 1945; Fellner 1945). New technologies in transportation and communications, such as transcontinental flight and more advanced telecommunications, allowed governments and international IFIs to orchestrate trade and developmental projects with an efficiency that had never been seen before. But despite all of the technological progress and resources that the newly formed Tunisian government had at its disposal, the patterns of exploitation that are commonly associated with periods of rapid economic development in agrarian societies did not deviate from usual course seen in other countries, both ancient and present; they were simply carried out with a greater level of efficiency and speed.

From Prophets to Profits

As soon as Tunisia gained its independence, and with the blessings and assistance of the IMF, the World Bank, the United Kingdom, the United States, and West Germany, the subsistence strategies and the institutions that supported the *habous* were abandoned, land was consolidated into latifundia, and the benefits of these changes were channelled into the coffers of the ruling elite and their supporters (Kleve 1971: 306–07; Entelis 1975:

538). Although the weapons that were used in mid-twentieth-century Tunisia may have been unique to their time (such as the structural adjustment programmes of the IMF and World Bank), the wounds that were inflicted on rural producers (economic and social displacement through land acquisition) were relatively common to those that were experienced in the Babylonian, Greek and Ottoman empires (Bosworth 2000: 276–79). It is the thread that connects these recurring societal patterns in the modern world that allows theories of cultural and world-systems evolution to move beyond abstract notions that become a tangible method for exploring the hidden contexts behind prophetic complaints against injustice in Judah, for which little other evidence is available. Such a realization raises an important consideration in addressing the ability of the ancient texts of the Bible to address modern forms of injustice; if the current economic abuses that are caused by corporate globalization are yet another phase of a recurring pattern that also took place in eighth-century Judah, prophetic texts that are attributed to that time find a previously unrecognized relevance in addressing the negative effects of the present cycle.

Despite the vast differences between Judah and Tunisia, as has been addressed above, Tunisia's entrance into corporate globalization in the mid-twentieth century CE and Judah's entrance into the Assyrian world system in the late eighth-century BCE appear to have produced some important similarities. Considering Tunisia's recent history in light of textual and archaeological evidence attributed to late eighth-century Judah, we are presented with two agrarian societies that were thrust into rapid economic development and increased trade activity and, as a result, were faced with a concerted effort to centralize their respective productive capabilities.

In the Judean context, rapid economic growth and centralization is evidenced through the development of a strengthened administrative core, expansion of agrarian activities into previously uncultivated regions, a state-sponsored centralization of Judah's olive-oil production, and prophetic complaints against land consolidation during the period in which Judah was absorbed into the Neo-Assyrian Empire.[18] While Tunisia experienced political independence from colonialism rather than acquisition by a foreign power in the mid-twentieth century, the effects of a developing world system with Western Europe and the United States at its core produced conditions akin to those experienced by the peripheral regions of previous world systems. The levels of efficiency that were required to compete in the international markets led Tunisia's ruling elite to marginalize the religious and subsistence traditions of those who had depended upon the *habous* endowments for centuries before embarking on various subsequent schemes to privatize Tunisia's arable lands throughout the 1970s and 1980s. As a rising political-elite minority prospered and hoarded the spoils of the increased revenue that was produced in Tunisia's evolving economic climate, millions of farmers and religious leaders suffered displacement, and unemployment, while some faced fatal levels of poverty. Both contexts appear to present a set of common goals that had been perused by elite members of society and, as a result of their actions, inflicted common consequences on those who would not benefit from their respective cultures' evolutionary changes.

Conclusion

While the exact nature of the agrarian centralization that took place in late eighth-century Judah cannot be known with certainty, the recurring patterns that cultural-evolutionary theorists attribute to rapid economic development in agrarian societies provides a link between ancient occurrences of economic abuse and those taking place in the most recent examples of the world-systems cycle. Chaney's and Premnath's work, coupled with modern-day case studies like the one given above, can help to shed light on the hidden contexts behind landownership abuse in ancient Judah and allow new questions to be asked of prophetic complaints against injustice. In addition to providing the field of biblical studies with a fresh interpretive approach in an area that had become relatively stagnant, this model for interpretation acts as a two-way street to offer the prophetic voice a previously unrecognized level of relevance in addressing the exploitative practices of corporate globalization on agrarian communities around the world. The cultural-evolutionary effects of the neoliberal policies of the IMF, World Bank, and the world's wealthiest nations, when seen as another turn in an ongoing socio-economic cycle of trade expansion and contraction, have not been limited to rural Tunisia, but have had adverse affects on the lives of farmers from East Asia to North and South America (Kumar 1962: 337; Parsons 1965: 304; Castillo and Nigh 1998: 240; Chossudovsky 2003: 180–83).

Although a detailed account of the complexities of cultural-evolutionary theory, the changes that took place in late eighth-century Judah, and those that Tunisia experienced in the mid-to-late twentieth century CE cannot fit into the confines of a chapter, this paper has attempted to illustrate the hypothesis that the landownership abuses to which prophetic texts like

Isa. 5:8–10 and Mic. 2:1–2 refer are not unique, but are rather *expected* in the socio-economic climate that developed during their supposed period of authorship.[19] A key question that such an argument presents is "how can revealing connections between prophetic complaints against landownership abuses stemming from corporate globalization be of practical use to individuals or faith-based organizations that draw upon biblical texts in order to confront exploitative economic practices? Revealing connections between the world system into which Judah was absorbed and the world system of corporate globalization can be useful in a couple of important ways.

A close analysis of the connections that appear to exist between the economic circumstances of eighth-century Judah and modern-day Tunisia can provide a better understanding of the exploitative effects of world-system expansion. In my hometown of Moorhead, Minnesota the Red River of the North can produce devastating floods when the snow that accumulates over the winter melts in the spring. Able to recognize this very simple and evident annual pattern, the Army Core of Engineers diverted the river in 1959 to mitigate the damage caused to both Moorhead and neighbouring Fargo, North Dakota. Through recognizing a recurring pattern and the problems that it posed, engineers were able to lessen its negative effects. Similarly, through understanding how the problems that stem from corporate globalization arise, like landownership abuse in agrarian societies, activists and conscientious policy-makers may find themselves in more advantageous positions to both recognize and address their root causes. It is even possible that such problems could be identified at an earlier stage and avoided before they arise.

Perhaps a more basic, yet an important way in which the model of cultural-evolutionary theory can be of assistance in the struggle against economic justice is as a rallying call. For those participating in various justice causes throughout the years, the Bible, like other religious texts, has given people a sense that they are not alone in their quests for a just world. During the nineteenth-century abolitionist movement in United States, both slaves and those who risked their lives to smuggle slaves to freedom found the Exodus narrative to be a source of strength (Kling 2004: 195). Similarly, Dietrich Bonhoeffer and the Confessing Church in Nazi Germany found strength in biblical texts like Psalm 119 as they resisted the Nazi regime in Germany (Brock 2005). The awareness of a common struggle as expressed in the Bible can be a powerful source of inspiration for those who confront injustices that are carried out by powers that can seem overwhelming.

Notes

1. "It has been told you, o human being, what is good and what the Lord requires of you: to perform justice, to love mercy, and to walk humbly with your God."
2. Conversely, they may find that a particular text does not relate at all.
3. Useful studies on the IMF and World Bank's influence on seemingly extraneous governmental functions to economic development that could endanger national sovereignty, such as national education and military policies, can also be found in "The Global Politics of Education: Brazil and the World Bank" (Kempner and Jurema 2002), "Globalization as a Mode of Thinking" (Biersteker 2000: 155–56), "The IMF Under Fire" (Amuzegar 1986: 118), "Security and Inequality" (Hurrell 1999), "The Meltzer Report" (Meltzer Commission 1999) and in *The Globalization of Poverty and the New World Order* (Chossudovsky 2003: 48).
4. Author's own translation
5. כי יש־לאל ידם Whether the power was of a political, legal, or a physical nature is not specified.
6. היו שרי יהודי כמסיגי גבול The verse does not specifically claim that the princes were involved in this activity, but it does suggest that the act was taking place, if not by them.
7. Conversely, the discovery of such answers may show that there is little comparison to be made.
8. Subsequent interpretations of archaeological evidence that have become commonly accepted render much of Kaiser's interpretation moot, such as a lack of any monetary system in eighth-century Judah.
9. For more on this process see Lenski (1966: 220), Johnson and Earle (2001: 22–37) and Berdan (2002: 79).
10. Although population levels of ancient sites are very difficult to determine, Liverani (2007: 152) estimates that the city grew from 1000 to 15,000 while Finkelstein and Silberman (2006: 265) suggest a growth rate of 1000 to 10,000 inhabitants in a single generation.
11. More on these developments can be found in Liverani (2007: 152–55), Avigad (1984: 46–53), McNutt (1999: 153–54), Shiloh (1984: 19), Jamieson-Drake (1991: 97) and in Elat (1978: 27).
12. Other indicators of trade include the import of fish and shellfish from distant regions. Henk Mienis (1992: 129) claims that shells discovered in Jerusalem originated from a variety of distant locations, including the Mediterranean Sea, the Red Sea, and the River Nile, indicating "intensive trade" between distant societies and Jerusalem. Other luxury items that were imported into Judah include luxury woods that were imported from as far away as South Arabia, North Syria, and perhaps even Greece, as addressed by Faust and Weiss (2005: 75).
13. Although modern globalization has roots dating further back than the twentieth century, for the purposes of this paper the author dates the beginnings of its most current form, which were developed with the creation of the International Monetary Fund and the International Bank for Reconstruction and Development (currently known as the World Bank) at the Bretton Woods Conference in 1944.
14. Prior to French colonization the *habous* covered one-third of Tunisia's arable lands. Also see McKay (1945: 387) for more information.

15. It should be noted that Bourguiba did take measures that were seen by many as open opposition to Muslim sensibilities, such as encouraging Tunisians to abandon the sacred fast of Ramadan on the grounds that it slowed productivity. See Boulby (1988: 592) and Anderson (1991: 107) for more information.
16. Unfortunately, there are no records on landownership. Landholding and landowning are different, and it is landholding that is represented in their study.
17. Or at least as European colonialism was in its previous form.
18. Even if these texts were written during a later period, perhaps addressing a similar boon in economic activity that brought about similar results, their setting in the eighth century suggests that such activities had taken place during Judah's absorption into the Neo-Assyrian Empire.
19. For a more in-depth analysis of these issues see Coomber, *Re-Reading the Prophets Through Corporate Globalization: A Cultural-Evolutionary Approach to Economic Injustice in the Hebrew Bible*. Biblical Intersections 4. Piscataway, New Jersey: Gorgias Press (2010).

Bibliography

Amuzegar, Jahangir. 1986. "The IMF Under Fire." *Foreign Policy* 64: 98–119.

Anderson, Lisa. 1986. *The State and Social Transformation in Tunisia and Libya: 1830– 1980*. Princeton, NJ: Princeton University Press.

_____1991. "Obligation and Accountability: Islamic Politics in North Africa." *Daedalus* 120 (3): 93–112.

Ashbel, D. 1971. "Israel, Land of (Geographical Survey): Climate." In *Encyclopaedia Judaica*, vol. 9: 181–94. Jerusalem: Keter Publishing House.

Ashford, Douglas E. 1973. "Succession and Social Change in Tunisia." *International Journal of Middle East Studies* 4 (1): 23–39.

Avigad, Nahman. 1984. *Discovering Jerusalem*. Oxford: Blackwell.

Bayly, C. A. 2002. "'Archaic' and 'Modern' Globalization in the Eurasian and African Arena: c. 1750–1850." In *Globalization in World History* ed. A.G. Hopkins: 47–73. London: Pimlico.

Berdan, Frances F. 2002. "Trade and Markets in Precapitalist States." In *Economic Anthropology*, ed. Stuart Plattner: 78–107. Stanford, CA: Stanford University Press.

Biersteker, Thomas. 2000. "Globalization as a Mode of Thinking." In *The Political Economy of Globalization*, ed. Ngaire Woods: 155–56. New York: St Martin's Press.

Borowski, Oded. 2002. *Agriculture in Iron Age Israel*. Boston, MA: American School of Oriental Research.

Bosworth, Andrew. 2000. "The Evolution of the World-City System." In *World System History: The Social Science of Long-Term Change*, eds Robert A. Denemark, Jonathan Friedman, Barry K. Gills and George Modelski: 273–83. London: Routledge.

Boulby, Marion. 1988. "The Islamic Challenge: Tunisia Since Independence." *Third World Quarterly* 10 (2), Islam & Politics: 590–614.

Bright, John. 1981. *A History of Israel*, 3rd edn. Philadelphia, PA: Westminster Press.

Brock, Brian. 2005. "Bonhoeffer and the Bible in Christian Ethics: Psalm 119, The Mandates, and Ethics as a 'Way'." *Studies in Christian Ethics* 18 (3): 7–29.

Castillo, Rosalva Aída Hernández and Ronald Nigh. 1998. "Global Processes and Local Identity Among Mayan Coffee Growers in Chiapas, Mexico." *American Anthropology* 100 (1): 136–47.

Chaney, Marvin L. 1989. "Bitter Bounty: The Dynamics of Political Economy Critiqued by the Eighth-Century Prophets." In *Reformed Faith and Economics*, ed. Robert L. Stivers: 15–30. Lanham, MD: University Press of America.

_____ 1999. "Whose Sour Grapes? The Addressees of Isaiah 5:1–7 in the Light of Political Economy." In *The Social World of the Hebrew Bible: Twenty-Five Years of the Social Sciences in the Academy* ([Semeia, 87], eds Ronald A. Simkins and Stephen L. Cook: 105–22. Atlanta, GA: Society of Biblical Literature.

_____ 2005. "Micah – Models Matter: Political Economy and Micah 6:9-15." In *Ancient Israel: The Old Testament in its Social Context*, ed. Philip F. Esler: 145–60. London: SCM Press.

Chossudovsky, Michel. 2003. *The Globalization of Poverty and the New World Order*, 2nd edn. Pincourt, Québec: Global Research.

Coomber, Matthew J.M. (2010). *Re-Reading the Prophets Through Corporate Globalization: A Cultural-Evolutionary Understanding of Economic Injustice in the Hebrew Bible*. Biblical Intersections 4. Piscataway, NJ: Gorgias Press.

Cowgill, George L. 1975. "On Causes and Consequences of Ancient and Modern Population Changes." *American Anthropologist* 77 (3): 505–25.

Crist, Raymond E. 1960. "Land for the Fellahin, XI: Land Tenure and Land Use in the Near East." *American Journal of Economics and Sociology* 19 (3): 311–22.

Debbasch, Charles. 1962. *La République Tunisienne*. Paris: CNRS.

Disney, Nigel. 1978. "The Working Class Revolt in Tunisia." *Middle East Research and Information Project Reports*, 67: 12–14.

Duwaji, Ghazi. 1968. "Land Ownership in Tunisia: An Obstacle to Agricultural Development." *Land Economics* 44 (1): 129–32.

Elat, Moshe. 1978. "The Economic Relations of the Neo-Assyrian Empire with Egypt." *Journal of the American Oriental Society* 98 (1): 20–34.

Entelis, John P. 1975. "Reformist Ideology in the Arab World: The Cases of Tunisia and Lebanon." *The Review of Politics* 37 (4): 513–46.

Faust, Avraham and Ehud Weiss. 2005. "Judah, Philistia, and the Mediterranean World: Reconstructing the Economic System of the Seventh Century B.C.E." *Bulletin of the American Schools of Oriental Research*, 338: 71–92.

Fellner, William. 1945. "The Commercial Policy Implications of the Fund and Bank." *The American Economic Review* 35 (2): 262–71.

Finkelstein, Israel and Nadav Na'aman. 2004. "The Judahite Shephelah in the Late 8th and Early 7th Centuries BCE." *Tel Aviv* 31 (1): 60–79.

Finkelstein, Israel and Neil Asher Silberman. 2006. "Temple and Dynasty: Hezekiah, the Remaking of Judah and the Rise of the Pan-Israelite Ideology." *Journal for the Study of the Old Testament* 30 (3): 259–85.

Hapke, Laura. 2004. *Sweatshop: The History of an American Idea*. London: Rutgers University Press.

Herbert, A. S. 1973. *The Book of the Prophet Isaiah: Chapters 1–39*. Cambridge: Cambridge University Press.

Hopkins, David C. 1985. *The Highlands of Canaan: Agricultural Life in the Early Iron Age* (The Social World of Biblical Antiquity, 3). Sheffield: Almond.

Hurrell, Andrew. 1999. "Security and Inequality." In *Inequality, Globalization, and World Politics*, eds Andrew Hurrell and Ngaire Woods: 248–353. Oxford: Oxford University Press.

Jamieson-Drake, David W. 1991. *Scribes and Schools in Monarchic Judah: A Socio-Archeological Approach*. Edited by David J. A. Clines and Philip R. Davies. Journal for the Study of the Old Testament Supplement Series 109. Sheffield: Almond Press.

Johnson, Allen W. and Timothy Earle. 1987. *The Evolution of Human Societies: From Foraging Group to Agrarian State*, 1st edn. Stanford, CA: Stanford University Press.

_____ 2001. *The Evolution of Human Societies: From Foraging Group to Agrarian State*, 2nd edn. Stanford, CA: Stanford University Press.

Kaiser, Otto. 1983. *Isaiah 1–12: A Commentary*. London: SCM Press Ltd.

Kautsky, John H. 1997. *The Politics of Aristocratic Empires*. London: Transaction Publishers.

Kempner, Ken and Ana Loureiro Jurema. 2002. "The Global Politics of Education: Brazil and the World Bank." *Higher Education* 43 (3): 331–54.

King, Martin Luther, Jr. 1991. "Letter From Birmingham Jail." In *A Testament of Hope: The Essential Writings and Speeches of Martin Luther King, Jr.*, ed. James M. Washington: 298–302. San Francisco, CA: HarperCollins.

King, Stephen J. 2003. *Liberalization Against Democracy: The Local Politics of Economic Reform in Tunisia*. Bloomington, IN: Indiana University Press.

Kissane, Edward J. 1941. *The Book of Isaiah: Translated from a Critically Revised Hebrew Text with Commentary* (vol. 1). Dublin: Browne and Nolan Limited.

Kleve, J. G. 1971. "The Control of Annual Plans: The Experience of Tunisia." *The Journal of Modern African Studies* 9 (2): 306–10.

Kling, D. W. 2004. *The Bible In History: How The Texts Have Shaped The Times*. Oxford: Oxford University Press.

Knapp, A. Bernard. 1988. "Copper Production and Eastern Mediterranean Trade: The Rise of Complex Society in Cyprus." In *State and Society: The Emergence and Development of Social Hierarchy and Political Centralization*, eds J. Gledhill, B. Bender, and M. T. Larsen: 149–72. London: Unwin Hyman.

Kumar, D. 1962. "Caste and Landlessness in South India." *Comparative Studies in Society and History* 4 (3): 337–63.

Lenski, Gerhard E. 1966. *Power and Privilege: A Theory of Social Stratification*. New York: McGraw-Hill Book Company.

_____ 2005. *Ecological-Evolutionary Theory: Principals and Applications*. Boulder, CO: Paradigm Publishers.

Levine, Baruch A. 1996. "Farewell to the Ancient Near East: Evaluating Biblical References of Ownership of Land in Comparative Perspective." In *Privatization in the Ancient Near East and Classical World*, eds Michael Hudson and Baruch A. Levine: 223–52. Cambridge: Peabody Museum of Archaeology and Ethnology.

Liverani, Mario. 2007. *Israel's History and the History of Israel*. Translated by Chiara Peri and Philip Davies. BibleWorld. London: Equinox.

MacGibbon, D. A. 1945. "International Monetary Control." *The Canadian Journal of Economics and Political Science* 11 (1): 1–13.

Mays, James Luther. 1976. *Micah: A Commentary*. London: SCM Press Ltd.

McKay, Donald Vernon. 1946. "The French in Tunisia." *Geographical Review* 35 (3): 368–90.

McNutt, Paula. 1999. *Reconstructing the Society of Ancient Israel*. Library of Ancient Israel. Louisville: Westminster John Knox Press.

Meinis, Henk K. 1992. "Molluscs." In *Excavations at the City of David 1978–1985*, eds A. de Groot and D. T. Ariel: 122–130. Jerusalem: Institute of Archaeology, Hebrew University of Jerusalem.

Meltzer Commission. 1999. *The Meltzer Report*. Washington DC: United States Congress.

Modelski, George and William R. Thompson. 1996. *Leading Sectors and World Powers: The Coevolution of Global Politics and Economics*. Columbia, SC: University of South Carolina Press.

Nussbaum, Fredrick L. 1933. *A History of the Economic Institutions of Modern Europe: An Introduction to "Der moderne Kapitalismus" of Werner Sombart*. New York: F. S. Crofts and Co.

Parsons, Kenneth H. 1965. "The Tunisian Program for Cooperative Farming." *Land Economics* 41 (4): 303–16.

Payne, Rhys. 1993. "Economic Crisis and Policy Reform in the 1980s." In *Polity and Society in Contemporary North Africa*, eds I. William Zartman and William Mark Habeeb: 139–67. Boulder, CO: Westview.

Plattner, Stuart. 2002. "Markets and Marketplaces." In *Economic Anthropology*, ed. Stuart Plattner: 171–208. Stanford, CA: Stanford University Press.

Pomeranz, Kenneth. 2000. *The Great Divergence: Europe, China, and the Making of the Modern World Economy*. Princeton, NJ: Princeton University Press.

Postgate, J. N. (ed.). 1969. *Neo-Assyrian Royal Grants and Degrees*. Rome: Pontifical Biblical Institute.

Powers, David S. 1989. "Orientalism, Colonialism, and Legal History." *Comparative Studies in Society and History* 31 (3): 535–71.

Premnath, D. N. 1997. "Latifundialization in Isaiah 5:8–10." In *Social-Scientific Old Testament Criticism*, ed. David J. Chalcraft: 301–12. Sheffield: Sheffield Academic Press.

_____ 2003. *Eighth Century Prophets: A Social Analysis*. St Louis, MO: Chalice.

Radwan, Samir, Vali Jamal and Ajit Ghose. 1991. *Tunisia: Rural Labour and Structural Transformation*. London: Routledge.

Rennstich, Joachim Karl. 2006. "Three Steps in Globalization: Global Networks from 1000 BCE to 2050 CE." In *Globalization and Global History*, vol. 2, eds Barry K. Gills and William R. Thompson: 203–31. London: Routledge.

Ronen, Yigal. 1996. "The Enigma of the Shekel Weights of the Judean Kingdom." *The American School of Oriental Research* 59 (2): 122–25.

Roy, A. 1971. "The Sacred in Human Evolution." *Annual Review of Ecology and Systematics* 2: 23–44.

Sanderson, Stephen K. 2001. *The Evolution of Human Sociality: A Darwinian Conflict Perspective*. Lanham, MD: Rowman & Littlefield Publishers.

Serotta, Gerry and Brian Walt. 2004. *Saving Homes and Humans in Gaza*. Available from http://www.shalomctr.org/node/611 [last accessed: 24/1/2010].

Sherratt, Susan and Andrew Sherratt. 1993. "The Growth of the Mediterranean Economy in the Early First Millennium BC." *World Archaeology* 24 (3): 361–78.

Shiloh, Yigal. 1984. *Excavations at the City of David: 1978-1982* (Qedem, 19). Jerusalem: Institute of Archaeology, Hebrew University of Jerusalem.

Shils, Edward. 1960. "Political Development in the New States." *Comparative Studies in Society and History* 2 (3): 265–92.

Smith, Ralph L. 1984. *Micah – Malachi*. Waco, TX: Word Books.

Smithies, Arthur. 1944. "The International Bank For Reconstruction and Development." *The American Economic Review* 43 (4): 785–97.

Thurow, Lester C. 1996. *The Future of Capitalism: How Today's Economic Forces Shape Tomorrow's World.* New York: William Morrow and Company, Inc.

Tozy, Mohammed. 1993. "Islam and the State." In *Polity and Society in Contemporary North Africa: State, Culture, and Society in Contemporary North Africa*, eds Zartman, William I. and William Mark Habeeb: 102–22. Boulder, CO: Westview Press.

United Nations Children's Fund. 1989. *The State of the World's Children.* New York: Oxford University Press.

Wallach, Lori and Patrick Woodall. 2004. *Whose Trade Organization?* New York: The New Press.

Woods, Ngaire. 2000. "The Challenge to International Institutions." In *The Political Economy of Globalization*, ed. Ngaire Woods: 202–20. New York: St Martin's Press.

Zaibet, Lokman T. and Elizabeth G. Dunn. 1998. "Land Tenure, Farm Size, and Rural Market Participation in Developing Countries: The Case of the Tunisian Olive Sector." *Economic Development and Cultural Change* 46 (4): 831–48.

Index of References

Index of Names and Subjects

Lightning Source UK Ltd.
Milton Keynes UK
UKOW051841230413

209648UK00002B/24/P